EXPLORATIONS

# Explorations 2

*New Language and Writing Skills for
Leaving Certificate
Higher Level*

---

ANNE GORMLEY

GILL & MACMILLAN

Gill & Macmillan Ltd
Goldenbridge
Dublin 8
with associated companies throughout the world
www.gillmacmillan.ie

© Anne Gormley 1999

0 7171 2652 8
Print origination by
Carrigboy Typesetting Services, County Cork.

*The paper used in this book is made from the wood pulp of managed forests.*
*For every tree felled, at least one tree is planted, thereby*
*renewing natural resources.*

All rights reserved. No part of this publication may be reproduced,
copied or transmitted in any form or by any means without written
permission of the publishers or else under the terms of any
licence permitting limited copying issued by the Irish
Copyright Licensing Agency, Irish Writers' Centre,
Parnell Square, Dublin 1.

# CONTENTS

| | |
|---|---|
| **PREFACE** | vii |
| **1. COMPREHENSION** | 1 |
| The characteristics of comprehension writing | 2 |
| Language and style | 6 |
| The language of information | 6 |
| The language of argument | 10 |
| The language of persuasion | 22 |
| The language of narration | 28 |
| The aesthetic use of language | 29 |
| Style | 34 |
| Tone or mood in writing | 39 |
| Comprehension or prose vocabulary | 43 |
| Literary terms | 43 |
| Reading | 48 |
| A review of newspaper articles | 54 |
| Approaching the comprehension passage | 61 |
| The summary | 70 |
| Characteristics of well-written answers | 74 |
| Exercises | 75 |
| **2. ENGLISH GRAMMAR** | 77 |
| What is grammar? | 77 |
| Syntax | 78 |
| Parts of speech | 78 |

| | |
|---|---:|
| Sentences, clauses, and phrases | 88 |
| Punctuation | 92 |
| Some confusing words | 99 |
| Common writing errors | 103 |
| Common spelling errors | 107 |
| Exercises | 108 |

## 3. THE ENGLISH COMPOSITION 115

| | |
|---|---:|
| Effective writing and what it involves | 115 |
| The hallmarks of a good writer in English | 118 |
| Check-list for precision in writing | 119 |
| Style | 119 |
| The English composition | 122 |
| The paragraph | 142 |
| Exercises on the paragraph | 165 |
| The language of narration | 170 |
| The aesthetic use of language | 182 |
| The language of argument | 188 |
| The language of persuasion | 191 |
| The language of information | 197 |

## 4. ANSWERS TO EXERCISES 232

# PREFACE

Although examination courses will vary considerably, the basic skills of writing will always remain the same. The Leaving Certificate English examination is still a written one, and success in this exam depends on the ability to write clear, grammatical English.

The aim of this book is to offer guidance on becoming a proficient writer. A series of examples and exercises are set out, all of which are designed to test and improve the basic writing skills. Sample exercises, paragraphs and compositions from actual pupils' work are analysed and assessed. The approach throughout is a practical one and should help pupils become more competent and more confident in a variety of writing genres.

As the new syllabus in English offers an opportunity to explore and write in many different styles and genres, the exercises and guidelines given here are structured in such a way as to make pupils familiar with all writing styles, from practical writing (reports, memos, and letters) to writing a narrative, an imaginative composition, or a short story.

## An approach to paper I

The mastering of writing skills demands a lot of hard work. Although pupils may acquire and develop insights and knowledge of the set texts, this knowledge is useless if they cannot communicate these insights in writing. Many able and even brilliant pupils are handicapped by a lack of the basic writing skills. Practice and more practice at writing is indispensable in becoming more adept at writing.

Time must be dedicated steadily throughout the school year to answering questions and learning how to tackle and construct exam-style questions. About half the time spent on studying English should be dedicated to writing, in learning to put information on paper.

Both fifth year and the first term of sixth year are good opportunities for developing writing skills. In fact the main thrust of an English class should be towards supplying pupils with information and then getting them to put it on paper. They should become familiar with the standard required by reading good compositions and sample answers in different genres: short story, narrative, factual writing, discursive writing, and so on.

There is no substitute for writing practice. Writing is a skill, and, like any other skill, it improves only with practice. It's no use trying to learn to swim simply by reading a book on swimming techniques and not going near the water, and it's the same with writing: to be a good composition writer, write compositions, and to be a very good composition writer, write more compositions. Pupils should write at least one paragraph a day, on any topic, in both fifth year and sixth year. The more they write the more confident and fluent their expression will become.

Time spent in class on writing practice is time well spent and will certainly reap its rewards when exam time comes.

## Acknowledgments

I wish to thank the following people for their encouragement and support: Margaret Kelly, Hazel Stanley, my brother John, and Margaret Roche.

I also want to thank the following pupils for allowing me to use their work as sample material: Jean Hegarty, Rachel Reilley, and Andrew Lavin.

Thanks to Four Courts Press for allowing some material to be reproduced.

Finally I wish to thank Hubert Mahony for helpful advice and support.

# One
# COMPREHENSION

To comprehend means to take in or to grasp with the mind. Comprehension in reading is a deep understanding that is arrived at by a close, accurate and imaginative reading of the passage. This includes the ability to identify the techniques used by the writer, to obtain a clear understanding of how individual writers make language work. To understand fully *what* is being said you must pay attention to *how* it is being said.

**Text** is the content of any written communication. Letters, reports, speeches, scripts, novels and poems are all texts and can be treated as examples of a specific **genre** or type, or a combination of different genres.

The following features must be identified and analysed in any piece of written communication to determine the genre or genres to which the writing belongs:

- the **register**—the vocabulary or kind of words that are used
- the **syntax**—the particular way in which the words are organised in a text
- the **style** of writing of the piece
- the **tone** or 'voice' of the writer
- the **structure** or layout of the writing
- the **format** or external form of the writing—whether it is written in verse, prose, or other form.

When you are confronted with a piece of unseen comprehension, it is important to be able to identify the purpose of the writing and to know how and why particular linguistic features are being used to serve that purpose. In other words, a good honours pupil has to be able to ask and answer the questions:

- What is the writer saying?
- How is the writer expressing himself or herself?
- Why is the writer saying this?

A sound and thorough comprehension can be attained when you fully understand the relation between a **statement** and an **implication**. A statement is an account of facts, whereas an implication is a subjective hint or opinion on a particular fact.

A writer may make a statement about a certain topic, for example '*Too much television viewing lessens concentration.*' They may then go on to make an implication on that particular statement, such as the following: '*That boy watches television every night. He must be illiterate.*' The implication here is that television is the cause of his lack of literacy.

The use of implication can serve many different functions. It can extend or reinforce a preceding statement; for example: '*That boy who watches television every night is top of his class.*'

Look at the following statement: '*The poor have been shifted from the inner cities and out to reservations in the badlands, where they are expected to stay put.*' The implication in this statement is that people are becoming less tolerant of the poor.

Remember always that a writer's implied meaning may extend, reinforce, modify or even negate the stated meaning.

## THE CHARACTERISTICS OF COMPREHENSION WRITING

### Theme

It is important to identify the theme or subject matter of the comprehension passage. The writer has something to say: this is the theme. Themes can be profound and serious, or light-hearted and entertaining.

### Intention

This is the *purpose* underlying the writing. A writer may have one of many different intentions; some of these are:

—**to inform.** The writer may wish to inform the reader of particular facts or a particular situation, or to give instructions.

—**to persuade.** Persuasive writing—unlike informative or factual writing—means that the writer is advancing a particular viewpoint. Good persuasive writing presupposes an acute awareness of the particular reader, together with the use of an appropriate tone and *register* to suit that reader. The type of argument and vocabulary used must also be suited to the content.

When confronted with a piece of persuasive writing, make sure you distinguish between a fact and an emotional appeal. The writer may wish to convince you about some issue. This can be done in many ways: by making a statement and supporting it with evidence and reasoning, or by using emotion and suggestion. In this case the use of emotive or rhetorical language would play a part.

While most persuasive writers are careful not to make blind assertions with no sound arguments, some still manage to present unsound arguments on the basis of a carefully orchestrated presentation and thereby win the reader more quickly.

—**to arouse.** The writer may wish to make the reader indignant or angry about something.
—**to teach, instruct, or moralise.** While these words are not strictly synonymous, sometimes a writer who wants to teach or impart some lesson may moralise or use a moralising tone.
—**to warn or alert** the reader to some danger.
—**to mock or satirise** somebody or something, for example an institution such as the Government or the Church.
—**to attack** somebody or something.
—**to amuse or entertain.**
—**to provoke a reaction**—of anger, sympathy, fear, or pity.

As we have seen, tone and intention are inseparable. So a writer wishing to mock something may adopt an ironic or satirical tone; similarly, a factual or persuasive tone can be adopted where the writer is trying to convince us that something is true.

A variety of tones can be used to serve one intention. A writer wishing to warn somebody of the dangers of drinking and driving might adopt a humorous approach at first and then present facts. They might also use irony to mock drunken drivers.

All these characteristics—theme, tone, and intention—are intimately related. Comprehension can be characterised as well written when the style, tone and feeling are all suited to the message the writer wishes to convey.

## *Tone*

Tone is the quality of speech and writing that reveals the writer's attitude towards the subject and the audience. It is the relationship they establish with the reader—*how* they are saying what they are saying.

The tone used will depend on the writer and on the purpose in writing. The writer could adopt a humorous, a satirical or an ironic tone to communicate the same ideas. On the other hand, the tone could simply be factual and informative.

## *Structure and form*

It is important to be able to understand clearly the particular layout or structure of a piece of comprehension writing. A prose passage is constructed on the basis of **sentences** and **paragraphs**.

SENTENCES

A sentence is a self-contained combination of words that makes complete sense. The way a writer constructs sentences can help to reveal certain attitudes towards the subject; it can also be a method of communicating what the writer wants to say in a more effective fashion.

The structure of sentences can contribute to the flow of thought in a passage. A series of terse sentences can give an impression of movement, tension or excitement in a piece of writing.

> Very slowly I brought the rifle up. The coyotes did not move. My finger was reluctant to touch the trigger. I must be getting old and my ancient conditioning worn thin. Coyotes are vermin. They steal chickens. They thin the ranks of quail and other game birds. They must be killed. They are the enemy. And I did not fire. My training said, Shoot, and my age replied, There is not a chicken within thirty miles. Why should I interfere?

A short sentence in the middle of longer ones can also have an arresting or dramatic effect.

> And there, if you please, is a conclusive comment upon the whole business—a final basis of comparison of all things, whether commercial or artistic; the bare dignity of the unadorned that may stand before the world all unashamed, panoplied rather than clothed in consciousness of perfection. We of this latter day, we painters and poets and writers—artists—must labour with all the wits of us, all the strength of us, and with all that we have of ingenuity and

perseverance to attain simplicity. <u>But it has not always been so.</u> At the very earliest, men—forgotten, ordinary men—were born with an easy unblurred vision that today we would hail as marvellous genius.

Simple sentences anchor the writer's thoughts securely. However, too many short sentences in succession can cause the writing to be jerky and monotonous.

> People have freedom. That was what everyone wanted. I think it was. That was the word they used. I used it too. I talked wildly about freedom. I felt briefly a longing to fight for freedom. I merely cried for freedom, however.

A writer who wants to be didactic or to moralise can use sentences in the form of commands.

> The drugs crisis must continue to get the same kind of concentrated attention it has received in the past.

> The new leadership must persuade the world that it really wants to be part of the democratic process.

> We need better-quality work with families and a programme of intervention in the schools. We also need a top-class foster-care system, and a residential care system that can help these children. We need to do these things now. We can afford to do them now—and, many would argue, we cannot afford not to do them now.

## PARAGRAPHS

Examine the structure and paragraphing in a comprehension passage: see whether it is presented in 'tabloid' style (with lots of short sentences, or with every sentence a new paragraph) or a continuous narrative, or somewhere in between. In well-written prose, every paragraph should contain a different point or deal with a distinct aspect of the topic.

Are the paragraphs proportionate to one another, or is there a disproportion in their length? Do the paragraphs develop logically?

Examine how the paragraphs are linked. Paragraphs can be linked through the repetition of key words and phrases. Examine the passage to see whether the linking or transitional devices are effective. The section on paragraphs in chapter 3 (page 142) deals with the different points that must be noted in constructing paragraphs and on the use of links and transitional devices.

## LANGUAGE AND STYLE

Language and the different modes in which it can be used may be classified under the following headings:

   (a) the language of *information*
   (b) the language of *argument*
   (c) the language of *persuasion*
   (d) the language of *narration*
   (e) the *aesthetic* use of language.

The use of language will not always be clear-cut and obvious, however. For example, a newspaper or television report may include a mixture of argument and persuasion. Similarly, an advertisement, while it is an example of the language of persuasion, may also contain information. So language forms can overlap and intermingle. It is important to recognise the different features of each of these uses of language.

## THE LANGUAGE OF INFORMATION

This type of language forms the basis of business reports and correspondence, textbooks, newspaper and television accounts of events, and documentary films.

The language of information is characterised by its emphasis on facts and the communication of information. It is usually terse and clear in approach.

The following newspaper extracts could be described as informative writing. Read them carefully, then answer the questions that follow.

### *Factual newspaper reports*

**Councils urged to declare war on litter louts**
Local authorities were ordered yesterday to hit litter louts where it hurt most—in their pockets.

Enforce the law, the Minister of State for the Environment, Danny Wallace, told local authority officials when he announced measures to end the blight of litter pollution.

Every local authority should have its own clean-up squad, he insisted. He reminded local authorities of their responsibilities under the Litter

Pollution Act, which was passed into law last July. Provisions of the Act include on-the-spot fines of £25, which can be imposed by litter wardens and by gardaí. Fines of up to £1,500 can be enforced under the Act.

He said: 'I am convinced that responsible action by the public is necessary to end the blight of litter pollution, but the primary management and enforcement responses to the problem must come from local authorities.'

His anti-litter programme includes a continuing regime to assist and review local authorities' enforcement action and to help litter black-spots. Mr Wallace said his department was also involved in a school information programme being developed by the environmental information office, ENFO.

The department was also joining business interests in jointly financing An Taisce's National Spring Clean, 1999, to raise public awareness and participation in anti-litter projects at local level.

The scheme, in which local authorities will play a central role, will be formally launched in the autumn. Mr Wallace intends to hold meetings with officials of the local authorities over the coming weeks to ensure that the momentum is not lost.

He pointed out that local authorities would be able to use some of the £125 million under the proposed Local Government Fund, which will come into operation next year, to tackle the litter problem. Everyone needed to adopt a responsible attitude if Ireland was to clean up its act, said Mr Wallace.

## Millions promised to fund huge countryside clean-up

Local authorities have been given the go-ahead for a multi-million-pound litter campaign. Yesterday the Minister of State for the Environment, Dan Wallace, announced a concerted plan of action to tidy up the country. He said the local authorities would be able to use some of the £125 million from the Local Government Fund to clean up their areas and focus on persistent litter black-spots.

A monitoring regime is also to be set up, together with a review of the local authority enforcement action, to identify the worst areas. Local authority public education and awareness initiatives will be financed for the litter black-spots.

Mr Wallace said a new schools information programme was also being set up to develop anti-litter awareness among young people, in co-operation with the Department of Education.

Business interests and the Government are joining together to provide financial support for a special An Taisce project, National Spring Clean, 1999, intended to raise public awareness and participation in anti-litter initiatives, with a central role for the local authorities.

The minister said that while responsible action was needed by the public to end the scourge of litter, primary management and enforcement responses had to come from the local authorities.

**City bosses told to take hard line on litter**
If the authorities were looking for just the right photo opportunity to illustrate Ireland's litter problem, they found it yesterday in Dublin's O'Connell Street, where soft-drink cans, fast-food cartons, bits of paper and even bottles were swirling around the Anna Livia fountain.

The Minister of State at the Department of the Environment, Mr Dan Wallace, obliged photographers by dipping his hand into the fountain—commonly known as the Floozie in the Jacuzzi—to fish out some of the detritus and pose glumly with what he caught.

The Dublin city manager, Mr John Fitzgerald, who was with him, said the fountain is 'cleaned all day, every day'—but the litter bugs still defeated the corporation's best efforts. 'Anywhere else in Europe, a fountain like this would be as clean as a whistle,' he added.

Three other city managers—Mr Jack Higgins (Cork), Mr Joe Galvin (Galway), and Mr Eddie Breen (Waterford)—were also present to hear Mr Wallace announcing yet another series of measures 'to combat the country's continuing litter problem.'

Though 'responsible action' by the public would be necessary to put an end to this 'blight', the minister made it clear that the primary response in tackling it 'must come from local authorities, using their enforcement powers under the 1997 Litter Pollution Act.

'We have to put the boot in,' Mr Wallace declared. 'The laws are there, but they just need to be implemented. We're also setting up a new monitoring regime to keep tabs on the performance of local authorities in this area, because some of them have no litter wardens.'

The number of litter wardens employed by Dublin Corporation will double this week, to fourteen. Most of them will be patrolling the city centre on foot, but there are also two vans to provide the wardens with greater mobility in detecting and apprehending offenders.

Mr Des Malone, one of the most active litter wardens in the city, said he had just 'done' three motorists yesterday morning for throwing cigarette butts out of their car windows. In each case he imposed an on-the-spot fine of £25, which must be paid within twenty-one days.

Mr Kevin O'Sullivan of the city's Cleansing Department said the wardens had issued three thousand on-the-spot fines since last July. 'We have forty-odd in court this Friday. Fines can be quite hefty—as much as £1,500 for serious offences, or £300 for throwing cigarette butts out of cars.'

The new monitoring regime for local authorities is intended to encourage them to take a more active role as well as to help identify and eliminate black-spots. Financing is to be provided for public education and awareness initiatives in the worst-polluted areas.

A new schools programme is being developed by ENFO, the environmental information service, and there will also be financial support for An Taisce's 'National Spring Clean' project next year, which will include a central role for local authorities.

Over the coming weeks Mr Wallace will be holding a series of meetings with city and county managers to stress the importance of taking stronger action on litter, by using some of the extra discretionary income they will receive from the local government fund.

Mr Jack Higgins, the Cork city manager, agreed it needed to be tackled, as evidenced by the ocean of litter left behind by crowds attending St Patrick's Day parades. 'We have to face up to the fact that we are a dirty people, and this is a cultural problem.'

## Questions

1. What type of information is being presented in each article?
2. Analyse in the case of each item how the organisation of the material affects the message.
3. Distinguish in each case the number of facts presented.
4. Identify the opinions in each article. Is evidence used to support these opinions in each case?
5. State whether the writer intrudes, and show how this is done.
6. What is the audience addressed in each case?
7. Discuss the significance of each of the headlines, and account for the difference in each case. In your answer take into account
   (a) the intended audience and
   (b) the purpose of each writer.
8. Identify *three* general statements made in each article and show how they are supported, whether by statistics, evidence, or illustrations.

## Expository writing

This type of writing falls within the category of the language of information. In expository writing the writer exposes or sets out clearly the subject matter, and then proceeds to develop it. *Clarity of expression* and *precision of detail* are features of this type of writing. Look at the following extract:

People seeing the headmaster for the first time often find him different from what they expected. Those who stay in the Deerfield community for any length of time quickly become aware that they are living in a monarchy and that the small man in the golf cart is the king; but visitors who have heard of him and know what a great man he is seem to insist that he ought to be a tall, white-haired patriarch. People see him picking up papers and assume it is his job. He has an infinite wisdom, which is as aggravating as hell. But anyone knowing him well who is faced with an important decision would go to him; that is, of course, most true of his students.

[John McPhee, 'The Headmaster']

## THE LANGUAGE OF ARGUMENT

Prose writing can also be structured on argument. Argument may be defined as a way of presenting information so as to convince or persuade the reader of some point of view. It is a type of informative writing, but it has persuasion as the basis of its structure.

Different types of writing can come under this heading, including

- *analytical* writing
- *discursive* writing.

In analysing writing, and particularly writing that is based on argument, it is important to distinguish between valid evidence and false evidence.

Argument is *valid* when the conclusion follows logically from the premise. To test the validity of an argument,

(a) assess the truth of the premise,
(b) assess the truth of each argument,
(c) assess the truth of each sub-argument.

Argument is *effective* when evidence and reasoning are both presented persuasively so as to convince the reader that certain opinions are preferable to others.

Look at the following points made on the subject of changes within the government of China.

Momentous change often comes wrapped in the garments of tradition in China. So it has been at the fifteenth party congress in Beijing, where the main announcement has been that state-owned companies may proceed with novel forms of ownership that could lead to mass privatisation. This is not new policy, since it has been anticipated by substantial changes throughout the main provinces in China. It was announced in a long speech by the president, Jiang Zemin, with a daunting title drawn from the nether reaches of bureaucratic prose. But it signals a decisive shift in China's economic reform programme, which will have many implications for its society and politics.

It is estimated that some 30 per cent of China's 124,000 state enterprises are losing money. Many millions of workers could lose their jobs, opening up the prospect of protest movements and therefore of political instability. But observers believe the timing of the announcement is well chosen. Growth is buoyant, and there are many examples of new forms of ownership that have turned companies around and secured employment. There is little or no evidence of a national rank-and-file trade unionism that might challenge party control, with most protests directed against local injustices and aberrant managements.

But another theme of the congress, corruption in senior party ranks, has been talked about quite openly and could prove as subversive of party control as more co-ordinated political opposition. As President Jiang put it, 'our party can never be daunted and vanquished by any enemy. But the easiest way to capture a fortress is from within, so in no way should we destroy ourselves.'

A slogan has been produced to justify the changes. It says that the forms of ownership do not matter so long as taxes are paid and development proceeds.

The Chinese Communist Party remains a large organisation, with some 58 million members and with sole responsibility for directing political life in China. Although its procedures are highly formalised on these occasions, it is capable of taking large-scale decisions with immense consequences for most Chinese citizens.

[Conor O'Clery, *Irish Times*, 16 September 1997]

*Comment*

In the argument above on the changes in the system of government in China, the writer outlines in a logical way the reasons that contribute to this change: the loss of money in the state enterprises and the existence of corruption in senior party ranks. To support the argument, he uses evidence in the form of statistics: the number of state enterprises that are losing money. There is a direct reference to points made by the president on the issue, together with the number of party members and the fact that a slogan has been produced to justify these changes.

## FACTS AND OPINION

In writing that is based on argument, the reader must learn to distinguish between a *fact* and an *opinion*. A fact is something that actually exists or occurs: it can be verified or proved to be true by an objective or detached observer.

Facts may be true in a particular context but false in another. 'With the growth in prosperity, poverty has rapidly disappeared in Ireland.' This statement may be true in some parts of Ireland, or for some people, but not for others.

'Access to the computer and the internet has made children more mature and literate.' This may be true in regions where technology is more accessible, but it is not true for all parts of the world.

An *opinion* is a judgment or a belief that is held by someone: it goes beyond a fact to make a judgment on the fact. An opinion can be based on a logical inference from the facts, or it can be a viewpoint based on subjective reasons or unwarranted assumptions.

To test factual statements we must examine the evidence. To test statements of opinion we must do two things:

(a) examine the evidence of fact;
(b) examine the inferences drawn from it.

In presenting an argument based on fact, it is enough to give evidence of the facts. In presenting an argument where we wish someone to adopt an opinion, we must present the underlying facts and then give the reasons for adopting, or not adopting, a particular view or opinion on it.

Identify the facts in the following extract:

---

Raf is the new force in men's fashion—a shy young Belgian, in fact, named Raf Simons. The 29-year-old's Paris show on Friday night confirmed his arrival on the international stage, where he joins his fellow-Belgians Dries van Noten, Dirk Bikkembergs and Walter van Beirendonck among the leading menswear designers. His sophisticated, well-made tailoring—shorn of all extraneous detail and cut long and sleek in jet black—had the fashion show packed with the ready-to-wear collections for next winter, which run until tomorrow.

The show traced the bleaker currents of youth culture over the past twenty years, but even the zips and frayed knits of the punk era came across as elegant rather than raw.

Peter Sidell, owner of the Library fashion store in London, said: 'These are the cultural reference points of the new generation. Raf fetches the past into the future. It is easy to tell when the fashion world has found a new star: twice as many people turn up at the show.'

But it was worth the scrum. The industry needs a shot in the arm, because the Far East's economic malaise has hit.

---

An opinion can be coherent and well informed, or it can be uninformed and woolly or convoluted. Look at the following statement: 'I think women are stronger than men. They suffer more physically; they generally work harder; and they usually end up as victims who are misunderstood.' This statement is based on **generalisations**; to be accepted as true it would need to be supported with specific facts.

## PROCESSES OF ARGUMENT

There are a number of different processes of argument or reasoning:

- deductive reasoning
- inductive reasoning
- a priori reasoning
- a posteriori reasoning.

Generally speaking, coherent opinions will use either deductive or inductive reasoning in their development of the argument.

The process of placing a general statement first and following it with supporting details is knows as the **deductive** method of reasoning. Reversing this procedure—opening a paragraph and making a statement with particular details that lead to a broad statement—is known as **inductive** reasoning. The inductive method is useful for leading the reader through a series of persuasive details to a conclusion.

### Deductive reasoning

Deduction means 'moving away from'. It begins with a general law and moves to a particular case. 'All men are mortal; John is a man; therefore John is mortal.' This formal pattern of deductive reasoning is called a **syllogism**. This is an argument consisting of three propositions that are constructed in such a way that if you admit the first and second proposition then you must agree with the third.

'All Irishmen are alcoholics; John is an Irishman; therefore John is an alcoholic.' The structure here is correct but the reasoning process and conclusion drawn are false. This is because the first premise is not true.

Look at the following statements. 'All animals are dangerous; our pet cat is an animal; therefore our cat is dangerous.' This appears to be a logical structure; the reasoning is false, however, because again the first premise is not a fact. 'All Spanish people are friendly; Concha is friendly; therefore Concha is Spanish.' The reasoning here is false because the first assertion is not a fact and because the conclusion does not logically follow from the preceding statements.

## Inductive reasoning

Induction means 'leading into'. This kind of reasoning begins by observing individual phenomena and then arriving at a general law. It is the kind of argument commonly used by scientists and by barristers. 'John is a man; John is mortal; therefore men are mortal.'

An inductive argument generally has the following structure: a proposition or statement of the thesis; the evidence presented; the conclusion. Here are some examples of inductive arguments:

'Water expands when it is frozen; the weather is freezing; therefore it is reasonable to suppose that the pipes may burst.'

'Regular meals are a requirement of good health; Margaret neglects her meals; so it can be presumed that she will fall ill.'

To be effective, both deductive and inductive arguments must be based on proven facts and demonstrable evidence.

## 'A priori' reasoning

This type of reasoning goes from cause to effect: it is a form of deductive reasoning. 'If water expands when it freezes, it follows that the pipes will burst when they are frozen.' 'He has been unemployed for five years, so therefore he has become poorer.'

## 'A posteriori' reasoning

This goes from the effect to the cause: it is a form of inductive reasoning. 'The pipes will burst when they are frozen, because water expands when it freezes.' 'He has less money now, because he has been unemployed for five years.'

## FALLACIES IN ARGUMENT

A **fallacy** is a false or misleading argument. It is important to be able to detect such errors in argument. They can be revealed in different ways: in statements that are not substantiated, in broad generalisations, in implication and innuendo, or through the use of allusion or indirect reference.

Here are some of the most common fallacies or errors in reasoning.

### Begging the question

Begging the question (i.e. 'appealing to the question', from the Latin term *petitio principii*) means taking for granted the point that is being disputed, or using the claim to support itself.

'We must believe that God exists, because it says so in the Bible, and the Bible is God's infallible word.' Here proof for the existence of God is based on an assumption of his existence, which is the question at issue, and so amounts to no proof at all.

'Democracy is the best form of government, because the majority are always right.' While it may be true, this is also a circular argument, because the alleged proof is an unsupported assertion that really means the same thing as the one that is being argued.

### False dilemma

This offers a choice between only two answers or two courses of action, ignoring alternative possibilities. 'The achievement of peace in the North requires that either the unionists or the nationalists give up their beliefs.' 'Unemployed people should either leave the country or be made to do community work.' This kind of argument is usually a mere assertion, put forward without any supporting evidence.

### Ignoring the question

This technique evades the point at issue altogether. One technique is to resort to the 'argument ad hominem' (against the person)—attempting to discredit the person who supports the other side.

### Non-sequitur

A non-sequitur (Latin, 'it does not follow') is a conclusion that cannot be validly inferred from the premise or assertion.

'All Africans are black; all Africans are men; therefore all men are black.' 'All Englishmen are Europeans; all Irishmen are Europeans; therefore all

Irishmen are Englishmen.' These are clear examples of non-sequiturs, where the conclusion does not follow logically from the preceding statements.

### Mere assertion

A common form of fallacious argument is the one that consists of a mere assertion, where something is stated in an authoritative way but without any supporting argument. A typical example would be a politician making such a statement as: 'Irish goods have a perfect right to be exempt from trade restrictions abroad.' The statement simply asserts that the situation can be no other way, without giving any reasons why it should be so.

### Emotional appeals

A writer can appeal to you in several ways. They can shock you or arouse you to a sense of indignation, pity, admiration, or rebellion. All of these are weapons or tactics of a clever writer. Examine them and learn to identify them: learn to recognise when the writer is appealing to your emotions rather than to your rational faculty.

Emotional appeals—including name-calling, labelling, and the use of loaded terms—can be regarded as a kind of non-sequitur. 'He's a red.' 'You're a reactionary.' 'She's a traditionalist.'

### Glittering generality

This is a sweeping statement, a broad generalisation, often in the form of a cliché: 'a gallant leader of men'; 'a woman of vision'; 'a pillar of progress'. These concepts are vague, as well as hackneyed. Get to the facts behind these statements. What exactly is the writer saying?

## Exercises

Examine the following articles, which are examples of the language of argument, and then answer the questions that follow.

PASSAGE 1

> High academic standards and high ethical standards are inseparably connected. According to a national poll, nearly 90 per cent of the American people believe that emphasising habits of discipline in school would make

a great difference in students' achievement. Several years ago the Department of Education wanted to find out why a group of award-winning schools was so successful. The study concluded that while academics remained the central mission, these effective schools were equally concerned about good character.

A good school is in fact always teaching values. A commitment to education rather than ignorance is a value. Working hard, getting to school on time, completing assignments and respecting teachers are all values that go to the very heart of education.

The author William Kilpatrick powerfully makes this point: 'If students don't learn habits of courage and justice, curriculums designed to improve their self-esteem won't stop the epidemic of extortion, bullying, and violence. Even academic reform depends on putting character first. Children need courage to tackle difficult assignments. They need self-discipline if they are going to devote their time to homework rather than television ... If they don't acquire intellectual virtues such as commitment to learning, objectivity, respect for the truth, and humility in the face of facts, then critical thinking strategies will only amount to one more gimmick in the curriculum.'

[Ernest Boyer, *The Basic School*]

## PASSAGE 2

Everything seems to indicate that television has awakened the enthusiasm of some and the animosity of others. There are probably as many in favour as against. It is undoubtedly the most polemical of all the mass media, possibly because it is the youngest.

For quite some time many people have maintained, and still maintain, that television is the way to mould, in a subtle or not so subtle way, the behaviour of the masses. This presupposition is maintained in spite of the findings of some sociologists who hold that television—and indeed other mass media—have little or no influence over public opinion.

An American researcher, William McGuire, states that the findings of a survey held over the past twenty years about the influence of the mass media are 'very embarrassing for those in positions of responsibility in these media, for there is little proof that any change has been effected in the general behaviour of audiences, and even less in activities such as who to vote for, or what brand to buy.'

However, those who pour vast quantities into advertising, and many sociologists, insist that television exercises an important influence on society. There are many examples of this supposed power of television to influence people. Another American, George Gebner, says that the topics that come up time and again in television serials produce, almost imperceptibly, a cumulative effect on the viewers. As proof, he alludes to different reports that indicate that the time of exposure to television is directly related to fears—exaggerated fears, let it be said—of being involved in violence, or being influenced in making political or personal decisions (sometimes important ones), or whether one should make a particular journey or not, or how the budget allocation for the police should be spent.

A small example of the false image that television serials give us is the fact that the police are continually being shown using their weapons, when in fact an armed policeman, on average, fires his pistol three times a year.

[Carlos Soria, *Television and Instant Images*]

## Questions

1. Outline the stages of argument in each article.
2. Identify the reasoning structure used in each case, i.e. whether deductive or inductive.
3. What is the attitude of the writer to the subject in each article?
4. Examine the evidence used by each writer to support their argument. Is this evidence valid? Refer to each article to support your answer.
5. Sum up the main arguments in each article. Would you agree with these arguments? Give reasons for your answer.

## Analytical writing

Analytical writing forms part of the language of argument. It asks the question 'why?'; it moves beyond description to look for reasons. Analysis involves breaking the topic down into different sections and seeing what is and is not important.

The following articles, from different types of publication, set out to analyse certain material. Examine these passages and then answer the questions that follow.

COMPREHENSION

## PASSAGE 1

A panoramic view of history reveals the fact that various peoples have practised some kind of euthanasia. Plato wrote: 'The state shall establish a discipline and laws that limit themselves to caring for citizens who are sound in mind and body. Those not sound in body shall be left to die.' Indeed, before Christian times there was, generally speaking, little or no respect for human life. There were exceptions, of course, like the Hippocratic oath (460 BC), which became the basis for all medical practice. In our times it has in large measure been dropped.

When we examine the statements made by defenders of euthanasia we can notice a definite crescendo in their arguments over the last few years. In 1974 forty well-known people (including the Nobel Prize winners Jacques Monod, Linus Pauling, and George Thompson) signed a statement saying: 'No rational morality can categorically forbid an individual from putting an end to his life if he is suffering from a horrible disease that known medical science can do nothing for.' From this position to 'mercy killing' and on to the need to eliminate 'useless lives' is not a very big step, since the jumping-off point is the same for all of them, namely the denial of the sacred character of all human life.

The great model for what can happen when the euthanasia mentality prevails is the Nazi experience. All the euthanasia policies at that time were not just the result of a sudden fatalism but were the culmination of an intellectual movement that began in the nineteen-twenties with the publication of *The Destruction of Worthless Life* by the psychiatrist Alfred Hoche and the lawyer Karl Binding. These two writers developed the thesis that there are human beings who have no value at all, and they thus championed the idea that the incurably ill should be eliminated. The crux of their argument rested on the economic drain these sick people caused. They dwelt long on the advantages of getting rid of them.

[Fernando Monge, *Position Papers*]

## PASSAGE 2

We live in an age of anxiety. We worry obsessively about the food we eat, and our fears are fanned by a new scare almost every week. At the same time we have never been more aspirational. We are consumed with a passion for the exotic, for experiment, and for novelty. If it's new we want it, and we want it now.

You mean you don't have ostrich steaks? What kind of a place are you running? Where's the polenta, the saffron potatoes, the balsamic vinegar and discreet dribble of truffle oil on the girolles? Bring out the lemon grass and lime leaf: bring on the seared tuna sashimi; astonish us with your basil-scented beurre blanc, your black-bean salsa, your minted couscous, and a taste of Pagnol tapenade.

Supermarkets are experts at detecting the slightest frisson on the gastronomic seismograph and search the world for tempting new tastes. They have skilfully laid their lines of supply on a global scale so that almost everything can now be had all year round.

These days, food has little to do with hunger, more to do with life-style. It was defined for me a few years ago in the Napa valley when I was on a tour around the latest fashionable boutique winery. 'My husband', said our guide, 'is into gerr-*may*. He's seriously organic.' She conjured up visions of a connoisseur spending quality time at the stove.

I suspect, now that food and wine have been turned into a hobby, we're all 'into gourmet.' Chefs on television dazzle us with their skill. There are food game-shows, food quizzes, food sitcoms, and wine documentaries. Everybody has a cellar these days, even if it's only the cupboard under the stairs.

Guides abound to every aspect of gourmet, for we are desperately keen on making the correct choices. Is it organic? Is it ethically acceptable? Were the peasants who grew the coffee paid enough?

Knowing exactly what we are eating and drinking has never been more essential. The BSE catastrophe has alerted us all to the high price we have to pay for cheap food produced not for its quality but for its quantity. We are, rightly, worried about the methods used by the food and farming industry to fill our trolleys.

Decades of chemically dependent intensive farming, the use of drugs and antibiotics in the animal sheds, the presence of pesticide residues in vegetables, the potential dangers of new technology such as irradiation and genetic engineering, the widespread use of cosmetic additives to tart up junk food, have created a new kind of shopper—one who scrutinises labels and walks warily down aisles.

Are we really happy to accept a situation in which there are two kinds of food: stuff produced cheaply that raises no expectations, and speciality products made in small quantities for a small market? Polarising food in this manner has produced a two-tier market, where the options are geared to price. You can have 'real cider' or industrial cider; 'real ice-cream' or a product made with vegetable oil; 'real cheese', properly matured, or slab cheese with no noticeable flavour; 'real sausages' or those made from slurry.

Food made properly, for those who care about how they feed their families, and junk for those who do not care or, more likely, cannot afford the option of good food—surely these options should not be embraced by a civilised society.

## Questions

1. What problems are set out in each article?
2. How has the writer structured his or her argument in each case?
3. What information is used in each case to develop the argument and to answer the leading questions?
4. How important is opinion or speculation in the development of the thought in each article?
5. What conclusions have been reached in each case? Are these conclusions valid? Give reasons for your answer.

## Discursive writing

Discursive writing forms part of the language of argument. It relies heavily on facts, balanced argument, and firm statement; it always demands the use of facts and argument to communicate ideas.

The method of the writer here is detached and logical. This type of writing is suited to a debate or a discussion.

The following is an extract from an article on the travelling people.

> In the year to last November, 211 extra families were accommodated by local authorities, making a total of 3,278 families in such accommodation. But 1,040 families were still living on the side of the road. And the traveller population is rising steadily. One of the problems facing travellers is that throughout the countryside, traditional, unserviced halting-sites are provided. But the anti-social and aggressive behaviour of some traveller families must also be recognised and dealt with in order to protect the larger community.

## Questions

1. Summarise the main thesis or idea here in one sentence.
2. What evidence is used in this extract to support the thesis?
3. What conclusion does the writer draw here?

# The Language of Persuasion

Where the language of argument will lean on various techniques such as logic, facts, and organised structure of thought, the language of persuasion may use implication, sensationalism, inference, generalisation and other techniques designed to manipulate a viewpoint.

Persuasive writing is used by writers to win you over to their side. It is a technique often used in advertising and in satirical or political speeches, and it makes use of a variety of devices to achieve its purpose. Persuasive writing may not depend on facts or logic: instead there is a heavy reliance on emotive language. The techniques used in this style of writing are designed to operate on the level of feeling and emotion, not logic or rational thought. The words that are used are chosen in order to manipulate the emotion and imagination of the reader, to elicit agreement on the basis of feeling or emotion.

Because the persuasive writer aims at manipulating the emotions and feelings of the audience, stress is placed on channelling feelings in a particular direction.

Persuasive writing is not limited to advertising: areas such as business, the media and politics employ persuasive means to achieve their purpose. The audience addressed will generally determine both the content and the quality, together with the type of language used in this type of writing.

Different types of writing come within the category of persuasive writing. Some of these are:

- emotive or affective writing
- rhetorical writing
- oratorical writing
- dogmatic or didactic writing.

Look at the following passages, which are taken from different sources, and then answer the questions that follow.

## PASSAGE 1

When the news finally came, they screamed and hugged each other. They had wanted her to come home, and when they heard the verdict it seemed almost unbelievable.

Once again Louise Woodward's supporters found themselves gathered around the television screens at the Rigger pub in Elton, Cheshire, last night. And when the verdict came they could hardly contain their delight.

COMPREHENSION

As villagers sent fireworks into the sky, the headquarters of the Louise Woodward Campaign for Justice erupted with whoops of delight and relief.

Speaking on Channel 5 news last night, a supporter said it was 'brilliant news. It's fantastic.' 'The village of Elton had been wholly behind the campaign to bring Louise Woodward back to Britain,' another said, 'but we won't rest until she is home. There may be an appeal, but we won't rest until she is with us. We don't know yet if we will have a party. It all depends on Louise.'

## PASSAGE 2

Bounded by hills in the north-east and south and facing the Pacific Ocean to the west, San Francisco is one of the most beautiful cities on earth. And, thanks to its inhabitants, it's also one of the most exciting.

The first rule when talking to a native is never, ever compare them to their cousins in Los Angeles. Somewhere between the two there's an invisible border. People from Los Angeles think everyone north of the border is a sandal-wearing, granola-munching hippie. Alternatively, San Franciscans think southern California, particularly LA-LA Land, is 'full of moussed-out dumb blondes—and that's just the boys.' Like all stereotypes, there's an element of truth in both. So you've been warned.

[*Ireland*, 8 March 1998]

## PASSAGE 3

'Untouchable.' That's the frightening idea Velmani has to live with. For many people like her, that label has meant violent harassment, verbal and physical abuse, and sometimes rape. 'Untouchable' is the word many people use to describe the Dalit people of Tamil Nadu in India. It's meant to keep them in their place.

The Dalits are considered to be at the very bottom of the now outlawed 3,000-year-old caste system. But despite the efforts of successive governments, sinister oppression and discrimination against Dalits continues.

The grinding poverty doesn't help either. Nearly half the population of this area live below the poverty line. The lower you are in the caste system, the poorer you are likely to be. Women and child labourers are the worst hit.

The effects of the caste system are shocking. Children are separated from higher-caste children at school. Women must use different wells. Men must drink from different cups at the tea-shop. Dalits must do all the toxic and hazardous tasks: sanitary work, processing leather, hides, and carcases, burying the dead. They must live in colonies on the edge of villages.

In many ways the sinister concept of 'untouchable' cuts to the core of Trócaire's work. Our commitment to human rights demands fairness and equality for all.

In Madurai, near where Velmani lives, Trócaire is working with a local Dalit organisation called the People's Education and Economic Development Society. It works to combat caste discrimination and helps Dalits learn about their legal rights.

## PASSAGE 4

*Macbeth*:
    We will proceed no further in this business.
    He hath honoured me of late, and I have bought
    Golden opinions from all sorts of people,
    Which would be worn now in their newest gloss,
    Not cast aside so soon.
*Lady Macbeth*:
                      Was the hope drunk
    Wherein you dressed yourself? Hath it slept since?
    And wakes it now to look so green and pale
    At what it did so freely? From this time
    Such I account thy love. Art thou afeared
    To be the same in thine own act and valour
    As thou art in desire? Wouldst thou have that
    Which thou esteem'st the ornament of life,
    And live a coward in thine own esteem,
    Letting 'I dare not' wait upon 'I would',
    Like the poor cat i' th'adage?
*Macbeth*:
                      Prithee, peace.
    I dare do all that may become a man;
    Who dares do more is none.
*Lady Macbeth*:
                      What beast was't then
    That made you break this enterprise to me?
    When you durst do it, then you were a man;

COMPREHENSION

And to be more than what you were, you would
Be so much more the man. Nor time nor place
Did then adhere, and yet you would make both.
They have made themselves, and that their fitness now
Does unmake you.

## Questions

1. What is the *purpose* of each extract?
2. Pick out *three* examples in each text where the writer (or character) appeals to emotion.
3. Who is the intended *audience* in each case?
4. What *techniques* are used in each case to convey the argument? Refer to sensationalism, implication, inference and innuendo in your answer.
5. What type of publication would you consider to be suitable for each passage? Give reasons for you answer.
6. Identify the *facts* in each article.
7. Write a note on the *language* in each extract, paying particular attention to the emotive or rhetorical use of words.

## *Emotive or affective writing*

Emotive writing is a kind of persuasive writing. The writer uses the emotional power of language to argue a point and to make the reader think in a way they want you to.

This kind of writing is characterised by the expression and overflow of powerful feelings, rather than the logical and rational development of thought. Words can sometimes be used like a drug, to sway the reader towards a certain opinion or viewpoint.

This style is a feature of marketing and advertising, and also of writing on politics. The following extract is an example.

> It is not mere journalese to say I knew something cataclysmic was happening that bright morning twenty-five years ago as I walked to the Belfast office of RTE, where I was a young journalist. It was just after dawn. I knew nothing of the internment operation but was groggy with fatigue. In the dark of the previous night I had seen a fat soldier, Gunner

Hatton, tumble and die in wild street-fighting in Ardoyne. Now, this August morning, the entire city was sinisterly transformed. Smoke rose in vast clouds from different areas, and there was the rattle of gunfire, like slates falling off roofs, from everywhere.

[Kevin Myers, *Irish Times*, 10 August 1996]

## Comment

Words such as 'cataclysmic', 'wild street-fighting', 'fat soldier tumbling' and 'rattle of gunfire' are emotive and designed to influence at the level of feeling.

## Rhetorical writing

This is a form of emotive writing. It tries to sway the reader to a certain viewpoint on the basis of feeling and emotion; like emotive writing, it is a striking feature of advertising.

Some of the features of rhetorical writing are:

(a) slogans
(b) catch-phrases and buzz-words
(c) name-calling
(d) metaphors or figurative language
(e) exclamation marks.

A dozen men were set aside for the most wicked part of the adventure: interrogation in depth, the systematic destruction of their central will by sensory deprivation. Spread-eagled against a wall, hooded, starved, exposed to a week-long regimen of white noise, denied the use of toilets, and beaten if they resisted—the only term that describes this treatment is torture. In those days, nobody had heard of the three vital elements employed: interrogation in depth, sensory deprivation, and white noise.

More than the English language changed that day. Nationalist areas rose in insurrection, and Belfast and much of Northern Ireland passed into a war mode. Insanity seized the city. Hundreds of vehicles were hijacked, and factories were burnt.

[Kevin Myers, *Irish Times*, 10 August 1996]

## *Oratorical writing*

This form of writing, also a form of persuasive writing, is more suited to speech than the written word.

> I am happy to join with you today in what will go down in history as the greatest demonstration for freedom in the history of our nation.
>
> Five score years ago, a great American, in whose symbolic shadow we stand today, signed the Emancipation Proclamation. This momentous decree came as the great beacon-light of hope for millions of Negro slaves who had been seared in the flames of injustice. It came as the joyous daybreak to end the long night of their captivity.
>
> But a hundred years later the Negro is still not free. One hundred years later, the life of the Negro is still badly crippled by the manacles of segregation and the chains of discrimination. One hundred years later, the Negro lives on a lonely island of poverty in the midst of a vast ocean of material prosperity. One hundred years later, the Negro is still languished in the corners of American society and finds himself an exile in his own land. So we have come here today to dramatise this shameful condition.
>
> [From a speech by Martin Luther King]

### *Comment*

The type of language used here is rich and colourful. It makes extensive use of imagery and metaphor.

## *Didactic or dogmatic writing*

This is also a form of persuasive writing. A writer who uses this style is trying to instruct readers in the way they ought to think and to accept ideas the writer is putting forward. The use of the imperative 'must' and 'have to' and of a dogmatic tone are features of this style.

The following lines take a distinctively dogmatic approach to their subject.

> The 'alcopops' controversy must be seen in the wider context of under-age drinking, which has been a serious and worsening problem for many years. Clearly, an effective education campaign about the use and abuse of alcohol is also essential—for adults as well as teenagers and children. In this area,

as in so many, children take their cues from their elders. That old-fashioned concept, good example, springs to mind.

[*Irish Times*, 9 August 1997]

## THE LANGUAGE OF NARRATION

In **narrative** prose, the writer is telling a story. There is a definite arrangement of ideas or sequence of events. Narrative prose puts an emphasis on description: describing people, actions and events in detail. (Chapter 3 shows both the features and the method of writing a narrative-style composition.)

**Anecdote** is a feature of narrative writing. Here, a single incident is told in the form of a short story. The incident almost always contains a definite point.

Look at the following example of a narrative style, which begins with an anecdote.

---

In my grandmother's dining-room there was a glass-fronted cabinet and in the cabinet a piece of skin. It was a small piece only, but thick and leathery, with strands of coarse reddish hair. It was stuck to a card with a rusty pin. On the card was some writing in some faded black ink, but I was too young then to read.

'What's that?'

'A piece of brontosaurus.'

My mother knew the names of two prehistoric animals, the brontosaurus and the mammoth. She knew it was not a mammoth. Mammoths came from Siberia.

The brontosaurus, I learnt, was an animal that had drowned in the flood, being too big for Noah to ship aboard the Ark. I pictured a shaggy, lumbering creature with claws and fangs and a malicious green light in its eyes. Sometimes the brontosaurus could crash through the bedroom wall and wake me from my sleep.

This particular brontosaurus had lived in Patagonia, a country in South America, at the far end of the world. Thousands of years before it had fallen into a glacier, travelled down a mountain in a prison of ice, and arrived in perfect condition at the bottom.

Charley Milward was captain of the merchant ship that sank at the entrance to the Strait of Magellan. He survived the wreck and settled

> nearby, at Punta Arenas, where he ran a ship-repairing yard. The Charley Milward of my imagination was a god among men—tall, silent, and strong, with black mutton-chop whiskers and fierce blue eyes. He wore his sailor's cap at an angle and the tops of his sea boots turned down.
>
> [Bruce Chatwin, *In Patagonia*]

The following extracts are examples of an autobiographical style, written in narrative form.

> I was born in Harlem thirty-one years ago. I began plotting novels at about the time I learnt to read. I read everything I could get my hands on—except the Bible, probably because it was the only book I was encouraged to read. I must also confess that I wrote a great deal.
>
> [James Baldwin, *Notes of a Native Son*]

Here is another passage from an autobiographical account:

> Of all sounds of all bells—most solemn and touching is the peal which rings out the New Year. I never hear it without a gathering-up of my mind to a concentration of all the images that have been diffused over the last twelve months; all I have done or suffered, performed or neglected in that regretted time. I begin to know its worth as when a person dies. I am naturally shy of novelties, new faces, new books, new years.
>
> [Charles Lamb, 'New Year's Eve']

## THE AESTHETIC USE OF LANGUAGE

The aesthetic use of language stresses those features that show the beauty in language. The emphasis here is on the nature of words and images and on how they function to broaden the imaginative faculty and reveal the richness and beauty underlying concepts. In this respect the use of images, the ability to create pictures through striking description and the use of language as an artistic medium are significant features.

The following types of writing fall under this heading:

- *imaginative* or impressionistic writing
- *descriptive* writing
- *ornate* writing.

To see how words work to create pictures, it is necessary to examine the nature of imagery.

## *Imagery*

Imagery can be used in prose writing for different reasons:

**—to illustrate a point** (in the following example the writer wishes to point out that African people are good at the art of mimicry. He uses images from animal life to illustrate his argument):

> In the shambas you would sometimes come upon a spurfowl which would run in front of your horse as if her wing was broken and she was terrified of being caught by the dogs. But her wing was not broken, and she was not afraid of the dogs—she would whir up before them the moment she chose—only she had got her brood of young chickens somewhere near by, and she was drawing our attention away from them. Like the spurfowl, the natives might be mimicking a fear of us because of some deeper dread, the nature of which we could not guess.

**—to evoke atmosphere:**

> Night after night in the villa during that tempestuous spring Copernicus groaned and sweated over his calculations, while outside the storm boomed and bellowed, tormenting the world. His dazed brain reeled, slipping and skidding in a frantic effort to marshal into some semblance of order the amorphous and apparently irreconcilable fragments of fact and speculation and fantastic dreaming ...

**—to provoke an emotional impact:**

> The scrappy skyline of Little Rock rises from the banks of the lazy Arkansas River and reads like the biography of a president fighting for survival.
>
> And doing so with uncanny success, thanks to the world hidden within this little cluster of skyscrapers and the huddle of buildings that cling to their feet like barnacles. This is Bill Clinton's fiefdom, a one-party town in which politics and business are entwined and fortunes made on politically influenced deals. These roots came dramatically back into play during Clinton's hour of need last week. His presidency and his place in history hung in the balance.
>
> [*Sunday Independent*, 1 February 1998]

There are different kinds of imagery:

**—simple:**

We stayed in a small hotel overlooking the bay. The price was reasonable, and it had a restaurant and a swimming-pool. You could lie at the side of the pool and look up at the mountains through the trees.

**—original:**

In his riding of the rolling level underneath him steady air ... how he rung upon the rein of a wimpling wing in his ecstasy ...

[Gerard Manley Hopkins]

**—vivid or clear:**

He is nearly as tall as a Dublin policeman, and, preaching literature he stood on the hearthrug, his feet set close together. Lifting his arms above his head (the very movement that Raphael gives to Paul when preaching at Athens), he said what he wanted to do was to gather up a great mass of speech.

[George Russell]

**—exotic:**

In the emptiness of the landscape, a cry arose whose shrillness pierced the still air like a sharp arrow flying straight to the very heart of the land; and, as if by enchantment, streams of human beings—of naked human beings—with spears in their hands, with bows, with shields, with wild glances and savage movements, were poured into the clearing by the dark-faced and pensive forest. The bushes shook, the grass swayed for a time, and then everything stood still in attentive mobility.

[Joseph Conrad, 'Heart of Darkness']

**—startling:**

Never shall I sow my salt seed in the least valley of sackcloth to mourn the majesty and burning of the child's death.

[Dylan Thomas]

When you see imagery in a prose passage, ask yourself the following questions:

- What does it say?
- Why is it used?
- How well does it function in the passage?
- Does it produce sound effects?

The ability to master description and to paint pictures is an important part of the aesthetic use of language.

## Descriptive writing

Where narrative writing tells us what people and things *do*, descriptive writing tells us what things are *like*. Descriptive writing

- gives a clear picture
- selects details with great care
- uses precise vocabulary and avoids exaggeration.

The following passage uses a keen sense of detail and a striking power of description.

> The flood of summer light had begun to ebb, the air had grown mellow, the shadows were long upon the smooth dense turf. The shadows on the lawn were straight and angular; they were the shadows of an old man sitting in a deep wicker chair near the low table on which the tea had been served, and of two younger men strolling to and fro, in desultory talk, in front of him. The old man had his cup in his hand; it was an unusually large cup, of a different pattern from the rest of the set and painted in brilliant colours.
>
> [Henry James, *Portrait of a Lady*]

## Imaginative writing

This is a style of writing that illustrates the power of the imagination to create unusual images, to juxtapose exciting and dynamic ideas. Imaginative writing differs from a factual or discursive approach because it links ideas through word repetition and image association, not through logic.

## COMPREHENSION

The following paragraphs are an example of imaginative writing with a strong focus on description.

> The sun rose. Bars of yellow and green fell on the shore, gilding the ribs of the eaten-out boat and making the sea holly and its mailed leaves gleam blue as steel. Light almost pierced the thin swift waves as they raced fan shaped over the beach. The girl who had taken her bead and made all the jewels, the topaz, the aquamarine, the water coloured jewels with sparks of fire in them, dance now bared her brows and with wide opened eyes drove a straight pathway over the waves. Their quivering mackerel sparkling was darkened; they massed themselves; their green hollows deepened and darkened and might be traversed by shoals of wandering fish.
>
> 'Let us now crawl', said Bernard, 'under the canopy of the currant leaves, and tell stories. Let us inhabit the underworld. Let us take possession of our secret territory, which is lit by pendant currants like candelabra, shining red on one side, black on the other. Here, Jinny, if we curl up close, we can sit under the canopy of the currant leaves and watch the censers swing. This is our universe. The others pass down the carriage-drive. The skirts of Miss Hudson and Miss Curry sweep by like candle extinguishers. Those are Susan's white socks. Those are Louis' neat sand shoes firmly printing the gravel. Here come warm gusts of decomposing leaves, of rotting vegetation. We are in a swamp now; in a malarial jungle. There is an elephant white with maggots, killed by an arrow shot dead in its eye. The bright eyes of hopping birds—eagles, vultures—are apparent. They take us for fallen trees. They pick at a worm—that is a hooded cobra—and leave it with a festering brown scar to be mauled by lions. This is our world, lit with crescents and stars of light; and great petals half transparent block the openings like purple windows. Everything is strange. Things are huge and very small. The stalks of flowers are thick as oak trees. Leaves are high as the domes of vast cathedrals. We are giants, lying here, who can make forests quiver.'
>
> [Virginia Woolf, *The Waves*]

## *Ornate writing*

This type of writing is flowery, elaborate and exalted in style. It makes use of colourful phrases, flowery expressions, and sometimes a verbose style.

> Once upon a time I had occasion to buy so uninteresting a thing as a silver soup ladle. The salesman at the silversmith's was obliging and for my inspection brought forth quite an array of ladles. But my purse was flaccid,

anaemic, and I must pick and choose with all the discrimination in the world. I wanted to make a brave showing with my gift—to get a great deal for my money. I went through a world of soup-ladles—ladles with gilded bowls, with embossed handles, with chased arabesques, but there were none to my taste.

As can be seen from all these examples, language can be used as an artistic medium to enrich imaginative perception and thus give aesthetic pleasure.

## STYLE

Style means presenting the subject in a way that is best suited to achieving the writer's aim. It is important to be able to identify the different styles used by a writer and to 'read between the lines,' to know how language and imagery work in writing to create tone and mood and to add up to a coherent style.

Words and their function in a piece of writing can be examined in a number of different ways.

### *Context*

How does the word affect other words? Words can contrast, harmonise, startle or arouse a reader. Take the following lines from an advertisement:

> BP, who bring billions of barrels from the back of beyond, now bake biscuits in Berlin.

The repetition of the consonant *b* here contributes to the impact of the slogan. Through the alliteration of certain consonants, different moods or emotions can be expressed by the writer.

Look at the following headlines:

> STRAINED STUDENTS SQUINT AND SQUIRM AS THEY OPEN THEIR LITTLE BROWN ENVELOPES
>
> SAILING BACK TO SANITY

The effect here is achieved by the repetition of the *s* sound—what is technically known as **sibilance**.

A writer can achieve a calm or a harsh effect depending on what particular combination of consonants or vowels they use. Examine the following headlines and comment on the techniques used in each case and the effect of such techniques:

> CAUGHT IN THE CROSS-FIRE
> BIG BOYS CAN RIDE BIKES
> TEARS AND TERROR
> TURTLE SURVIVAL AT LOGGERHEADS WITH LAGER LOUTS ON GREEK BEACH
> KNOCK YOUR SOCKS OFF

## *Connotations*

The connotation of a word is its emotive impact or associations—whether positive or negative—in addition to its strict meaning. The connotations of certain words need to be examined: the words 'yuppie', 'soap opera', 'terrorist' all suggest certain attitudes to an idea.

Look at the following terms and identify which have positive connotations, which have negative connotations, and which have none:

> 'the fat boy'
> 'the obese boy'
> 'the big boy'
> 'the overweight boy'.

### *Alliteration*

This is the repetition of consonant sounds, especially the initial consonants of words. Through the alliteration of certain consonants, various moods or emotions can be conveyed. Take, for example, these lines from T. S. Eliot:

> I should have been a pair of ragged claws
> Scuttling across the floors of silent seas.

The alliteration of the *l* sounds here depicts a tone of self-contempt or uselessness.

> Fleeing from the foreign faces and the foreign swords.
> Wait for the wind that chills towards the dead land.

The effects here are also achieved through alliteration. The rhyming of the consonant *f* in the first line conveys the fear in the people.

A calmer and more subdued effect can also be achieved through alliteration:

> leafy-with-love banks and the green waters of the canal
> Pouring redemption for me, that I do
> The will of God, wallow in the habitual, the banal.

## Assonance

This is the repetition of vowel sounds, which can convey a musical or sensuous impact or a sense of harmony. Many writers make use of the technique of assonance.

> Now as I was young and easy under the apple boughs
> About the lilting house and happy as the grass was green,
> And as I was green and carefree, famous among the barns
> About the happy yard and singing as the farm was home.

The effect of the repetition of the o sound conveys a rich musicality and gives a deep, sensuous quality to the verse.

## Cacophony or dissonance

This is the opposite of assonance and consists of the repetition of 'hard' sounds, such as *k*, to suggest a harsh or grating mood to the reader. This is especially vivid in the following lines from Emily Dickinson:

> And creak across my soul …

and from Yeats:

> the clever man who cries the catch cries of the clown.

## Sibilance

This is the repetition of *s* and *z* sounds, and it conveys a deep appeal to the senses. A writer wishing to convey the notion of gentleness might choose words that emphasise these sounds, as in the following lines from Keats:

> Of beechen green, and shadows numberless,
> Singest of summer in full-throated ease …
> Where palsy shakes a few, sad, last grey hairs,
> Where youth grows pale, and spectre-thin and dies;
> Where but to think is to be full of sorrow
> And leaden-eyed despair …

## Simile

Similes offer the reader an opportunity to travel in the imagination between two different things. They lend a colour and power to writing.

> There are masterpieces of dry, limpid, organised thought that provoke in us an artistic quiver quite as strongly as a novel like *Mansfield Park* does or as any rich flow of Dickensian sensual imagery.

> He brought out a soup-ladle that was as plain and as unadorned as the unclouded sky—and about as beautiful.

> It was as if the channels of his brain had been sluiced with an icy drench of water.

## Metaphor

A metaphor fuses two things in a few words; it draws a comparison between two different things in a vivid and economical way.

Look at the following sentences:

> The snow came down like a sheet.
> The sheet of snow came down.

In the first, the writer is using a simile to describe how the snow was falling. The second sentence makes use of a metaphor to convey the same idea.

Metaphors are immediate and economic in their impact. In the following extract from an article on modern technology, the writer uses a distinctive metaphorical approach to the subject.

> Satellite and cable television have allowed us to import the American phenomenon of 'channel-surfers'—people who never really watch any one programme, because they are constantly scanning the alternatives, either in sequence or in simultaneous 'mosaic' format. The new technology will offer vastly more possibilities to those who can 'navigate the net'. Imagine being cast into an endlessly variable labyrinth, in which we know there are caves of gold and libraries of treasure but most of the twists and turns leave us lost in a maze of suburban high streets.

## Comment

The use of the colourful metaphor of being plunged into a rich labyrinth filled with gold and treasure cleverly parallels the ability to make use of the modern computer.

## Influencing the reader

We have seen earlier that the particular way in which words are used enables the reader to form an assumption, make an inference, form a judgment, extract evidence, or develop a perception on something.

It is important, therefore, to distinguish all the ways in which words can be used to influence the reader and to recognise when an assumption, an inference or an implication is being made in writing.

### Assumption

An assumption is the acceptance of something without having proof. If we are repeatedly exposed to examples of corruption within the Government, we may assume that everybody in the Government is corrupt. We make assumptions on the basis of our experience or our prior knowledge that something is true or false, logical or illogical, right or wrong.

### Perception

Perception is the truth as we see it, or the intuitive recognition of a truth. It is the apprehension of truth mainly through the senses; for example, after reading a newspaper report about a suicide, a reader may be able to form a perception that a person was harassed or suffered from depression.

### Implication and inference

An *implication* is something that is hinted at or suggested but is not explicitly stated. For example: 'Her husband has not been seen since last summer.' The implication here could be that the marriage is in trouble.

An *inference* is an interpretation of a fact. If we saw someone running along the road crying we might infer that some accident had occurred; for all we know they may have won the lottery and be crying with joy. Remember that the writer *implies*, the reader *infers*.

### Judgment

A judgment is an evaluation made on certain facts or beliefs. Judgments may be subjective: for example, someone may make the judgment that the driver was drunk and that that is why the car crashed.

## Use of personal pronouns

Another way in which a writer can use words to influence a reader is the use of the first-person pronouns 'I' and 'we'. Many times this can be used as a subtle and persuasive device on the part of the writer to elicit the full involvement and therefore agreement of the reader.

> The first premise that I would like to postulate is that all thinking about language is emotional. The linguistic faculty is such an integral and mysterious part of the personality that it could not be otherwise. Nor must we fall into the error of thinking that only the language learnt at the mother's knee can evoke intense feeling. We have seen governments prepared to take life rather than abandon the imposition of a largely artificial dialect on their people, and people prepared to die rather than accept it.

## TONE OR MOOD IN WRITING

A writer can also use the **syntax** or arrangement of words in a sentence to convey a tone or mood in the writing.

Tone is the relationship the writer establishes with the reader: it is the particular voice of the writer, and it can play a central part in communicating the message. As we have seen, there are as many tones as there are intentions.

We will examine the following types of tones and see how they can be used in writing:

- comic or humorous
- ironic
- satirical
- colloquial or conversational.

## Comic or humorous tone

The purpose of this tone in writing is to entertain the reader. Sometimes the writer will use humour as a tool in writing to drive home a point, or to illustrate an argument, or to teach some lesson. A humorous tone can also heighten the implications of a more serious message: for example, in the following paragraph on computers the writer uses a series of humorous anecdotes to illustrate how computers can still betray us.

Perhaps the definitive statement on our superiority over machines was inadvertently made by a computer. The machine was asked to rewrite a passage that included the phrase 'out of sight, out of mind.' The computer chugged away and translated the cliché as 'invisible idiot.'

The following is a description of the person who borrows:

What a careless, even deportment has your borrower! What rosy gills! What a beautiful reliance on Providence does he manifest!—taking no more thought than lilies! What contempt for money—accounting it (yours and mine especially) no better than dross!

[Charles Lamb, 'The Two Races of Men']

## *Ironic tone*

Ironic writing—the employment of **irony**—communicates a meaning that is the opposite of what is written. Its purpose can be either to entertain or to ridicule; it can also be a means of *satirising* a person or institution, using scorn to expose injustice or folly.

In ironic writing the writer emphasises discrepancies in human behaviour. Jane Austen is one of the most celebrated ironists of the English language.

The following paragraph on the travelling community is an example of ironic writing.

There are fewer travellers in Ireland than there are Irish people in Germany. The latest estimates I have seen for the latter category is 25,000, for the former 22,000. The figures suggest the paradox of Irish attitudes to travellers. We are one of the most unsettled people in Europe, yet we are also one of the societies least tolerant of unsettled people.

Paradoxically, at a time of vastly greater ease of travel and communication, we have constructed a division of space in which the haves and the have-nots see much less of each other than they would have done in pre-war Ireland.

The greatest paradox of the travellers' situation, indeed, is that the contempt for them in parts of the settled community is self-contempt.

Travellers are the closest group in Ireland to the way the whole country was before the industrial revolution of the nineteen-sixties.

We know how much our achievement of a settled and stable nation owes to the movement of some of us to positions on the physical and economic outskirts, out of sight, out of mind. Travellers have the bad grace to remind settled society of what much of it was like before the sixties and to transgress against the ultimate social etiquette of modern Ireland, the requirement that the poor not appear except as abstract statistics.

That is why a society that supposedly embraces restlessness and the fall of national borders still can't cope with people who will not stay put. That is why a society that likes to think of itself as part of a world in which satellites send images around the world in the blink of an eye is thrown into confusion when a single family moves from Athlone to Moate.

We have made ourselves into a place in which anything is acceptable except the truth of our own recent past and how we left it behind.

## *Comment*

This passage is a striking example of ironic writing. The writer undermines the attitude of people towards the travelling community; he ironically maintains that many of the prejudices held by Irish people are hypocritical and self-condemnatory. Any real objections to travellers are made by people who themselves come from a similar background; Irish people are so neurotic about maintaining their present position within Europe that the continued presence of travellers in our society is disturbing.

The writer also ironically states that while our society claims to embrace restlessness and a free spirit, it still cannot cope with people who will not stay put.

## *Satirical tone*

Satirical writing exposes the folly and vice of humans to ridicule. Look at the following satirical commentary on the rich.

Now, the different thing is what they eat. Think about it. You pay upwards of four thousand pounds to bring the family on a fortnight's holiday in the south of France, the place that gave the salivating world bouillabaisse, bourride, and a thousand other incomparable dishes. What do you eat? I'll tell you what you eat: you slowly masticate frozen hamburger and oven chips and tinned sweet corn, or face-flannel fried chicken with oven chips and ketchup and a side order of taco chips with bottled guacamole followed by muesli ice cream and Diet Coke.

In the early evening there are dozens of little dinner parties serving the most expensive junk food in the world.

I have a theory about why the rich hanker after cheap food. They want the one thing the poor have that they never can: hunger. The rich are never hungry. Once in a while they can rise to peckish; but the rich man yearns for the savour of a poor man's ravenous appetite, and this the rich man can't manage, even if he does dress up like a cabin boy from the *Bounty*.

Now, down here, when the bobbing flotsam want to go out and eat on dryish land, like as not they'll go to a beach restaurant called the Voile Rouge. The coast here is parcelled up into little private stretches, and each has a slightly different nuance and style. Some are tasteless, naff and common and some are tasteless, naff and chic. This one is the chien's rognons blancs.

[*Style*, 25 August 1996]

## Colloquial tone

This type of writing is more conversational or informal in approach. The purpose may be to involve the reader more in the subject matter, or the writer may wish to communicate with a wider readership. A colloquial style uses vocabulary that is familiar to the reader; the diction is simple, and examples are homely and precise. The writer may use popular expressions that are more suited to everyday speech.

> Sometimes known as 'the net', usually shortspeak for the internet but also including rivals such as Compuserve, the term 'cyberspace' owes much of its vogue to William Gibson, the classy American scribbler of thrillers set only pixels away in a near future where constellations of accessible information can be stored in a pair of designer sunglasses and influenced by eye movement. Do not scoff: that much is already here, even if largely deployed in the development of the cutting edge of the virtual reality games market.

The writer here relies on buzz-words and Americanisms to convey the message.

## Comprehension or Prose Vocabulary

To answer questions on comprehension you must be aware of the meaning of the following words:

**analyse:** to 'take apart' an idea or a statement in order to consider all its aspects.
**compare:** to show the similarities and the differences between things (*compare with*: to make a comparison; *compare to*: to suggest a similarity).
**contrast:** to show the differences between things.
**criticise:** to point out mistakes and weaknesses in a balanced way.
**define:** to give the precise meaning of a concept.
**discuss:** to explain an item and give details, with examples.
**disprove:** to refute or produce arguments that show something to be false.
**evaluate:** to discuss, but to go on and judge for and against.
**explain:** to offer a detailed and exact explanation of an idea or principle.
**illustrate:** to give examples that demonstrate and prove.
**justify:** to give the reasons for a position.
**prove:** to give answers that demonstrate the logical arguments.
**state:** to express the points, briefly and clearly.
**summarise, outline:** give only the main points, not details.
**trace:** to give a description in logical or chronological order of the stages of a process.

## Literary Terms

You must also have a good understanding of the meaning of the following words:

**alliteration:** the repetition of the same initial consonant. 'The day dawns ... dry bedroom air ... a dark exhausted eye, a dry downturning mouth ...'
**allusion:** a reference. Allusions can be

—**scientific:** 'Darwin suggested in a letter written in 1871 that life arose in a warm little pond'
—**literary:** 'I wondered whether he knew the legend of Diarmaid and Gráinne ...'
—**historical:** 'During the Napoleonic wars the squirearchy were a strong social system in England'

—**political:** 'Was it for this the Wild Geese spread the grey wing on every tide? For this that all the blood was shed?'
—**Biblical or religious:** 'Christ's temptations in the desert are an example to us for all time'
—**mythical:** 'Parnassian islands'; 'no second Troy.'

**ambiguity:** the use of an expression or word that has a number of possible meanings in such a way that it is difficult to tell which meaning is intended. 'Love is blind'; 'For men were born to pray and save'; 'Fair is foul and foul is fair'. Unintentional ambiguity: 'Woman acts to keep her husband from unemployment.' Ambiguity can also be created by deliberately punning on words that have similar sounds but different meanings.

**analogy:** a comparison that points out a relationship or similarity between two things. Analogies compare things from different classes: for example, a writer wishing to show the corrupting effect of power could draw an analogy between political power and spiritual power.

**antithesis:** the balance of opposing ideas in a sentence. 'Kings will be tyrants from policy when subjects are rebels from principle'; 'To advocate unsuccessfully what he wants seems to him more futile than to advocate successfully what he does not want.'

**aphorism:** a short, powerful maxim; a concise statement of truth: 'Hamlet is the prince of philosophical speculators'; "'Tis better to have loved and lost | Than never to have loved at all'; 'Life's but a walking shadow, a poor player | That struts and frets his hour upon the stage, | And then is heard no more.'

**archaic:** obsolete, no longer in use: 'irksome' (tiresome), 'felicity' (happiness), 'thou' (you), 'henceforth' (from now on).

**assonance:** the rhyming of vowel sounds within words: shade, grain, hail … 'and the watery hazes of the hazel …'

**atmosphere:** the feelings or emotions evoked by a scene, by a work of art or music, etc.

**balance:** the placing of two parts of a sentence, or words within a sentence, in such a way as to be in opposition to one another. 'To make us love our country, our country ought to be lovely'; 'They renounced coercive power, but not the power that rests upon persuasion.'

**bias:** a prejudice; favouring one side in an argument.

**cadence:** the rhythmical rising and falling of language in writing or speech.

**caricature:** the portrayal of a character in which certain characteristics are exaggerated so that the person appears ridiculous.
**clause:** a division of a sentence containing its own subject and predicate (verb).
**cliché:** a hackneyed expression so overused as to have lost its impact. 'Each and every one of us'; 'few and far between'; 'it's up for grabs.'
**climax:** the culminating moment in a poem, play, or piece of prose.
**colloquial:** belonging to common or ordinary speech; informal language.
**connotations:** reverberations; what is implied by a word; nuances or suggestions that stem from a word.
**cynicism:** having little or no faith in human goodness.
**diction:** the writer's choice of words.
**digression:** turning aside from the main subject.
**ellipsis:** the omission of words, usually indicated by *omission points* (...).
**emotive:** tending to arouse emotion or feelings.
**empathy:** the complete association of the self with another being.
**epigram:** a short sentence expressing a witty thought or shrewd comment. 'Too many people expect wonders from democracy, when the most wonderful thing of all is just having it'; 'Genius begins great works; labour alone finishes them.'
**euphemism:** a mild expression in place of a harsh one. 'He was rough' (a tyrant); 'she's in care' (in a mental home); 'he's down' (depressed).
**figurative language:** language that contains many *figures of speech*— metaphors, similes, etc. 'He flowed out into a torrent of argument and explanation, very ingenious but impossible to follow. Phrase after phrase rose and turned and went out like a wreath of smoke'; 'He feared he would go mad, or fall ill, yet he could not rest, for if he once let go his fierce hold, the elaborate scaffolding he had so painfully erected would fall asunder.'
**hyperbole:** deliberate exaggeration to achieve a certain effect. 'The world is filled with gross, stupid, ferocious and sordid barbarians who are alien from religion and civilisation'; 'a thousand million thanks.'
**idiom, idiomatic expression:** an expression peculiar to a certain language, especially one with a meaning that cannot be deduced from the individual words: 'over the moon' (delighted); 'down in the dumps' (depressed), 'a feather in his cap' (a recognised achievement).
**implication:** something that is hinted at or suggested rather than stated explicitly. 'The bond between the human and the horse ends with the human partner coming out on top, both literally and metaphorically.'

The implication here is that the human is superior at every stage to the horse.

**inference:** a judgment or conclusion derived from a statement. An *implication* is made by a writer; an *inference* is drawn by the reader.

**invective:** wordy abuse or denunciation. The following sentence (suggesting that peace should be waged with the same intensity as war) is an example: 'The killers and maimers, the kneecappers and torturers, the bombers and snipers, the gung-ho enforcers and righteous crusaders, have shown more courage, more fixity of purpose, more willingness to sacrifice and endure, than almost all of the rest of us put together.'

**irony:** an incongruous contrast between the words used and their implications. 'In an age of computer-literacy, the level of illiteracy has increased.' 'The qualities that make public monuments so valuable in building support for established regimes also make them useful to groups who want to overthrow such regimes.'

**lucid:** vivid or clear.

**lyrical:** literally: like a song; figuratively: enthusiastic, full of praise.

**maxim:** an adage; an established principle or truth expressed in a concise form. 'Renewal is not relaxation'; 'He who has a *why* to live for can bear with almost any *how*.'

**metaphor:** making a comparison between two things without using the words 'like' or 'as'. 'Politicians are wedded to the status quo'; 'the very marrow of thought'; 'her eyes are stars.'

**mood:** the particular feeling or atmosphere created by a piece of writing.

**moral:** concerned with the good or bad of human behaviour. 'Bullfighting belongs more to the decadence of imperial Rome. At the Roman city of Morida in Estremadura there is a huge amphitheatre in which you can still see the sluices and channels through which the water was conducted for shipwreck scenes. A favourite entertainment was to launch a toy ship on the miniature sea, man it with a crew of wild beasts and Christians, and allow it to sink. The Romans were a highly developed people, and in this spectacle there was much to please the eye of the artist and delight the connoisseur of technical innovations. There was sportsmanship in it too. The Christians were given swords, and those who pleased the audience by their resistance would, of course, be fished out of the water and allowed to compete in the next spectacle. The audience would talk with knowledge and charm about stage sets and navigation and costumes and traditional ceremonies and Numidian lions. The ordinary spectator, listening to this discourse, would be shy of disparaging an entertainment that such an expert found edifying. Only some very crude provincial would venture to suggest that it was tough on the Christians.' The moral here is that people can fool themselves in the name of art and culture and forget about such things as violence and cruelty.

**oratorical:** eloquent.

**paradox:** a statement that is apparently contradictory but might be true in a way. 'The child is father to the man'; 'tremendous silence'; 'dying generations.'

**parenthesis:** an aside; a remark inserted into a sentence, like an afterthought. It can be indicated by *commas*, *dashes*, or *parentheses*, but always in pairs. 'The doctor—he was a little bald man, with gleaming eyes and an excitable manner—rubbed his hands'; 'The average rise and fall of the tide (depending of course on the season) is about three feet.'

**pathos:** pity, sadness or tenderness created by the writer.

**personification:** investing inanimate things with human qualities: 'sad Russia'; 'sleeping Jerusalem'; 'his instincts threw up their defences'; 'sullen waterscape'; 'then the idea sauntered up to him, humming happily, and tapped him on the back, wanting to know what all the uproar was about.'

**platitude:** a trite or commonplace remark, especially when presented as if it is significant. 'He who goes a-borrowing goes a-sorrowing'; 'The team that gets its act together will come out on top at the end of the day.'

**polemics:** the art of controversial discussion.

**précis:** a summary.

**pun:** a play on words that are similar in sound but different in meaning: 'king of every blooming thing' (Kavanagh).

**quip:** a sharp retort or short sarcastic remark. 'Takes one to know one'; 'Men—can't live with them, can't live without them'; 'It takes two to tango.'

**rhetoric:** persuasive and impressive speech or writing.

**sarcasm:** a bitter or wounding remark made at the expense of another.

**sardonic:** derisive, mocking, or sneering.

**satire:** the ridiculing of folly. 'The Irish middle classes have long been uncomfortable with the symptoms of Mariolatry in Irish life: Knock and Ballinspittle have seemed to us to be evidence of an embarrassing peasant backwardness. But we have seen in the past week that the need for a single icon of virtue is not confined to the Irish; and in post-Christian England, the figure of Diana, playgirl, adulteress and society star, is surely no less ridiculous as a spiritual assurance than a gable end or moving statue in Ireland' (Kevin Myers, *Irish Times*, 30 August 1997).

**simile:** the direct comparison of two things, using the words 'like' or 'as'. 'It was as natural as a cat playing with a mouse'; 'It is noble but untameable, like a giraffe'; 'The sea heaves like a mighty animal.'

**slang:** extremely informal spoken language, generally cultivated by uneducated people in order to create an effect, enjoying a brief burst of popularity before being replaced by a newer fashion. In the written language, slang may be used when it is necessary to convey dialogue accurately, or in certain types of journalism, but it is not generally acceptable in serious writing.

**syntax:** word order: the arrangement of words according to the established conventions of a language.

**tone:** the 'tone of voice' of the writer.

**verbosity:** wordiness; using more words (or longer or more formal words) than is necessary. 'Our story would be as commensurate with the subject as the flippant smartness of a bright reporter in the Sistine Chapel: we would be striving to cover up our innate incompetence by elaborateness of design and intricacy of rhetoric.' In other words, 'Our story would be as irrelevant as a smart reporter writing about the Sistine Chapel: we would be covering up our lack of knowledge by exaggeration.'

# READING

Reading is one of the most basic and most essential life skills and at the same time is one of the crowning achievements of human culture. Reading feeds the imagination; it stimulates the creative response, while at the same time providing endless hours of enjoyment.

Reading has several different purposes. We can read to obtain information on something, to get instructions or to know what is happening. Written language is still the principal means of conveying information: even with text on a computer, we have to be able to read it, and perhaps also to write it. We also read for pleasure—to learn of other lives and other worlds.

To understand and master the skills of writing, reading is indispensable. Style, fluency and flow of language, precision in conveying meaning—all are improved by careful and selective reading.

Successful reading involves using different techniques for different purposes. These include skimming, or scanning for essential information or key words. It also involves the ability to identify the *functional* or *rhetorical* intention of individual sentences or fragments of text.

Reading is an active skill that is essential for anyone who wishes to be an effective communicator. Reading makes 'a full man', according to Bacon—a complete person. Reading can help you develop interesting and new ways of expression; it can broaden and enrich your thought. Try to assimilate new facts from your reading, and afterwards make an effort to recall these to yourself. Reading in this way will also ensure that your critical ability, and your speed, will improve.

A concise writer will be a discriminate reader who is able to organise information clearly, to filter the relevant from the irrelevant, to group and classify information, and to find relationships between different parts.

## *Efficient reading*

The Leaving Certificate examination imposes deadlines. Targets have to be met, and time is all-important. It is essential, therefore, to choose the reading material for your composition both carefully and selectively.

Learning to read efficiently and knowing what to read is as important a skill as learning to write effectively. Effective reading has to be both active and purposeful; in other words, reading involves not only mental alertness but also a certain purpose in the reader's mind.

Ask yourself why you are reading that book or article. Know your purpose in reading. See whether or not you agree with what you are reading.

If the passage is a descriptive piece of writing, look at the way language is used to get the ideas across. See whether the language is effective and, if so, how that effect is achieved. If the language is not clear and effective, know how to identify this. This ability to identify purpose in language is all part of the process of active and purposeful reading.

Jot down new words, new phrases, new ideas, and descriptive modes of expression, and keep them in a special notebook for that purpose.

Choose some topics that you are interested in—music, sports, education, women's questions, history—and select your reading matter accordingly. It is a good idea to have material prepared on several different topics, so that you can have enough content to choose from at the time of the examination.

Effective reading involves *comprehension* or understanding of the material being read. Learn to survey the work: sometimes a quick glance will give you a clear overview. A look at the title can often tell you the subject being dealt with by the writer.

Look at the writer's argument and see first of all how it is laid out and what type of structure it has. The author of a book will normally organise their thoughts into *paragraphs* and *chapters*, and sometimes also in *sections*, with sub-headings.

Effective reading involves being able to answer the following questions:

- What does the writer hope to accomplish?
- What does the order of chapters tell me?
- Why are the chapters arranged as they are?
- Is there a logical development between chapters, and if not, why not?
- How are paragraphs constructed?
- Does each paragraph flow on naturally from the preceding one?
- What kind of style is the writer using? Why is this particular style used? The use of lengthy sentences, unfamiliar words or archaic diction will obscure the writer's meaning.
- Is the tone serious, light-hearted, ironic, or patronising?
- Does the writer show any bias or prejudice in the way in which evidence is selected and interpreted?
- Are there places where the writer is making an assumption or an implication?

Being able to remember and recall some of these questions while reading will not only ensure that your reading is more alert and critical but will also help you to assimilate better what you are reading.

The final stage in effective reading is the ability to retain and reproduce what you read.

## *Purposeful reading*

Purposeful reading is similar to study. It involves

    (a) comprehension of the writing;
    (b) reacting to or interacting with the material;

(c) the retention of new material and new facts;
(d) incorporating new material into your existing knowledge.

All this will accelerate your fluency in communicating more effectively through writing.

Remember the following guidelines for effective reading:

- Preview—check the number of chapters; look at the titles of chapters and any sub-headings. Many times this can tell you a great deal about the content.
- Learn how to recognise the difference between a fact and an opinion.
- State the central ideas, either orally or in writing.
- Re-read difficult material in order to understand it fully.
- Ask questions about what you are reading.
- When reading arguments that are based on logic, ask yourself the following questions:
  —What is the evidence prompting the claim?
  —Has the writer used appropriate analogies and definitions?
  —What provision has been made for rebuttal?
- Become a more active reader by paying attention to the way in which the writer appeals to logic or to emotion in arguing a case.

## *Exercise on critical reading*

Read the following newspaper editorials and note any instances of faulty reasoning or rhetorical devices used to sway the reader. Look for emotive language, assumptions, unsupported generalisations, begging the question, and other devices. How has the particular perspective of the writers shaped their selection of evidence? How might a different writer have presented the same facts?

PASSAGE 1

> Back in the days when a little restraint with regard to the private life of a deceased public person was regarded as a good thing, and a sense of respect for the recently dead was instinctively given, biographies—that formerly most enjoyable of literary genres—concentrated on those events and actions nearly all of which—apart from diaries and letters made available to the biographer—were in the public domain.

Side by side, however, with such biographies there has always gone a very different approach to biography. That old gossip Suetonius, in his classic *The Twelve Caesars*, dug up the dirt on Julius and his successors and laid it all out for his fascinated readers, all of it presented of course in the morally disapproving tone of a *Sun* editorial.

Something new, however, has happened in the late twentieth century. Whereas there had obviously been too much of a tendency on the part of the older-style biographies that sometimes read like saints' lives, the latest approach takes the shovel provided by Suetonius, sharpens it against the whetstone of Freud, and proceeds to give us an unsparing and breathtakingly presumptuous 'inside' look at the subject under the microscope, or tied down on the psychoanalyst's couch.

Previously, biographers gave us heroes, with one or two warts, just for the purposes of contrast. Now biographers refuse to entertain even the possibility that anyone, living or dead, might have shown heroic qualities. Every motive is now suspect, every action open to the kind of analysis that leaves it looking either self-serving or morally suspect. Every truth that can be unearthed must be presented in the most unforgiving light.

The title of this biography is *The Life and Death of a Crime Reporter*, written by Emily O'Reilly, a journalist. In her book she levels a number of extremely damaging accusations at Ms Guerin: that she forged documents to advance her career, that she lied about her qualifications, that she betrayed contacts, and—perhaps most damaging to her memory—that she got a thrill out of 'fencing' with the Dublin crime bosses, that she forgot or ignored the boundary between the work of a journalist and that of a private detective.

She also accuses the editor of the *Sunday Independent*, for whom Ms Guerin worked, of 'dereliction of duty and responsibility' in not exercising due caution in allowing her to continue the kind of potentially dangerous investigative journalism in which she was engaged.

Not surprisingly, Emily O'Reilly this week has been on the receiving end of a considerable amount of criticism. Her book has been sharply condemned by Veronica Guerin's family. She has been accused of being tactless, tasteless, cruel, vindictive, and deceitful.

Her own motives, based on the theory that there was rivalry between these two women journalists, have been questioned. In fact she is being subjected to a barrage of criticism almost equal in intensity to the kind she allegedly makes of Veronica Guerin.

[*Galway Advertiser*, 30 April 1998]

## PASSAGE 2

This has been a pitiful, squalid week for British journalism; a shaming week for British politics. With one lurch, the Mary Bell episode has hauled back a world of mediaeval unreason, where the rule of law, redemption and rehabilitation are impossible and the basest of human instincts are given free reign. Worse, our political leaders, anxious to curry favour with the tabloids, have endorsed those populist, unreasoning values and joined the wolf pack baying for blood. We are all diminished, and an innocent fourteen-year-old—Mary Bell's daughter—has been consigned to a life on the run and in personal torment.

When the press outcry began, newspapers in their hysteria suggested banning the book. Notwithstanding that she was condemned for manslaughter with responsibility, and had served her time, Bell was routinely called a child-killer and a child-murderer. A witch-hunt was launched for the 41-year-old Bell—whose identity the author, Gitta Sereny, had taken vast care to protect—and for her wholly innocent daughter. Their lives, what they had made of them, were about to be ruined. What was needed, and fast, was sense, courage, and leadership.

Instead, Blair played to the tabloid gallery, betraying his own Christian values by offering an instant and populist judgment of a book, which he had not read, as 'inherently repugnant ... I can't justify it. We must look at whether the law needs to be tightened.' The kangaroo court was given the nod. Jack Straw wrote: 'Mary Bell, by bringing herself into the public arena in such a dramatic way, has compromised her own claim for her own privacy.'

But Straw is our Home Secretary. One of his main responsibilities is upholding the laws of the land. An exemplar of these is the so-called 'Mary Bell Order', a law expressly designed to prevent vulnerable children (including those of criminals) from being identified, exposed, or vilified. Straw wrote his words for the *Sun*—the paper that was happily leading its front page that same day with the fact it had found Mary Bell and her daughter, hidden in their 'lair'. Clues to both identities were scattered like confetti. Journalists and their editors weighed up the arguments: to obey a fair law and leave a rehabilitated woman and an innocent girl alone, or to trample over justice, raise the mob, jerk the knee, follow the pack. They descended. The lives of Bell and her daughter have been ruined, as comprehensively—if not as tragically, then as finally—as Bell ruined the lives of the families of Martin Brown and Brian Howe all those years ago.

[*Observer*, 3 May 1998]

# A REVIEW OF NEWSPAPER ARTICLES

Look at the following four newspaper headlines, which show different attitudes on the part of the editors. They reveal the strikingly different way in which each paper approaches the reporting of a murder case.

> WARRANTS FOR GUERIN MURDER
> GILLIGAN EXTRADITION PROCEEDINGS ADJOURNED PENDING AN APPEAL
> GILLIGAN TO FACE EIGHTEEN NEW CHARGES
> ACCUSED OF MURDER—COPS WANT GILLIGAN BROUGHT HOME

The first headline strikes an imperious and forceful note, while the second introduces the topic on a pragmatic note. The third headline is cool, clear-cut, and factual; while the fourth is an example of sensationalism.

## *Exercises*

1. Below are four different reports of a political event. Each article, taken from a different newspaper, reveals a different attitude towards the event. Read the four articles, paying particular attention to the writer's use of language in each case, then answer the questions that follow.

   **Blair will offer hand of peace to Adams**
   The British Prime Minister, Tony Blair, will today extend the hand of peace to the Sinn Féin leader, Gerry Adams.
   The symbolic gesture will take place behind closed doors at Castle Buildings, Stormont, and no cameras will be allowed to capture the historic moment. The only witnesses to the encounter will be the delegates at the peace table.
   The government is keen to make Mr Blair's meeting with Mr Adams as low-key as possible. Mr Blair is anxious not to enrage loyalists. But it will be the first meeting between a British Prime Minister and a Sinn Féin leader since Lloyd George met Michael Collins in 1921.
   Mr Blair will spend about ten minutes in talks with Sinn Féin and each of the other parties at the talks. He will also meet the chairman of the talks, ex-Senator George Mitchell. At least two other Sinn Féin members will be introduced to the Prime Minister.
   The Ulster Unionist Party's security spokesman, Ken Maginnis MP, made it clear last night that he was against the meeting but said it was

'inevitable'. He predicted: 'It will end in tears—as it did the last time. I wish I felt otherwise.'

[*Daily Mirror*, 13 October 1997]

## Blair to make history with talks handshake

The first face-to-face meeting between a British Prime Minister and a Sinn Féin leader for more than seventy-five years will take place in Belfast today.

Tony Blair will take another historic step in the peace process when he shakes hands with Sinn Féin's president, Gerry Adams. He is also expected to meet all the participants in the talks process at Stormont.

Contrary to some reports, there were never any plans for the Taoiseach, Bertie Ahern, who met Mr Blair in Strasbourg on Friday, to travel north today.

There is an expectation that Mr Blair will make an important policy statement on the negotiations and announce 'confidence-building measures' that would make support for participation by some parties in the talks process more secure. No cameras will be present to record his meeting with Mr Adams and two other members of the republican leadership, probably Martin McGuinness MP and Gerry Kelly.

It is also expected that Mr Blair will announce measures that will meet with general approval within the unionist constituency.

The low-key nature of the meeting being organised by the British is directly related to the apprehension about how it will be received within the unionist community. Not since the meeting of Lloyd George and Michael Collins to sign the treaty giving twenty-six counties freedom from British rule in 1921 has any similar meeting been thought either likely or possible.

While Mr Blair has to be seen to treat the Sinn Féin delegation no differently from any other political party participating in the talks process, he will have to take account of unionist sensitivities. He has had several crucial meetings with the UUP leader, David Trimble, and knows the pressure Mr Trimble is under from within and without his party to leave the talks.

Meanwhile, Sinn Féin is making no big play of a statement by the new Minister for Foreign Affairs, David Andrews, although it did say it was 'unhelpful'. The controversial remark came during a BBC interview in which Mr Andrews said: 'My party aspirationally seeks a united Ireland, but I would imagine that in my lifetime it is not achievable.'

[*Irish Independent*, 13 October 1997]

### Blair and Adams in gesture of hope
Tony Blair will today exchange a historic handshake with the Sinn Féin leader, Gerry Adams. The British prime minister will meet Mr Adams when he calls in on the peace talks in Belfast.

But the handshake will take place behind closed doors—so Mr Blair avoids giving Mr Adams a public seal of approval.

The move is sure to outrage some Tories and Unionists. The shadow Secretary of State for Northern Ireland, Andrew Mackay, yesterday warned what happened just before the IRA ended its last ceasefire in February last year. He said: 'Shaking hands is premature. The ceasefire is new, and Mr Adams and his colleagues are still to prove their democratic credentials.

'I would remind Mr Blair that President Clinton shook hands with Mr Adams, and shortly afterwards that ceasefire ended with the bombing of London's docklands.'

The Democratic Unionist Party is already boycotting the talks in protest at Sinn Féin's presence. And the Ulster Unionist Party leader, David Trimble, is under increasing pressure to pull out.

The meeting of Mr Blair and Mr Adams is the first between a British prime minister and a Sinn Féin leader since 1969. Mr Blair will also meet other Ulster leaders.

[*Sun*, 13 October 1997]

### Blair-Adams handshake to be in secret
Tony Blair will become the first British Prime Minister in modern times to meet a Sinn Féin leader when he has talks in Belfast with Gerry Adams today.

The meeting will take place behind closed doors when Mr Blair visits the multi-party talks at Stormont. No camera will capture the expected historic handshake between Mr Blair and the Sinn Féin president.

Mr Blair will spend about ten minutes in talks with Sinn Féin and each of the other parties. The meeting will be the first between a British premier and a Sinn Féin leader since Lloyd George met Michael Collins to sign the 1921 treaty.

Ken Maginnis of the UUP is against the meeting but said it is 'inevitable'. 'It's going to happen, and nothing I feel about it is going to make it not happen,' he said.

The SDLP said it was right that the Prime Minister met Sinn Féin. 'I think it will be an important building block to the talks process,' a spokesman said.

COMPREHENSION

## *Questions*

1. Comment on the headlines, and show how they indicate different attitudes on the part of each paper.
2. Which of these articles makes use of evidence in a convincing manner?
3. Show examples from each of the articles of the emotive use of language.
4. Pick out examples of facts from each article.
5. Which article relies more on opinion?
6. Examine how each writer reveals different attitudes through the choice of language.
7. Do you detect bias in any of these articles? Give an example.

## *Further exercises*

The following extracts from various newspapers give an account of plans to introduce internet access to schools.

1. Discuss the structure of each passage, and give an account of the reason for that particular structure.
2. Identify in each article the audience that is being addressed.
3. What differences are there in the language of each article? Give a reason for these differences.
4. What is the writer's purpose in each of the articles? Identify *three* different techniques in each article by means of which the writer achieves this purpose. Refer to word choice, selection of vocabulary, and language used.
5. Point out the *facts* in each article.
6. Which article relies more heavily on *opinion*?
7. Comment on the different headlines, and show how they illustrate the different purpose of each writer.
8. Comment on the use of *statistics* in each article.

---

**Telecom plans to provide every school with link to internet**

Telecom Éireann is to invest £10 million over the next three years in providing internet connections to every school in the country and other communications and computer services to some schools. This represents the largest investment in schools by any body other than the Department of Education.

Introducing the initiative in Dublin yesterday, the Taoiseach said that Telecom Éireann's decision was an important step towards ensuring 'that every school-leaver has computer literacy as a basic skill.'

The Telecom initiative will provide a free internet connection for every school; advanced ISDN telecommunications links to some larger schools; free internet use up to a certain level; assistance to some schools in disadvantaged areas in obtaining computers; and a special worldwide web site to provide information and services of particular relevance to schools.

Telecom Éireann also plans to select about forty primary and second-level schools to pilot emerging technologies in education.

Mr Ahern said that now was the time to reap the benefits of the opportunities offered by the new technologies. 'Telecom Éireann's massive contribution through this education project and through their highly successful Information Age Town competition are perfect examples of how essential it is to foster a partnership approach to the development of the information society in Ireland.'

It is understood that the Telecom plan was initiated just three weeks ago and emerged largely from its experience of the huge impact of its Information Age Town competition. The chief executive, Mr Alfie Kane, said that 'the importance and urgency of developing information technology in schools' had been emphasised in all fifty-one submissions received in that competition.

The Minister for Education, Mr Martin, said he would soon publish a 'comprehensive policy framework' for IT in schools, which would include effective support services and in-service training for teachers. He said the Government's policy was to encourage the private sector to invest in IT in education. Until now there had been no structure within the department to drive this forward, but two months ago he had set up an IT co-ordinating unit under a senior inspector.

Yesterday's announcement was welcomed by the unions. However, the primary teachers' union, the INTO, said there had not been enough consultation and called on the Government to set up a council for information technology in education.

The main secondary teachers' union, the ASTI, called on the Department of Education to match Telecom Éireann's investment. 'Our schools need modern equipment so that pupils can avail of the full range of information technology facilities provided by Telecom Éireann,' said the ASTI general secretary, Mr Charlie Lennon.

[*Irish Times*, 17 September 1997]

---

### £30 million to put every school on internet

The Government is to pour £30 million into the provision of information technology in schools in an initiative that will put all schools on the internet within two years.

The move follows the announcement yesterday that Telecom Éireann is to invest £10 million in the programme—the largest amount by any body outside the Department of Education. It is understood that a Government decision earlier this year to invest about £30 million in introducing sophisticated information technology into schools, at all levels of the education system, will be implemented shortly.

Teacher, parent and management bodies have been expecting a formal announcement of the plan for some time. This announcement is expected to be made in the coming weeks.

Announcing the Telecom investment initiative, called Telecom Éireann Information Age Schools, Mr Martin said it would involve at least £10 million being spent over the next three years and would work in tandem with the department's own plans in this area. The minister said it was his intention that within two years every school would be connected to the internet.

Telecom Éireann's initiative will provide free internet connections to every school; free use of the internet; and the establishment of a central server, which will provide information and services for schools. Training will be provided for teachers.

Another dimension is that schools will be linked to schools on the Continent in a new cross-Europe Schools Network.

However, while the initiative was welcomed by the main teachers' organisations, the primary teachers' union, the INTO, said there had not been 'sufficient consultation' before the announcement of the project and called on the Government to establish a Council for Information Technology in Education.

Mr Martin said Ireland had lagged significantly behind other countries in its development of information and communication technologies in schools. 'Tackling this situation is of major national significance,' he said, adding that in recognition of this, the Programme for Government committed the department to giving every child the opportunity to develop computer literacy while at school and to using the technology to enhance the learning environment.

Meanwhile, in a separate development last night, the Construction Industry Federation said that industry needed ten thousand new apprentices over the next three years—and that the present apprenticeship system was failing the sector.

A new approach was required by the state and by FÁS if the high standards demanded of the construction industry were to be met in the future, said Peter McCabe, director of the CIF.

Mr McCabe said there was 'widespread dissatisfaction among CIF members with many aspects of the present system, and nothing would be gained by vested interests blaming the construction industry for something regarding which they themselves had serious questions to answer.

'This industry needs ten thousand new apprentices in the next three years. Can the state agency with responsibility for training deal effectively with this? Why is the current system not meeting industry needs?'

[*Examiner*, 17 September 1997]

### £10 million boost will give schools access to internet

The country's four thousand primary and second-level schools are to get a £10 million investment to bring them into the Information Age.

The Taoiseach, Bertie Ahern, joined ministers Mary O'Rourke and Michael Martin yesterday to announce the link-up with Telecom Éireann that will bring advanced information and communications technologies to all schools over the next three years.

The initiative will provide:
- free internet connection to every school;
- free usage of the internet up to a certain level;
- assistance in providing computers in schools; and
- support for a central service that will provide specialised information and services for schools.

It is understood that disadvantaged schools will be given assistance in buying computers, and that a national centre for technology in education will be established.

The Taoiseach said that the £10 million would be in addition to a major funding programme, the full details of which would be announced in the coming weeks.

He said that the reputation of our education system had always been excellent. 'We must now make sure that every school-leaver has computer literacy as a basic skill.'

The Minister for Education said that the contribution of £10 million was the largest investment in schools by an organisation outside the Department of Education. He said the connection of the schools to the internet would make a huge range of learning instruments available to teachers and pupils. Irish schools will be linked to a new Europe Schools Network, and a new on-line advice and support service will also be established.

The ASTI general secretary, Charlie Lennon, welcomed the £10 million announcement but said it should be matched by a similar investment by the Department of Education.

A survey carried out by Lansdowne Market Research for the past year showed that 38 per cent of post-primary schools were connected to the internet and that a similar number had access to e-mail facilities. 'One in five schools had no computer room, and one in ten schools said they could not offer computer science as an option because of staffing restrictions.'

## APPROACHING THE COMPREHENSION PASSAGE

Questions on unseen prose are designed to test your ability to understand the passage and to reflect on the significance of the layout and the relationship between the different ideas. You must be able to follow and develop a line of argument and to draw logical conclusions from stated facts.

You must be able to identify the particular structure and form of the passage, to examine why it is written in a particular way. You must also be able to respond imaginatively to the implications of content and style, for example to understand metaphors and a metaphorical approach.

The answers to all factual question are in the passage itself. Non-factual questions test your imaginative response to the language: they test whether you understand the difference between *implication*, *statement*, *assumption*, and *inference*.

The questions on the comprehension passage may test you in some or all of the following ways:

1. They may test whether you understand the subject and the content of the passage: in other words, do you understand exactly what the writer is saying?
2. Questions can also test your ability to draw conclusions, to follow a line of argument, or to recognise the use of evidence.
3. Some of the questions may also test your assessment of the style or language used in the passage. Questions on style test the ways in which language is used in the passage: they are designed to test your understanding of how the writer expresses the content. In answering questions of this type you must first of all
    (a) identify the feature,
    (b) give an example from the passage, and
    (c) comment on its effectiveness within the passage, i.e. its effect in communicating the theme.
4. Questions may also test your imaginative response to the passage.

## EXPLORATIONS 2

Study the following passages for examples of some of these features.

## PASSAGE 1

A different kind of conservatism was represented by Robert Bridges (1844–1930), an elegantly craftsmanlike poet with considerable metrical skill. Possessed of a sensitively idealising mind, yet interested in the sciences (he was trained as a doctor) as well as in music and in language, he produced some finely chiselled lyrics and in *The Testament of Beauty* (1929), written in 'loose Alexandrines', achieved qualified success in a form the Victorians had rarely been able to manage: the long philosophical poem. In spite of its date, *The Testament of Beauty* may be regarded as the last significant English poem in the Victorian tradition. Bridges' metrical experiments were not radical, as were Hopkins', and his interest in language was in favour of 'purity' rather than new kinds of excitement. In Bridges' poetry the Victorian Muse makes its last formal appearance, appropriately enough as a scholar and a gentleman.

The publication by Bridges of Gerard Manley Hopkins' poems in 1918, long after Hopkins' death, was another significant factor in developing the new poetic style. Hopkins' experiments with words and rhythms, his attempts to forge language to a more direct and explosive conveyance of meaning than the usual nineteenth-century modes allowed, the intense individuality of his poems and their air of being shaped to contain unique experience, and perhaps most of all the way the meanings of his words and phrases did not work outward to the building up of a generalised emotion but inward, to build up a complex pattern of meaning within the poem—all this attracted the admiring attention of the younger poets. Eliot admired but was not radically influenced: he had already gone too far along his own road. But the poets who began to write in the late nineteen-twenties and thirties saw both Hopkins and Eliot as their masters, as well as the metaphysicals, the Jacobean dramatists (whose poetic idiom had influenced Eliot), the French Symbolists and ironists, Wilfred Owen, John Skelton, with his rough, jogging metre, and the popular singers of the English music-hall.

That the metaphysical poets and the English music-hall should both figure among the influences on modern poetry reflects the emphasis on irony, on the development of simultaneous meanings, on the deliberate counterpointing of the colloquial and the formal, that are part of the modern poet's refusal of solemnity. The reintroduction of wit into serious poetry not only meant the revival of the pun as a serious poetic device, after its banishment from all but comic poetry for over two centuries, but also the realisation that truly serious art transcends the vulgar and the everyday by including it, not by rejecting it. The narrowing of attitude to a feverish insistence on the importance of high seriousness of what is treated, the treatment of the poet himself as the single-minded hero of his poems, came to be regarded as a characteristic romantic error, making the poet vulnerable to parody and constricting the exploratory range of the imagination. Love between the sexes, for example, treated in a spirit of Platonic elevation by Shelley, is more likely to be seen by the modern poet as both physical and spiritual, both comic and profound, both ridiculous and splendid, and he will seek for devices to convey both attitudes simultaneously. One of the reasons why Shelley has been the chief whipping-boy of modern anti-romantic criticism has been because he makes himself the naïve hero of his own poems and never insures himself, as it were, against the operation of the comic spirit. It is only by including the comic spirit, the modern poet would maintain, that its mocking element can be exorcised from serious poetry.

## Questions

*Questions to test your understanding of the subject or content*

1. What are the elements of the new 'poetic style' described in the second paragraph above?
2. How did the English music-hall influence modern poetry?
3. Show how Robert Bridges represented a new kind of conservatism.

*Questions to test your ability to draw conclusions or recognise the use of evidence*

1. How does the writer develop his point that a different kind of conservatism was represented by Robert Bridges?
2. What arguments does the writer use in the third paragraph to support his assertion that paradox is considered a criterion of good poetry?
3. In your opinion, what is the writer's purpose in writing the passage?

*Questions to test your assessment of the style or language used*

1. Write a note on the tone and linguistic style of the passage.
2. What techniques does the writer use in the first paragraph to argue his point?
3. Discuss any feature of the writer's style that impressed you.

EXPLORATIONS 2

*Questions to test your imaginative response to the passage*

1. What impression do you form of the writer from the passage? Justify your answer by referring to the passage.
2. Show how the statement made in the last sentence—'It is only by including the comic spirit that its mocking element can be exorcised from serious poetry'—is effective in the context of this passage.
3. Show how, in your opinion, Hopkins influenced modern poetry.

## PASSAGE 2

Sectarian practices among the young are too often approached from a perspective of high moralism—the reverse side of which is usually a deficit model of working-class culture. Orange popular culture certainly fosters hostility towards Catholics. But it does more than this. It also functions to encourage localistic loyalties, to provide public and recreational space for the marginalised young, and to furnish the symbolic resources for the construction by the young of a distinctively Protestant sense of community for an increasingly beleaguered people. That is why the young cling to its arcane representations.

The central role that the marginalised young now play in the maintenance and renewal of loyalist tradition has been explored previously. Hopefully, we are now in a better position to understand their resistance to the existing cultural studies programmes.

Teachers and youth workers have up to now experienced a real dilemma when faced with the expressed sectarian views of their charges. Should they attempt to banish all political argument and sectarian display from the hallowed walls of the educational precincts? Or have they a social responsibility to engage with populist sectarianism and encourage a critical dialogue between and within the two 'traditions', with all their strengths and shibboleths? Should school provide a neutral and civilised haven from the political rancour and sectarian bigotry of the adult world by banishing all political discussion? Or should young people be facilitated by the educational system in their critical interrogation of their culture of origin?

In effect, the prohibition of 'political talk' and evasion of controversial issues are the preferred strategies of most schools and youth clubs when confronted with the popular cultural 'politics' of their pupils or members. After all, argue many teachers, the adult world has not shown itself to be particularly adept at addressing or living with the very real political and cultural differences that separate the two communities. Why, these teachers ask, should the school or youth club be expected to tackle the apparently irresolvable? Education cannot compensate for society; is it not better that schools and youth clubs function as the 'time out' of Ulster society?

The problem remains of how to critically engage with sectarian behaviour and attitudes that are enshrined in popular cultural forms, like the marching bands, and that daily threaten the order of the classroom and the playground. The problem remains that for most of these people, the official culture of tolerance stops at the classroom door.

Teachers and youth workers know well enough that their pupils invest much time and energy in the sub-culture arena. Despite this, any mention of politics and identity is generally banned from the school and youth club. In English schools, with their multi-racial and multi-national composition, silencing racist discourse in the classroom is entirely justifiable in order to marginalise racist elements and to show solidarity with black children who are at the receiving end of racist jibes. In Northern Ireland's already segregated schools, where people of the other religion are not usually present to be offended and where patterns of sectarian differentiation are more porous and have less ideological underpinning, I suspect that such a strategy of control is not justified.

Perhaps rather than demanding that young Protestants abandon overnight their popular cultural 'tradition' it might be more appropriate for educationalists to provide a learning context within which young Protestants have the opportunity to explore and question their own culture of tradition. History teaches us that Protestant experience in Ireland is more complex than most loyalists acknowledge. For instance, few young loyalists realise that the creation of the idea of an Irish nation and indeed of revolutionary republicanism was largely a 'Protestant' invention. In contemporary Ulster, history must be redeemed. As we have seen, the young people are implicitly engaged in an exploration of the limits and contradictions of their parental culture through their sub-culture activity. Can critical youth work practice assist them in making this exploration a more reflexive process?

## Questions

*Questions to test your understanding of the content or subject of this passage*

1. What are the important questions that the writer examines in this passage?
2. How does the writer view the role of teachers and youth workers in the Northern Ireland situation? Support your answer by reference to the passage.

3. What dilemmas face those who have to deal with racism and its effects?

*Questions to test your ability to follow a line of argument or to draw conclusions*

1. What solutions does the writer propose to facilitate teachers and youth workers?
2. In your opinion, does the writer present a balanced view of the problems faced by teachers in dealing with young people who are involved in sectarian issues?
3. Show how the writer structures his argument in the passage.

*Questions to test your analysis of the style*

1. Identify the type of writing in the passage, and comment on its effectiveness in serving the writer's purpose.
2. Would you agree that this passage is well argued? Give reasons for your answer.
3. What techniques does the writer use in this passage to gain our attention?

*Questions to test your imaginative response to the passage:*

1. Comment on the effectiveness of the writer's use of comparison and contrast in the passage.
2. Would you agree with the writer's vision of youth as represented here?
3. What do you understand by the writer's statement that 'schools and youth clubs should function as the "time out" in Ulster society'?

## Methods of answering comprehension questions

1. Read first all the questions to be answered. Very often one question can throw light on another.
2. Divide your time between the questions, making sure to note the number of marks allotted to each question.
3. Read the passage through very carefully two or three times in order to understand fully the meaning of what is written. Don't worry about or waste time trying to unravel the meaning of difficult or awkward words: the main idea is to get a general idea or gist of the arguments in the passage.

4. It can often help to jot down a title or a heading in order to identify the main theme of the passage.
5. Start on the easiest questions first, and begin to work on a rough draft. Get down notes and ideas related to the question.
6. At Honours level, the questions in this section demand interpretation of material rather than explanation—for example, 'What evidence do you find in the passage to support the view that the writer has mixed feelings about the subject?' or 'The writer of this passage could hardly be described as a detached observer. Discuss this view, supporting your points by reference to the passage.' Both of these questions demand a clear understanding of the content of the passage and not merely a restatement of the ideas expressed.
7. Read the passage for each question. If four questions are asked, read it four times. Jot down ideas and points as you go along, all the time organising and forming a rough draft. Read the questions *carefully*. Note the difference between such terms as 'analyse', 'discuss', 'compare', 'contrast', 'criticise'. In a question such as 'Discuss how the language conveys the writer's argument,' not only must examples of where language reflects the argument be taken from the passage but you must also show the techniques used by the writer to forge their argument. In other words, you must be able to ask and answer the questions *what?* and *how?*
8. Write out your answers clearly, factually, and logically. Make your answers as crisp and clear as possible.
9. Use your own words where possible.
10. Keep control of the time: don't let it control you. Dedicate an equal amount of time to each question. Stop writing when your five or ten minutes are up. Leave a space if necessary and come back later if you can. The main thing is to tackle every question and every aspect of every question.
11. Don't waste time trying to puzzle out the answer to a difficult question. Leave it for later. Do the composition, and possibly the answer will come to you.
12. When reading back, read with a purpose. Check that you have answered the actual question. Is your answer logical, relevant, and orderly? Are the examples that are given relevant and useful?

A good Honours pupil must be able to ask and answer the following questions: Do the language, style and tone suit the subject? Do they advance the thought or, on the contrary, make the thought convoluted? Remember that the language and imagery should emphasise and express the subject, not conflict with it.

Know how to recognise the kind of tone, and know the reason why it is used. Know the relation between the tone and the subject. Know how to establish the logic of the argument (if any) in the piece of writing.

Know how to identify underlying attitudes, to 'read between the lines.' Know the writer's attitude to the subject in question. Know how to distinguish between a fact and an opinion.

Analyse whether the writer proves the point, and how. This can be done in several different ways: logically, with examples, by means of anecdotes, through facts, comparisons, contrasts, statistics, etc.

- How does each paragraph fit in to the scheme of the composition as a whole?
- Is the writer appealing to our emotions or to our intellect? Know how to discern what emotions dominate the writing.
- Does the nature of the subject justify the use of such emotions by the writer?
- How does the style help to further the writer's aims?
- Is the style uniform? Does it vary? Why?
- Is the diction simple? ornate? archaic?
- Discuss the writer's choice of words.
- What do the style, ideas and attitudes tell us about the writer?
- Do you find the arguments convincing? If so, why?

Look at the following passage for examples of some of these features.

With blithe lightness of mind, we assumed that the world was moving irrevocably beyond nationalism, beyond tribalism, beyond the provincial confines of the identities inscribed in our passports, towards a global market culture that was to be our new home. In retrospect, we were whistling in the dark. The repressed has returned, and its name is nationalism.

It takes two forms. One, which applies to most Western states, maintains that the nation should be composed of all those who subscribe to the nation's political creed, regardless of race, colour, creed, sex, or language. This is called civic nationalism, because it envisages the nation as a community of equal citizens, united in patriotic attachment to a shared set of political practices and values. It is necessarily democratic, since it vests sovereignty in all the people.

By contrast, ethnic nationalism claims that an individual's deepest attachments are inherited, not chosen. It is the national community that defines the individual, not the individuals who define the national community. As a result, it tends to be authoritarian, maintaining unity by force rather than by consent.

With the collapse of the Soviet empire and its satellites, none of the nationalities over which it had held sway had any experience of conciliating their disagreements by democratic discussion. Violence or force became their arbiter. Nationalist rhetoric swept through these regions like wildfire, because it provided warlords and gunmen with a vocabulary of opportunist self-justification. In the fear and panic that swept the ruins of the communist states, people began to ask: so who will protect me now? Ethnic nationalism provided an intuitive answer: trust those only of your own blood.

And so, in the name of nationalism, dozens of viable states have been shattered beyond repair. In the name of state-building, we have returned large portions of Europe to the pre-political chaos that existed before the emergence of the modern state.

Much of the former Yugoslavia is now ruled by warlords, figures who have not been seen in Europe for six hundred years. They appear wherever nation-states disintegrate: in Lebanon, Somalia, northern India, Armenia, Georgia, Ossetia, Cambodia. With their car phones, faxes, and exquisite personal weaponry, they look post-modern, but the reality is early mediaeval. Their vehicle of choice is a four-wheel drive Cherokee Chief, with a policeman's blue light to flash when speeding through a check-point. They pack a pistol, but they don't wave it about. They leave vulgar intimidation to the bodyguards in the back, the ones with shades, designer jeans, and Zastava machine-pistols. They themselves dress in the leather jackets, floral ties and pressed corduroy trousers favoured by German television producers. They bear no resemblance whatever to Rambo. The ones I met at the check-points on the roads of Croatia and Serbia were short, stubby men who in a former life had been small-time hoods, small-town policemen, or both. Spend a day with them, touring their world, and you'd hardly know that most of them are serial killers.

---

## Comment

The writer appeals to the reader's emotions by using phrases such as 'whistling in the dark,' 'you'd hardly know that most of them are serial killers,' 'the reality is early mediaeval.'

The writer makes use of contrast effectively to convey his message clearly. Look, for example, at the following sentence: 'With their car phones, faxes, and exquisite personal weaponry, they look post-modern, but the reality is early mediaeval.'

The writer strikes a deeply ironic note in the last paragraph, when he talks of a government of warlords who dress in expensive clothes but most of whom are serial killers. Examine this paragraph and consider how effectively it conveys the writer's message.

*Paragraph structure*: The second paragraph opens in a completely different manner from the first. In the first paragraph the writer uses a dramatic and emotive approach to introduce his theme; the second paragraph takes a more factual and logical approach to the subject.

## The summary

All aspects of the comprehension passages demand a clear understanding of what the writer is saying. Summary writing is an accurate measure of your ability to understand a particular passage and to communicate this understanding in writing. The art of writing a summary tests you in two ways: it tests your comprehension of what you read; it also tests your ability to express that understanding in writing.

### *Writing a summary*

In writing a summary, you are expected to retain the shape and emphasis of the original text, while reducing it substantially. You are required to work within a specified number of words; this limit is designed to test your ability to work within constraints.

You are not asked to comment or to add information from your own experience.

Summaries test your ability to

- condense material, choose the main points, and express these in appropriate language
- organise the content in a coherent and logical manner.

#### METHOD OF WRITING A SUMMARY

1. Read the passage through three or four times in order to grasp the gist or central points that are being made. At this stage, ask exactly

what the writer is saying. How is the writer expressing the content? It is important to understand not only what is being said but also how it is being said. In other words, examine the writer's purpose in the passage.
2. Don't worry or waste time trying to work out the meaning of difficult words. First get the main ideas of the passage into your head.
3. Notice how the passage is developed, the particular stages through which it moves. Note the number of paragraphs (if any) in the passage. Trace the different stages through which the writer develops their thoughts.
4. Work at getting the main points down in the form of a rough draft.
5. Read the passage through again, and compare it with your draft. Fill in any gaps or essential points that are missing.
6. Write out your summary in prose form as one main paragraph.
7. Count the number of words, and check them against what is asked.
8. Check that all the main points in the original passage are included in your draft.
9. Include all dates, numbers and statistics in the summary.
10. Leave out examples or illustrations, unless they are essential.
11. Write your summary in the past tense.
11. Direct quotations must be changed to indirect speech. '"I've been out all day," said John,' becomes 'John said he had been out all day.' Remember that the tense changes to the past here, and that you use the word 'that' when reporting speech. Commands and requests must be rephrased. 'The people said, "Stop the war"' becomes 'The people told them to stop the war.'
12. Make sure to write the number of words at the end of your summary.

## SAMPLE EXERCISE 1

Write a summary of about sixty words of the following article.

> With a thorough knowledge of your firm and its products, its markets and marketing policy, your previous advertising, the various constraints imposed, the competition you face, and changes in business background, you can now commence more positive action-problem analysis and determination of your specific advertising objective.
>
> Advertising is a means of achieving an objective. Your firm may have more than one reason for advertising and therefore need to run two or more

concurrent campaigns. The underlying purpose of these campaigns may also change from time to time with circumstances.

There is a remarkably wide range of reasons for advertising: one well-known analysis contains a check-list of fifty-two advertising tasks! Even the more fundamental reasons are, surprisingly enough, a blind spot to many advertising people, who are so engrossed in the detail of their work that they overlook the need to define clearly the basic purpose of their advertising. Many times, when you enquire about the objective of a proposed advertising campaign, you receive a surprised look and the answer, 'Why, it's to increase sales, of course'—as though you had asked a foolish question. But how are these increased sales to be achieved? 'Increased sales' is not a business objective but only an optimistic hope for the future. If these increased sales are in fact to be realised, then there must be a definite objective; for, as you will see later, this will affect the type of advertising campaign, the media used, and its creative content.

[Martin Davis, *The Effective Use of Advertising Media*]

Here is a sample summary:

Advertising is a means of achieving an objective. Your specific advertising objective can be determined by means of a greater knowledge of your firm and the competition you face. Many advertisers fail to define a clear purpose. To achieve increased sales, a definite objective must be organised that will affect the content and the media used in the advertising campaign. [60 words]

SAMPLE EXERCISE 2

Write a summary of the following article in about seventy words.

The Campbell-Bewley group has taken its first sip of the American coffee market, acquiring a Boston café company, Rebecca's Café.

Mr Patrick Campbell, the group's chairman, said yesterday that the decision to buy the company's eleven cafés and its corporate and contract catering business was part of a strategy to introduce the Bewley's brand name to the United States.

The Rebecca's Café name will be maintained, however, and, with the backing of Campbell-Bewley, the chain will expand. Its expected sales in 1997 are about $20 million (£13.5 million), according to Campbell-Bewley. The acquisition cost is believed to be in the region of £5 million.

## COMPREHENSION

'We have paid what we consider a good price for it but one that will give us a good return,' Mr Campbell said. He said Rebecca's had established its own reputation, despite aggressive competition from such chains as Starbuck's. 'We see this as a springboard for the American market. The first thing we need to do is get comfortable with Rebecca's. We would hope to open a Bewley's café within the Boston area this year,' he said.

Campbell-Bewley has been seeking an American foothold for the past two years, after establishing eight outlets in England in addition to its twenty-five in Ireland.

The president of Rebecca's Café, Bob Tyack, said that neither he nor his two partners had been seeking to sell the eleven-year-old company, but they had been approached by an investment banker. It had helped that his company's chief financial officer, Conor Creedon, from County Cork, was familiar with the Bewley name.

Because of its size, Rebecca's Café had been frustrated by the limited growth rate it could achieve, Mr Tyack added. It employs three hundred people in nine Boston locations and two locations in nearby Cambridge and Burlington.

[*Irish Times*, 29 August 1997]

Here is a sample summary:

> Bewley's group has acquired Rebecca's Café, a Boston café company. The name will remain the same. According to the chairman of Campbell-Bewley, expected sales in 1997 will be about $20 million. The acquisition cost is roughly £5 million. Campbell-Bewley has established eight outlets in England, as well as twenty-five in Ireland. Rebecca's Café had a limited growth rate because of its size. It employs three hundred people in nine Boston cafés. [74 words]

Check-list on writing summaries

1. Have you got the correct number of words?
2. Is the summary a connected and readable piece of prose?
3. Have you checked for any errors in punctuation, spelling, and grammar?

Common errors in comprehension answers

1. *Misunderstanding the content*: incorrect facts, or a lack of factual information.

2. *Misunderstanding the questions*: failure to distinguish between simple terms such as 'How does the writer reach the conclusion that ...?' and 'Why does the writer claim that ...?' In the first question you are asked about the *method*, the techniques used by the writer, while in the second you are asked for the *reason* underlying the writer's claim.
3. *Not giving reasons for answers* when asked to do so.
4. *Failure to analyse the effect and impact of examples.* Take, for example, a question such as 'Give two examples of the writer's use of effective argument, and justify your choice in each case.' Merely *quoting* two examples, without justifying or showing their use and effect in the passage, will result in a loss of marks.
5. *Badly structured answers*, where minor or irrelevant points are developed and the main point is ignored.
6. *Badly written answers*: answers with faulty grammar or punctuation and weak expression.
7. *Irrelevancies* and information that has no bearing on the question asked: not coming to grips with what is really asked in the question.

## CHARACTERISTICS OF WELL-WRITTEN ANSWERS

Any judgment on the quality of a particular prose style must take account of the purposes of the writer and whether the style used is adequate to those purposes.

1. There must be *a clear analysis and understanding of the content* in the passage.
2. The answers must *focus directly on the questions asked* and make detailed reference to the passage. This is particularly important when the question uses terms such as 'justify your answer' or 'refer to the passage.'
3. A good Honours pupil must be able to *grasp the writer's intention* in the passage and to follow their argument, weighing it up objectively all the time.
4. You must show *a basic knowledge of the fundamental elements of prose*, for example tone, structure, and kinds of sentences used. You must be able to discern why these features are used, and what part they play in communicating the theme.
5. Your answers should display *lucidity* or clarity of argument and expression: they should be written in clear, correct English, with good organisation of thought.

6. Answers must be *clear*, *logical*, *factual*, and *precise*. Avoid summaries of the passage, repetition, and padding: focus exactly on what is asked, and answer it as crisply and simply as possible, all the time referring to the passage itself.

## *Exercises*

1. Distinguish facts from opinions in the following statements.
   (a) Experts are worth listening to, because they have special knowledge.
   (b) A syllogism is an argument consisting of three propositions.
   (c) The research department is in no position to preach against overspending, since it exceeded the budget last month.
   (d) When an argument is reduced to three propositions you can detect whether it is valid or invalid.
   (e) The practice of using euphemisms in speech was more prevalent in the nineteenth century.
2. Distinguish opinion from evidence in the following passages:
   (a) Mother Teresa was one of the best-known and most-loved religious personalities in Christianity. Mother Teresa was well known in ireland, north and south, but in the early seventies her attempt to establish a mission in Belfast ran up against the hostility of the local church establishment.
   (b) Harryville, a small suburb of Ballymena, may become a watershed in the conflict in Northern Ireland. For the last three months loyalist thugs have waylaid local Catholics on their way to Mass at the weekend.
   (c) The French authorities have reacted cautiously to speculation that the bomb outrage in the Paris metro on Tuesday evening was the work of Algerian militants. It is a situation that France, with its large and increasingly restive North African population, is ill equipped to deal with.
   (d) There are cities in the world that are always hard to leave, and Prague is definitely one of them.
   (e) Camping in the desert is another invigorating change from ordinary life. The Wahiba Sands, a great sand sea inland from Oman's eastern coast, consists of wave after wave of precipitous ridges leading to moonscape plateaus.
3. Identify those of the following deductive arguments that are false. Give your reasons.

(a) All Europeans eat rice; John is a European; therefore John eats rice.
(b) All wise men are virtuous; Plato was a wise man; therefore Plato was virtuous.
(c) All birds have feathers; the sparrow is a bird; therefore the sparrow has feathers.
(d) All humans will die; Harry is a human; therefore Harry will die.

4. Identify the arguments in the following extract, and pick out the evidence to support them.

> For some time, those who deal with homelessness have been telling us that the problem is getting worse. They point to the scarcity of local authority housing, to the overcrowding of hostels and to rising rents in the private sector as factors that leave increasing numbers of people without a roof over their heads.
>
> More recent years have seen the appearance on the streets of young men and women wrapped in blankets and sleeping in doorways—images that many have thought belonged more properly to the England of Margaret Thatcher. Even the Simon Community has expressed surprise at the number of people it found sleeping rough in a one-week survey last December—and the public must surely be surprised at the proportion of teenagers, some very young, among that number.
>
> In a separate development, the Children's Court was told last week that one fourteen-year-old boy has been living on the streets for nearly a year. The court heard that he has a mental age of eight. He is now in the care of St Michael's Assessment and Remand Centre, pending another court appearance next week.

5. Identify what is opinion and what is fact in the following extract.

> Before despairing about the current crisis in the peace process and giving up on the IRA, it is worth remembering how hard that process inevitably is. It is an attempt to end a conflict. But conflicts normally end in one of two ways: victory or compromise. And neither of those endings is available in the story of the last thirty years. Nobody can win.
>
> For unionists, the desired outcome—a copperfastening of the United Kingdom *in saecula saeculorum*—is impossible, since that state is changing, whatever they do. For nationalists, the goal of a united Ireland is unreachable, because the population of the Republic is not willing to pay the price in economic costs, political instability, and possible civil war.

# Two
# ENGLISH GRAMMAR

The Leaving Certificate examination is a written one. While you may be able to *discuss* the texts with a great deal of depth and imaginative insight, if you cannot *write* about them in the same way, the whole experience has been useless.

As we have seen earlier, people become proficient writers *through writing*, and there is no substitute for this. But the mechanics of writing—including spelling, grammar, and punctuation—are an essential foundation of clear expression, and without a thorough knowledge of them you will never be able to write properly, not even the simplest text.

## WHAT IS GRAMMAR?

Strictly speaking, 'grammar' means the analysis and description of the conventions of a language, though it is loosely used to mean these conventions themselves. These are widely accepted practices that have developed over a very long time among the speakers of a language; and to depart significantly from them will mark you (rightly or wrongly) as an uneducated or ignorant person whose views will not be taken seriously. Nevertheless, these conventions are valid only as long as the majority of speakers and writers accept them. There are no 'rules' of grammar other than these accepted conventions.

Remember too that the study of the conventions of English is only a means to an end. Languages are flexible: they constantly change and adapt to the needs of the societies that speak them. However, *a thorough knowledge of current best practice* lies at the foundation of all study that leads to good, clear, striking expression in English. A detailed knowledge of these conventions helps us to choose and use the forms of language best suited to each particular situation.

Grammar teaches us how to look at words in sentences in an analytical way. It shows us how to discover what each word is doing, and how sentences are built.

## SYNTAX

Words do not operate on their own but in groups. We combine words to form sentences; groups of sentences can be combined in paragraphs. A group of paragraphs can constitute a composition or an article, a thesis, or the chapter of a book.

Each word in a sentence carries out a particular function. It is important to know the particular function of each word before embarking on the job of structuring a sentence. This relationship between words in a sentence, the arrangement of words to create meaning, is called **syntax**. Our ability to communicate effectively in language depends on our capacity to manage words—to establish a meaningful relationship between words and to arrange particular words in a suitable context.

## PARTS OF SPEECH

Words must be examined in the context of a particular sentence to find out what function they carry out. A word can perform one function in one sentence and a different function in another.

> She was the driving force in the business.
> He must have been driving too fast.
>
> They live beside a park.
> She decided to park the car at the door.
>
> If you fall off that wall you'll break your leg!
> The teacher gave us a break between the classes.

Examine the words in the following sentence:

> The man and his dog walked slowly.

'the': this is a type of word that makes something *definite*.
'man': this type of word *identifies* a thing (in this case a person).
'and': this word connects the two things referred to ('man' and 'dog').
'his': this type of word tells us *whose* dog is referred to.

'dog': this word also identifies a thing.
'walked': this type of word tells us what the person *did*; it functions as an 'action word'.
'slowly': this type of word describes the *manner* in which an action was performed.

When we classify words in this way according to their function in a sentence, we describe them as belonging to particular **parts of speech**. There are eight principal parts of speech:

- noun
- verb
- pronoun
- adjective
- adverb
- preposition
- conjunction
- interjection.

## *Nouns*

A noun identifies something that is referred to: 'man', 'dog', 'Ireland', 'loneliness'. A group of words can also function as a noun; this is called a **noun phrase**: 'Leaving Certificate', 'Dublin Fire Brigade'.
There are four kinds of nouns:

- common nouns
- proper nouns
- abstract nouns
- collective nouns.

### COMMON NOUNS

These nouns identify the *kind of thing* something is, and generally (though not always) refer to something concrete or physical: 'bicycle', 'father', 'pencil', 'sister', 'woman'.

## PROPER NOUNS

These nouns identify a *specific* person, place, or thing: 'John', 'Siobhán', 'Blackrock', 'Canada'. While a common noun identifies or *characterises* a thing, a proper noun *names* it. Proper nouns are distinguished in writing by beginning with a capital letter.

## ABSTRACT NOUNS

These nouns refer to non-material or intangible states or things: 'courage', 'heroism', 'joy', 'grief', 'health', 'happiness'.

## COLLECTIVE NOUNS

These nouns refer to groups of people or collections of things: 'crew', 'fleet', 'team', 'crowd', 'horde'.

## THE PLURAL OF NOUNS

The plural of nouns is normally made by adding *s* to the singular:

> day—days
> month—months
> mother—mothers

Nouns endding in *o*, and nouns ending in a *sibilant* (*s*, *x*, or *z*), usually add *es* in the plural:

> potato—potatoes        success—successes
> tomato—tomatoes        box—boxes
> hero—heroes            fizz—fizzes

Nouns ending in *y* preceded by a consonant drop the *y* and add *ies*:

> baby—babies
> country—countries
> fly—flies

But proper nouns just add *s*:

> There are two Marys in my class.

With a few exceptions, English nouns of foreign origin form the plural according to the normal conventions of English:

    appendix—appendixes
    dogma—dogmas
    formula—formulas
    genius—geniuses
    index—indexes

## Verbs

A verb is a word that describes an action (including the action of being): the function of the verb is to tell us what the subject *does* or *is* in the particular sentence.

Examine the action in the following sentences in order to find the verbs:

    Can you wait three minutes?
    He did not see the man.
    They are going to Italy.

### VOICES OF VERBS

A verb has two voices: active and passive. The **active voice** indicates that the subject of the verb acts; the **passive voice** shows that the subject of the verb is acted upon.

    The Government planned a campaign.
    A campaign was planned by the Government.

In the first sentence, the subject—the Government—carries out the action. In the second sentence, the subject is *acted upon*: it undergoes the action.

Here are some more examples of the passive voice:

    The pupils <u>were delighted</u> with their results.
    Lithuania <u>was overwhelmed</u> with the result of the election.
    The satellite <u>will be seen</u> at midnight.

## TENSES OF VERBS

'Tense' means 'time'. The tense of a verb indicates whether the action takes place in the present, the past, or the future.

> I write every day [**present tense**].
> I wrote letters yesterday [**past tense**].
> I will write a chapter tomorrow [**future tense**].

**Continuous tenses** show that an action is, was or will be continuing. They are formed by combining the **present participle** of the verb—the form that ends in *ing* ('going', 'eating', 'sleeping', etc.)—with the verb 'be'.

> I am writing every day.
> I was writing letters yesterday.
> I will be writing a chapter tomorrow.

## MOODS OF VERBS

A verb can have four **moods**:

- indicative
- imperative
- subjunctive
- infinitive.

A verb in the **indicative mood** simply states a fact, or asks a question.

> She broke the vase.
> Has she broken the vase?

A verb in the **imperative mood** expresses a command or a request.

> Don't do that!
> Please put out the light.

The **subjunctive mood** expresses a wish, a supposition, or a doubt. It is not much used in present-day English, except in very formal constructions.

> If he <u>were</u> twenty years younger he would make a marvellous actor.
> If I <u>were</u> you I would not accept that part.
> It is very important that he <u>give</u> the right answer.

The ***infinitive mood*** expresses a general statement, with no reference to a subject of its own.

> To <u>serve</u> on a jury is a privilege.
> I must <u>go</u> and <u>meet</u> my sister at the airport.

# Pronouns

A pronoun is a word used in place of a noun—generally to avoid repeating the noun itself. It carries out the same function as a noun: it identifies a person or thing.

> Mary and Jim have moved house, and <u>they</u> are now very happy.
> The thief tried to escape from the gardaí, but <u>they</u> saw him.
> Bring in your boots and put <u>them</u> away.

There are a number of different kinds of pronoun. Here are the most common kinds.

### PERSONAL PRONOUNS

'I', 'you', 'he', 'she', 'we', 'you', 'they' (subject); 'me', 'you', 'him', 'her', 'us', 'you', 'them' (object).

### POSSESSIVE PRONOUNS

These are personal pronouns that indicate possession: 'mine', 'yours', 'his', 'hers', 'ours', 'yours', 'theirs'.

### DEMONSTRATIVE PRONOUNS

These point out or identify the thing or person they refer to: 'this', 'that', 'these', 'those'.

### INTERROGATIVE PRONOUNS

These are used in asking question: 'who?' 'which?' 'what?' 'where?'

## RELATIVE PRONOUNS

These are linking or introducing words: 'who', 'that', 'which'.
'That' and 'which' are used to relate to things; 'who' relates to people.

The clause following a relative pronoun is called a **relative clause**. There are two types of relative clause—**defining** and **non-defining**—and it is essential that you understand the difference between them.

> The dancers who have worked abroad should get a visa immediately.
> The dancers, who have worked abroad, should get a visa immediately.

The subordinate clause in the first sentence is *defining*—that is to say, its purpose is to define the subject of the sentence. (Which dancers should get a visa? The ones who worked abroad.) *A defining clause is not separated from the rest of the sentence by commas.*

The relative clause in the second sentence is *non-defining*. We are presumed to know already what dancers are being referred to; in this sentence the clause 'who have worked abroad' is an additional piece of information added by way of parenthesis. *A non-defining clause is separated from the rest of the sentence by commas.*

When a relative clause refers to things rather than to people, we use 'that' or 'which' instead of 'who'. In addition to the distinction made by the use of commas, 'that' is used with defining clauses and 'which' is used with non-defining clauses.

> It was philosophy that caused him most trouble.
> This is the house that is for sale.
> This is Tom's house, which is for sale.

## *Adjectives*

An adjective is a word that modifies the meaning of a noun. There are five different kinds of adjectives:

- descriptive adjectives
- possessive adjectives
- demonstrative adjectives
- relative adjectives
- interrogative adjectives.

The definite article ('the') and the indefinite article ('a', 'an') can be thought of also as special kinds of adjectives.

## DESCRIPTIVE ADJECTIVES

These qualify the noun by describing some quality or attribute attached to the person or thing denoted by the noun: 'a blue table', 'twinkling eyes', 'golden stars', 'a pale face'.

## POSSESSIVE ADJECTIVES

Possessive adjectives (not to be confused with *possessive pronouns*) always qualify a noun. They tell us who the owner of the object is: 'my pen', 'her house', 'their books', 'our caravan'.

## DEMONSTRATIVE ADJECTIVES

These point out things, just like demonstrative pronouns: 'that question', 'those melons', 'these books'.

## RELATIVE ADJECTIVES

These are the words 'what', 'which' and 'that' when they are used to introduce relative clauses:

> You can take what money you can find.
> I don't know which book you prefer.
> You can have that one over there.

## INTERROGATIVE ADJECTIVES

These are 'which', 'what' and 'whose' when they introduce questions.

> Which car will I take?
> What alternatives are there?
> Whose results are these?

## DEGREES OF COMPARISON

Adjectives can have three degrees of comparison:

- positive
- comparative
- superlative.

The **positive degree** is the ordinary form of the adjective: 'dark', 'high', 'industrious'. The **comparative degree** makes a comparison with something else: 'darker', 'higher', 'more industrious'. The **superlative degree** marks the greatest comparison possible: 'darkest, 'highest', 'most industrious'.

The comparative degree is usually formed by adding *er* to the positive degree or basic form, while the superlative degree adds *est*. Adjectives of three or more syllables form their comparative and superlative by putting the word 'more' and 'most', respectively, before the positive degree.

> interesting—more interesting—most interesting
> frightening—more frightening—most frightening

Here are some irregular adjectives:

> bad—worse—worst
> far—further—furthest
> good—better—best
> little—less—least
> many—more—most
> much—more—most

## *Adverbs*

Just as an adjective modifies or limits a noun, so an adverb modifies or limits a verb. It can also modify an adjective, or another adverb.

Many adverbs are formed by adding *ly* to an adjective: 'unique—uniquely', 'short—shortly', 'happy—happily'.

> He got an exceptionally good result in his examination.
> [The adverb 'exceptionally' modifies the adjective 'good'.]
> They left late. [The adverb 'late' modifies the verb 'left'.]
> Those plants are almost fresh.
> [The adverb 'almost' modifies the adjective 'fresh'.]
> She drove so fast that they nearly crashed.
> [The adverb 'so' modifies the adverb 'fast'.]

Adverbs may be classified as

- simple
- interrogative
- relative.

## SIMPLE ADVERBS

These indicate *manner, degree, time,* or *place.*

> April came in <u>swiftly</u>. [manner]
> The coach arrived <u>late</u>. [time]
> The pilot landed <u>there</u>. [place]
> The weather was <u>extremely</u> close. [degree]

## INTERROGATIVE ADVERBS

These are the words 'how', 'where' and 'why' when used to introduce questions.

> How did she go?
> Where is she going?
> Why did she do that?

## RELATIVE ADVERBS

These are like relative pronouns, because they function as linking words.

> She visited Stratford, <u>where</u> Shakespeare was born.
> Spring is the season <u>when</u> plants begin to blossom.

Remember that 'good' is an adjective, while 'well' is an adverb.

> She has good skills.
> He is doing it well.

# *Prepositions*

Prepositions are words that identify the relative position of something: 'on', 'under', 'over', 'beside', 'with', etc. They relate one word—either a noun or a pronoun—to another word.

> She wrote to me <u>from</u> France.
> He booked a room <u>at</u> the hotel.
> The garden is full <u>of</u> roses.

There is no basis for the assertion that a sentence should not end with a preposition.

That is the garden we sat in.
This is the pen he invariably wrote with.

## *Conjunctions*

A conjunction is a *joining* word: it links words or clauses together.

> The family went to Canada <u>and</u> they will not return.
> I have sent them a letter, <u>but</u> I have received no reply.

## SENTENCES, CLAUSES, AND PHRASES

## *Sentences*

A sentence is a group of words that makes complete sense; it is an independent statement and does not need other words to complete its meaning. Each sentence starts with a capital letter and ends with a full stop.

Sentences can be analysed according to

- their purpose
- their syntax
- their form.

According to its purpose or mood, a sentence may be

—**declarative:** this type of sentence is a statement or assertion: 'All men are mortal.' 'Blades are sharp.'
—**interrogative:** this type of sentence asks a question
—**imperative:** this type of sentence makes a command: 'Stop that shouting.' 'Slow down, please.' 'Close the door.' 'Stop talking.' The imperative form is also used in making a request or an exhortation: 'Please turn the television off.' 'I beg you to tell him.'
—**exclamatory:** this type of sentence expresses surprise, shock, etc.

> What a dreadful day!
> How can you say that!
> What an awful dress!

## TYPES OF SENTENCE

According to their syntax, sentences may be

- simple
- compound
- complex.

According to their form, sentences may be

- periodic
- loose
- balanced
- inverted
- antithetical.

### *Simple sentence*

This type of sentence is made up of one subject, one verb, and one object.

>The boy read the book.

### *Compound sentence*

A compound sentence is made up of two simple sentences connected by means of a conjunction.

>They returned in the afternoon, and they ate their dinner.

### *Complex sentence*

This type of sentence consists of a simple sentence followed by one or two qualifying clauses. Complex sentences can be used to refine or qualify a writer's thoughts.

>There was an air of tension about the man, which was unusual, as he had always been a person of absolute serenity.

### *Periodic sentence*

In this type of sentence, the main idea comes at the end.

>The parade was spectacular, and it attracted thousands.
>Professors of poetry, apologists for it, practitioners of it—all sooner or later are tempted to show how poetry's existence as a form of art relates to our existence as citizens of society.

*Loose sentence*

In this type of sentence the main point comes at the beginning.

> The modern city is impersonal and anonymous, with endless suburban houses, spreading continuously.

> The south-west endured torrential rainfall, with a month's rain falling in hours, leaving burst river banks and flooded homes in its wake.

*Balanced sentence*

This type of sentence has a similarity of thought, or an equal weight of thought, and a similarity of structure.

> Christ is offered all the kingdoms of the Earth if he will fall down and worship Satan: that is to say, he is offered power to achieve certain objectives, but not those he has in view.

> There are three points of view from which a writer can be considered: he may be considered as a storyteller, as a teacher, and as an enchanter.

*Inverted sentence*

In this type of sentence the subject is placed at the end, or perhaps in the middle. This gives the sentence strength and can create a dramatic effect.

> Of all my books, that one on horses was my favourite.

*Antithetical sentence*

An antithetical sentence or statement (from 'antithesis') is similar to a balanced sentence, except that the balance is made up of opposing ideas.

> The king was an unruly tyrant, while his subjects were docile and obedient.

> The teacher was conscientious and diligent, while the pupils were idle and undisciplined.

## *Clauses*

A clause is a sequence of words that contains a subject and a verb but is not a sentence.

A clause can be either dependent or independent. An ***independent clause*** or main clause is a finished statement: it stands on its own and makes complete sense. It is the main part of a complex sentence. A ***subordinate clause*** or dependent clause is not a sentence: it does not express a finished thought.

Here are some examples of independent clauses and subordinate clauses.

> The board of directors have mooted the idea [independent clause] of opening a factory in the region [subordinate clause].
>
> When we arrived at the old house [subordinate clause] it was deserted [independent clause], except for the butler [subordinate clause].
>
> You should finish that composition now [independent clause], unless you really want to be in trouble [subordinate clause].

## *Phrases*

A phrase is any sequence of words other than a clause; it generally does not contain a verb.

## *Co-ordination*

Co-ordination governs all writing. It is the scaffolding on which sentences, paragraphs and compositions are built. There must be co-ordination in a sentence, in a paragraph, and in a composition.

### CO-ORDINATING CONJUNCTIONS

There are seven co-ordinating conjunctions: 'and', 'but', 'yet', 'for', so', 'or', 'nor'. These are used to link ideas of equal value or to add ideas together.
  'And' indicates addition.

> He went to Dublin and then saw his mother.
> She wrote a letter and made a phone call.

  'But' and 'yet' indicate opposition or contrast.

> He got the job, but he discovered he hated it.
> She enjoyed the match, yet it rained all the time.

'For' indicates the cause of an effect.

> Charlie had to type the whole composition again, for his computer had erased the original.

'So' introduces the effect after the cause.

> She never came in on time or did her work properly, so she has no-one to blame but herself.

'Or' indicates alternatives.

> To be or not to be: that is the question.

'Nor' indicates negative addition.

> They could find no fault in the system, nor did any signs appear on the surface.

Occasionally starting a sentence with one of these conjunctions can make an impact on the reader.

### SUBORDINATING CONJUNCTIONS

Subordination is the relation between ideas that are unequal in rank. It compels otherwise isolated ideas to interact and thereby to show their dominant or submissive positions in the sentence.

> Because she is sick, he is not working.
> Although they write often, they don't know each other well.
> He reads so that he can converse with her.
> He visits her frequently, although she lives far away.

Conjunctions such as 'because,' 'although,' 'when' and 'where' may introduce elements of time, cause, purpose or condition into a sentence. In other words, these conjunctions can illustrate and define the hierarchy of a sentence by showing the *when, how* and *if* of an idea.

## PUNCTUATION

Punctuation is a vital element in clear writing—and the most neglected. Accurate punctuation is essential in conveying the meaning of a sentence.

Up to the end of the nineteenth century, punctuation was 'oratorical', based on the idea that its function was to indicate pauses in speech.

Nowadays it is accepted that the role of punctuation is to reveal the *structure* of a sentence—although this is also reflected in speech.

## The full stop

The full stop (technically called 'full point') marks the end of a sentence. If the sentence is a question, however, you use a question mark instead; if the sentence is an exclamation, use an exclamation mark!

The full stop is also used after abbreviations—

> Co. [County]; Nov. [November]—

but is not required when the abbreviation includes the last letter of the word:

> Dr; Mr; Ltd;

nor with groups of initials:

> UNICEF; RTE; PhD.

## The comma

The comma has a number of different uses. The principal ones are as follows.

A comma is used to separate independent clauses, i.e. those in which the subject is named:

> The abbey was situated beside the river, and the grounds were extensive.

but not when the second clause shares the first subject:

> The abbey was situated beside the river and had extensive grounds.

A comma is used to separate a *series* of terms.

> He took with him his hunting tackle, gun, leather belt, arrows, and flask.

The same applies to a series of clauses:

> She got off the bus, crossed the road, looked swiftly behind her, and walked across to Main Street.

The last comma in a series should be dropped when any *following* terms or clause *qualify the whole series*.

> She speaks English, Irish, and French.

but

> English, Irish and French are the languages she speaks.

A comma is used to mark off a *parenthesis* (a non-essential element or afterthought) in a sentence.

> This device, constructed last year, works very well.

Note that parentheses or dashes can also be used for the same purpose, depending on the degree of separation of the parenthesis and the emphasis you wish to give it.

> This device (constructed last year) works very well.
> This device—constructed last year—works very well.

A comma is used to mark off phrases or words in apposition.

> Séamus Heaney, the Irish writer, won the Nobel Prize.

A comma is used to mark off the name of a person addressed.

> Milton, thou shouldst be living at this hour.
> Mary, come over here.
> Come over here, Mary.

A comma is used to mark off a *non-defining relative clause* (see above under 'Relative pronouns', page 84).

> The dancers, who have worked abroad, should get a visa immediately.

Commas are used in introducing direct speech, and following it.

> Then she said, 'I know.'
> 'I've known about it for some time,' he replied.

## **The semi-colon**

A semi-colon creates a greater degree of separation between clauses than a comma.

> I knew he would fail; and he did.
> I've neither father nor mother; I'm poor and of a serious disposition; I'm not pretty.

Semi-colons are used especially to separate clauses that themselves contain commas.

> I studied maths, science, and engineering; I've worked as a fitter, an engineer, a shop assistant, and a salesman; and I've lived in Greece, Turkey, and Spain.

Note that when a semi-colon is used, a conjunction is not required between clauses, whereas it is essential with clauses separated by a comma. In fact you will notice that careful writers often use a semi-colon deliberately instead of the conjunction 'and' (or sometimes 'but') as an alternative to the rather limp effect of linking them with 'and'.

> The company will expand its operations to the Netherlands next year; this venture will increase employment by 50 per cent.

## *The colon*

A colon is used to introduce a significant point or conclusion.

> Only one person could possibly have stolen the money: the foreman.

Similarly it is used to introduce a list.

> Here's what you must bring: your train fare, a waterproof coat, a change of shoes, a packed lunch, and a notebook.

A colon is used before a clause that amplifies, justifies or explains what went before.

> Languages are flexible: they constantly change and adapt.

A colon is also used (instead of a comma) to introduce direct speech if you are not using one of the conventional expressions such as 'he said'.

> The manager then announced: 'Here follows the report of the committee …'

## *The question mark*

A question mark is used after every *direct* question.

> Would you like some tea?
> What day is this?

It is not used in reported speech:

> She asked me if I would like some tea.
> He asked me what day it was.

Nor is it used in *rhetorical questions* (questions to which an answer is not required or expected); these usually have an exclamation mark instead.

## The exclamation mark

An exclamation mark is used to identify exclamations and interjections.

> I'm awfully cold!
> How insufferable!
> What a piece of work is man!

An exclamation mark is also generally used instead of a question mark after *rhetorical questions*, i.e. those to which you do not really expect an answer.

> Do you expect me to go up in that thing!

Exclamation marks are mainly used in dialogue and in informal writing. They can be used (carefully and sparingly) in imaginative writing, such as compositions; they are almost never used in formal writing, such as letters or memos.

## The apostrophe

The *possessive case* is normally marked by the addition of an apostrophe and s.

> the girl's hat
> the boy's coat
> the mother's job

Indefinite pronouns use the apostrophe and s to show possession in the normal way.

> one's rights
> somebody else's car

To plural nouns ending in *s*, an apostrophe on its own is added.

a girls' school
the pupils' hostel
the eagles' nest

An apostrophe is also used to show the omission of letters.

Don't do that.
He won't be there.
He hasn't come back yet.
It's hard to tell.

Remember that **it's** is a contraction of 'it is,' while **its** is a possessive adjective.

The cat is licking its fur.
The world is using up its resources.

*Never add an apostrophe to a possessive adjective or possessive pronoun.*

That house is theirs [*not* their's].
That phone is ours.
Those records are hers.

## The hyphen

A hyphen is used to create compound words, including compound adjectives.

father-in-law
down-and-out
flat-footed
state-sponsored
a well-meaning intervention
a French-speaking Canadian

A hyphen is also used to join certain prefixes and suffixes to a word.

pro-Irish
anti-war
north-bound

## *The dash*

A dash creates an abrubt *separation* within a sentence, such as a parenthesis or afterthought.

> Mortgage rates are lower this year—and that's definite.

As we have already seen, commas can also be used to mark a parenthesis, though in a gentler way. One marked off by dashes usually represents a more abrupt break in the sentence.

> Those pupils who have passed—and they are few enough—have gone on to university.
>
> People who knew her—and who in the town did not know her?—respected her highly.

A dash can also be used to add a summing-up statement after a series.

> Money, power, fame—these were the goals of her life.

## *Quotation marks*

Quotation marks—"like this"—are used to mark direct quotations or the actual words that have been spoken. (Sometimes 'single quotation marks' are used instead, as in this book.)

> As Hamlet said, 'To be or not to be: that is the question.'
> She said, 'Let me know tomorrow about that matter.'

Quotation marks are also used to clarify a word or term that should stand apart.

> When you click on 'File', a menu will drop down.
> Please send an application form to everyone who chose 'very interested'.

## *Parentheses*

These are used to mark off a strong parenthesis or afterthought.

> Hamlet's antic disposition (erected as a defence mechanism) enabled him to cope with the events that ensued.

Campaigning for next week's devolution in Scotland and Wales (but not next week's voting) was postponed.

## SOME CONFUSING WORDS

### Agree with, agree to

To agree *with* means to approve of a suggestion or a proposed action.

>I don't agree with the Government's policy on tax.

To agree *to* means to give your consent to something.

>She was forced to agree to the plans for the extension.

### Between, among

The word 'between' can refer to more than two things, just like the word 'among'.

>The three pupils collected over a hundred bags between them.

'Among' always relates a person or thing to more than two things.

>A village among the hills.
>A cat among the pigeons.

### Both, either, each

'Both' means one *and* the other; it takes a plural verb.

>Both sides of the stream were covered in slime.

'Either' means *any one* of two; it takes a singular verb. 'Each' means the same as 'both'; but it takes a singular verb.

>If either of you cares to call, I'll be in this evening.
>There was a pillar on each [*not* 'either'] side of the gate.

### Compare with, compare to

To compare something *with* something is to invite the reader to contrast them, to consider all the points of resemblance and difference between them.

>His marks are surprisingly good, compared with last year's.

To compare something *to* something is to suggest that they are similar.

>Her work has been compared to that of George Eliot.
>Shall I compare thee to a summer's day?

## *Consists of, consists in*

'Consist of' refers to what something is made of.

>The drink consists of water with a little flavouring added.

'Consist in' means to have as its essential element.

>Courage consists in overcoming one's fears.

## *Different*

'Different' should be followed by 'from', not 'to' or 'than'.

>The bread is different from what it used to be.
>The exam system is no different from what it was last year.

## *Every day, everyday*

'Everyday' (one word) is an adjective; 'every day' (two words) is an adverbial phrase.

>everyday conversation
>an everyday occurrence
>He comes to the office every day.

'Sometime' (one word) is also an adjective, meaning 'former'; 'some time' (two words) is an adverbial phrase.

>John O'Brien, sometime mayor of Wexford, was the guest of honour.
>The bus eventually arrived some time later.

All other compounds of 'any', 'every' and 'some' with 'day' and 'time' are adverbial phrases, consisting of two separate words.

Remember that 'every' takes a singular verb.

>Every one of the boys is sick.

## *He, she, they*

The English language has always used the plural pronouns—'they', 'them', 'their', and 'theirs'—as a convenient way of referring to a person of either sex, or where the sex of the person is not known. With the emphasis now placed on avoiding discrimination in language, this natural practice has undergone a revival. Some people assert that this is 'ungrammatical', that these pronouns can only be used in the plural and that we must specify 'he or she', 'his or her', every time. This assertion is contradicted both by the spoken language and by the masters of English prose of all centuries.

## Like, as

'Like' may be used as a noun or an adjective but *never* as a conjunction.

> Fiona came in and looked like she couldn't wait to tell us something. ✗
> I felt like I was turning into a psychiatrist. ✗
> It was like she was in a trance. ✗
> Do it like I told you. ✗
> Please leave the room like you found it. ✗

These sentences are unacceptable, because 'like' is being used as a conjunction. It should be replaced in each case with 'as'.

'Like' can be used as a noun—

> I never saw his like

or as a verb—

> I like the theatre

or as an adjective—

> in like manner.

## Little, few

Both these words denote scarcity or lack of something and have almost the force of a negative.

> There is little hope of fine weather.
> Few examples have been seen there.

'A little' is used before uncountable nouns.

> a little time
> a little rest

'Few' is used before the *plural* of countable nouns.

> There were few tennis players on the court.
> Few women read those magazines.

## Many, much

'Many' is used before the plural of countable nouns.

> He didn't make many mistakes.

'Much' is used before uncountable nouns.

> We haven't much milk.

## Neither

'Neither' means not one *and* not the other. It takes an affirmative singular verb.

> Neither of them smokes.
> Neither of them takes sugar.

## One another, each other

Both these expressions can be used about two or more things, but 'one another' is frequently used when there are more than two.

## Only

The word 'only' should be placed directly before what you want to emphasise.

> I only bought a tennis racket. [All I did was buy a tennis racket.]
> I bought only a tennis racket. [I bought only a tennis racket and nothing else.]

## Some, any

Each of these words can be a pronoun or an adjective. Both mean a certain number or amount. 'Some' is used with affirmative sentences, or offers or requests.

> Would you like some coffee?
> They took some money.

'Any' is used in negative sentences.

>I haven't any meat.
>She hasn't any money left.
>They haven't any things to sell.

### *Who, which, that*

These are all *relative pronouns*. 'Who' is used only of people. 'That' and 'which' are used of things, 'that' in *defining* relative clauses and 'which' in *non-defining* relative clauses (see page 84).

## COMMON WRITING ERRORS

### *Non-parallel structure*

This means breaking the pattern of a series by introducing a different part of speech.

>My uncle enjoys tennis, swimming, and to water-ski. ✗

In this series, two nouns are followed by a verb in the infinitive.

>It is important to get good marks as well as having fun. ✗

In this sentence the series consists of an infinitive followed by a present participle.

>She asked me whether I could do shorthand and my office experience. ✗

In this sentence an attempt is made to create a parallel series, but although both items are governed by 'she asked me', the first is an adverbial clause (*'whether* I could …') and the second is a noun phrase ('my office experience').

Here are corrected versions:

>My uncle enjoys tennis, swimming, and water-skiing.

>It is important to get good marks as well as to have fun.

>She asked me whether I could do shorthand and what office experience I had.

## *Ambiguity*

Another common error is ambiguity, or the use of confusing words and statements. Ambiguity can be 'lexical': that is to say, a word can have more than one meaning in the context. 'She cannot bear children' can mean either that she cannot have children or that she cannot tolerate children.

'The man in the black coat took the picture' could mean that he stole the picture or that he simply took away the picture after buying it, or it could mean that he took a photograph.

Ambiguity is most often caused by inaccurate (or missing) punctuation.

> The fire was started by local children and their parents called the Fire Brigade. ✗

> In considering the art of teaching the first requirement is the teaching process itself the skill of passing on to the pupil the benefit of the teacher's own experience. ✗

Correct punctuation will clarify such sentences:

> The fire was started by local children, and their parents called the Fire Brigade.

> In considering the art of teaching, the first requirement is the teaching process itself: the skill of passing on to the pupil the benefit of the teacher's own experience.

Another source of ambiguity is poor *reference*, the incorrect use of pronouns. It must be clear which noun a pronoun refers to.

> Siobhán came top in English and went on to study journalism, encouraged by her family all the time. It's paying off now, because her career as a journalist is well under way. ✗

It is not clear from this sentence what exactly is paying off, her grade in English or the encouragement from her family. The pronoun 'it' in the second sentence does not relate clearly to any noun in the first sentence.

> Siobhán came top in English and went on to study journalism, encouraged by her family all the time. This good work is paying off now, because her career as a journalist is well under way.

## Sentence fragments

A sentence fragment is an incomplete statement, lacking some part of what makes a complete sentence.

> All too often the teacher considers himself a passer-on of information. A middleman between the recognised authorities and the pupils. A facilitator in the process of learning. The most important function of the teacher is making the pupil think.

The two middle elements (beginning 'A middleman ...' and 'A facilitator ...') are sentence fragments rather than full sentences: in this example they have no subject and no verb (though the subject 'the teacher' is implied).

Sentence fragments are acceptable in certain contexts—in conversation, for example, and as answers to questions—and can also be used effectively as a stylistic device. They are wrong only when the writer cannot tell the difference!

> The girl who lost her money. [sentence fragment]
> Feeling awful. [sentence fragment]
> I woke early. [sentence]
> A drugs crisis uncontained will surely grow and spread. [sentence]
> Many thanks for your invitation to lunch. [sentence fragment]

## Dangling participle

A sentence can begin with the *present participle* of a verb ('walking', 'talking', 'thinking', 'looking', etc.) if the main clause begins with the subject, thus telling us who was doing the walking, talking, etc. Otherwise the participle hangs in mid-air, often with incongruous results.

> Standing at the top of the road, the car was scarcely visible. ✗

It is not clear who exactly was standing—certainly not the car. Sentences like this must be rewritten to eliminate this ambiguity.

> Standing at the top of the road, we could scarcely see the car.

Analyse and correct the following sentences containing dangling participles:

> Coming down to breakfast, the aroma of the coffee could be smelt throughout the house.

Mowing the lawn, a new idea popped into the writer's head.

Cycling home from school, the cows looked peaceful in the light of the evening sun.

## Misplaced modifiers

Modifiers are adjectives and adverbs—words that alter the meaning of other words in a sentence. Modifiers must be placed as close as possible to the words they are intended to modify, otherwise they can distort the meaning of the sentence.

> The teacher kept the child who was troublesome in the corner. ✗

Was the child troublesome only when in the corner?

> The teacher kept the troublesome child in the corner.

Note the difference in meaning in these two sentences according to the placement of the modifier 'also':

> The Government also must have a definite policy on this problem. ['Also' qualifies 'the Government', meaning that the Government—in addition to some other body—must have such a policy.]

> The Government must also have a definite policy on this problem. ['Also' qualifies 'must', meaning that the Government must have a policy on this question—in addition to having something else.]

## Redundancy

Redundancies are expressions that repeat the same idea.

> each and every
> first and foremost
> fair, just, and equitable
> final outcome [the outcome]
> end result [the result]
> co-operate together
> deeds and actions

## Jargon and slang

Jargon is the inappropriate use of technical vocabulary—language from specialised areas of life such as science, technology, medicine, or the legal world. Jargon makes writing unclear and abstract. The best way to avoid jargon is to remember the rule, 'Write to communicate, not to impress.'

Slang—extremely informal language—is more suited to colloquial speech than to the written word. The use of slang gives a casual or informal tone to writing.

The particular purpose and context of the writing determine the suitability of such types of language. For example, slang may be appropriate in introducing dialogue into a composition; however, it would not suit the formal or discursive writing style.

## COMMON SPELLING ERRORS

Study and learn the correct spelling of the following words:

| | |
|---|---|
| acceptable | hypocrisy |
| accommodation | hypocrite |
| adolescence | immense |
| alliteration | ironically |
| argument | loose [adjective] |
| beginning | lose [verb] |
| benefit | metaphor |
| definite | originated |
| description | portrayed |
| descriptive | repetition |
| despise | repetitive |
| ecstatic | rhetorical |
| emphasis | sentence |
| emphasise | simile, similes |
| exaggeration | soliloquy, soliloquies |
| familiar | tragedy |
| fulfil | tragic |
| gullible | whereas |

EXPLORATIONS 2

## *Exercises*

EXERCISES ON SENTENCES

(Suggested answers on page 232.)

1. Identify the following sentences as *compound, simple, complex*, or *balanced*.
    (a) I spoke to the man who delivered the milk.
    (b) Aer Lingus has made substantial progress over the last couple of years.
    (c) These days food has little to do with hunger: it has more to do with life-style.
    (d) From that moment we have no compass to govern us; nor can we know distinctly to what port we steer.
    (e) The river was at some distance; where the ground began to slope, the lawn, properly speaking, ceased.
    (f) I have already referred to scientific research, which is an important part of the activities carried out in our institution.
    (g) We live in an age of anxiety.
    (h) Disappointed in ambition, I had recourse to love.
    (i) The politician in power is wedded to the status quo, while art is forever disrupting it.
    (j) Recreations are not education; accomplishments are not education.

2. Rewrite the following sentences to eliminate unnecessary repetition.
    (a) Pupils get bored easily in the summer holidays, so pupils should get summer jobs.
    (b) If you cannot see how serious this issue is, I'd seriously think you should consider retiring.
    (c) Life is at best a wonderful experience, but to experience life one must experience happiness and suffering.
    (d) The worst fear has to be the fear of failure, which is a tremendous fear.
    (e) This great story would darken anyone's mind and open anyone's eyes.
    (f) Big cities are overpopulated, overdiseased and so so dirty.
    (g) How can these people know any other way when there's nothing there to teach them another way of life!
    (h) What we've got here is failure: failure to relate, failure to see, failure to communicate—in short failure in life.

(i) Society today tends to accept these problems as everyday happenings and does not do everything it could to act as a bulwark against these problems.

**3.** Shorten and increase the vigour of the following sentences, and make any other corrections necessary.
 (a) I have nothing to offer but blood, toil, sweating, and crying.
 (b) The manager described the department's problems succinctly, clearly, and with candour.
 (c) Reviewing the records daily is as important as to collect accurate information.
 (d) Society has come to the conclusion that law-abiding citizens, who perhaps have a speeding fine at the top of their law-breaking activities, are the exception to the rule in modern society.
 (e) Charles Jarvis is an excellent lecturer, personable conversationalist, and he writes well also.
 (f) Sport has been alive in the world for as long as the history books can tell, and there is no sign of its death.
 (g) People who you might never expect to be interested in soccer could have been washed away by the sea of emotion that swept through Ireland when Ray Houghton scored in the one-nil victory over Italy.
 (h) Life, with its abundance of trials and tribulations, has dealt yet another obstacle that I must overcome, this takes the form of my parents, the bane of my life.
 (i) That night while I was cleaning my room I heard somebody roaring, so I looked out the window; it was the same man throwing stones at everything he saw and roaring at the same time and luckily no-one was outside.
 (j) The amount of young people devoting their lives to youth work and the work and effort that is put in is amazing.

**4.** Say whether the following groups of words are whole sentences or sentence fragments.
 (a) Although it rained.
 (b) On the way.
 (c) The apostrophe is also used to denote ownership or possession.
 (d) You can add the page to a particular folder.
 (e) Take a look around.
 (f) Happy surfing!

5. Rewrite the following sentences, making them more terse and concise.
   (a) Down through the years I have been graced in contact with a diverse and deep lagoon of people, from every possible race and creed.
   (b) Enclosed is a copy of last year's annual report for the fiscal year 1996.
   (c) It is my opinion that the co-operation shown by the employees and the co-operation shown by the management was responsible for last year's increase in sales.
   (d) At some point in time we must decide on whether or not we are going to build the new addition.
   (e) Beacuse all the data is not available, we will withhold making a decision until such time as all the data is accessible.
   (f) The power of love is all around and cannot be challenged by any other emotional or physical feeling.
   (g) The writer's purpose in writing this passage is to show that the people of society today are very careful to keep the status quo of this society.
   (h) The beeping of horns, the screech of brakes, the clatter of bags, briefcases, and boxes, the high-pitched chitter-chatter of people big and small whizzed by them as they made their way down O'Connell Street.
   (i) The writer's use of statistics, facts and references conveys a clear, persuasive tone.
   (j) There was a period of expansion in new areas and then more slowly until it reached a peak in 1998.

EXERCISES ON GRAMMAR

(Suggested answers on page 234.)

1. Pick out the nouns in each of the following sentences and say what kind they are.
   (a) Jane went to France with a group of pupils.
   (b) The women returned from Madrid in fear.
   (c) The team were praised for their courage.
   (d) Mrs Smith saw the crowd in Lisbon.
   (e) Charity is a strong virtue.

2. Rewrite the following sentences to eliminate all grammatical errors.
   (a) After researching the topic for five months my supervisor cancelled the project.
   (b) After being rejected by three companies my employment counsellor suggested I rewrite my CV.
   (c) To learn the technique thoroughly the first three exercises must be completed.
   (d) Joan is the cleverest of the two.
   (e) Entering the golf course the lightning struck.
   (f) Their is no hatred among Jack and Mary.
   (g) Each of the boys must wear their uniform.
   (h) Never before in our great history have we needed the art of conversation to grace our lives more than now.
   (i) Is anyone going to be their?
   (j) I cannot work like I used to.

3. Rewrite the following sentences and add apostrophes where necessary to show possession.
   (a) The towns main street is very narrow.
   (b) The boys ties are in a bad state.
   (c) After yesterdays events I feel very hopeful.
   (d) The typist finds Dr Thorntons letters very hard to understand.
   (e) Womens rights in this century have been a point of contention.

4. Rewrite the following sentences and add apostrophes where necessary to show where letters have been omitted.
   (a) Wouldnt it be marvellous to go!
   (b) Its not going to rain yet.
   (c) Youll find it in the press under the stairs.
   (d) Hurry up or well never get there on time.
   (e) I didnt say theyre mad.

5. Insert appropriate prepositions in the following sentences.
   (a) You will have to allow ... some extra expenses in college.
   (b) They carried ... their work in spite of the interruptions.
   (c) Watch ... the sign: I don't want to get lost.
   (d) Have you heard ... Nora ... her return?
   (e) She insisted ... reading the report.
   (f) I'll have to work harder ... it, and spend more time ... it.

6. Fill in the gaps with appropriate conjunctions.
   (a) Her cat is small ... wild.
   (b) She was treated with respect ... with fear.
   (c) The film was funny ... simple.
   (d) Did you take the train ... the bus?
   (e) The electrician turned the key ... the motor started.
   (f) The detectives searched the warehouse ... they did not find the file.

7. Correct any dangling participles and misplaced modifiers in the following sentences.
   (a) Working too hard and playing too little, my ulcer is acting up again.
   (b) Before leaving for Africa, a new visa will have to go into my passport.
   (c) Waving frantically, the taxi went right past me.
   (d) The manager spoke to the secretary with a harsh voice.
   (e) The new product was developed in two weeks, which doubled the company's gross sales.
   (f) The primary problem is the emphasis placed on satellite programmes, which are launched on boosters.
   (g) Based on her recent inspection of the plant, the safety director decided to revise the safety procedures.
   (h) The meat was tough, besides the pie being tasteless.
   (i) She arrived at the school in a flood of emotion and a Ford Capri.
   (j) He both adored biology and his French teacher.

8. Distinguish between the following pairs of words by using them in sentences.
   (a) accepted, excepted
   (b) lose, loose
   (c) practice, practise
   (d) principal, principle
   (e) prophecy, prophesy
   (f) stationery, stationary
   (g) thought, taught.

## EXERCISES ON CO-ORDINATING CONJUNCTIONS

1. Join the following sentences by using co-ordinating conjunctions to indicate the logical relationship between the two independent clauses.
   (a) Mark shouted out. Nobody heard him.

(b) He tried to swim to shore. His clothes dragged him down.
(c) John had a hard time. He wanted to leave the country.
(d) The teacher handed her a piece of paper. She began to write much better.
(e) The wind began to howl. The rain began to pour down.
(f) The Gardaí arrived in ten minutes. It was then too late.
(g) The sun shone on the house next door. It lit up the glasshouse plants.
(h) He did not wear an overcoat. He did not carry a briefcase.
(i) I felt very glad. My letter had been accepted by the company.
(j) The principal arrived late. The meeting was cancelled.
(k) The river was clear. The team had worked intensely.

2. Identify the methods of co-ordination in the following paragraph.

With some exceptions, most of those seeking the nomination from the main political parties will probably fail to enthuse the majority of voters. Some are well-established party political figures for whom the presidency might be seen as a kind of political consolation prize. Others are well regarded and respected within the party rooms, but their ability to inspire and captivate the public at large is, at best, uncertain. Yet there is a clear danger that the presidential election campaign will be fought out on familiar ground—on allegation and counter-allegation about the past—instead of being used to articulate a vision for the future.

3. Combine the following pairs of sentences to indicate relationships of time, condition, purpose, or cause. In each case show the meaning of the sentence arising from that particular subordination. Examine how subordination brings out ideas that are not present in the sentences as they stand in isolation.
   (a) The girl took a business studies course. The teacher assigned a term composition.
   (b) A woman is elected President. The country is excited over this.
   (c) She swallowed her tooth. Her sister screamed.
   (d) They ran a tourist business. It was on a small scale.
   (e) There must have been an accident. There was so much debris.
   (f) They had reached the outpost. They heard a scream.
   (g) She wanted to prove herself. Previously she had failed.
   (h) They sent birthday greetings. They had not been in contact for years.
   (i) The chairman resigned. The report was read.

## EXERCISES ON PUNCTUATION

Rewrite the following sentences, putting in the correct punctuation and making any other corrections necessary. (Suggested answers on page 236.)

(a) And now ladies and gentlemen we come to the most interesting exhibit of all.
(b) Your dinner is on the table she shouted all right he replied Im coming now.
(c) He entered the room locked the door took out his papers and seated himself at the desk.
(d) Faith family and football in that order are the most important things in my life but keeping the balance is not easy.
(e) Has she injured you he asked.
(f) Eat more meat otherwise you will regret it.
(g) He said Im going out now and I will be in by nine dont wait up for me.
(h) My younger brother who is a tax inspector knows all about this matter he will advise you best.
(i) Were waiting for the school bus said the children its late again weve made a terrible mistake to wait so long.

# Three
# THE ENGLISH COMPOSITION

## EFFECTIVE WRITING AND WHAT IT INVOLVES

The two basic aims of all writing are

  (a) to express your meaning clearly and
  (b) to persuade your reader to respond in the way you want.

Writing, as we have seen, is a skill, and therefore it improves with practice. The more you write, the better your writing turns out; the more you write, the more your expression improves.

Writing is a form of communication. Good, effective writing is crafted with a combination of skills and a vocabulary that is accessible to all.

Writing is a craft: it requires a lot of hard work and apprenticeship. Good writing demands a mastery of the basics. It is an exacting skill, which requires a great deal of application. Writing can be mastered, with effort and practice; it is essential to be systematic and patient in the process of writing.

Successful writing involves a number of elements. It means organising your content at the level of the paragraph and the complete text. It means selecting an appropriate style for your reader and mastering the conventions of spelling and punctuation, together with the ability to polish and revise what you have written.

All forms of communication must take into account the following elements:

  (a) a speaker or a writer;
  (b) an audience or a receiver—the person who is at the receiving end of the communication; and
  (c) the purpose of that communication—the reason behind or underlying the particular piece of writing: what particular context can this mode of communication fit into?

Before you start writing, it is important to ascertain these facts, because the language, style, tone, structure and form of the writing will depend on them.

When you are answering exam questions that involve the use of the written word, make sure you are communicating. Forget about the results or marks at the end.

Before you start writing, establish clearly what your purpose is, what your subject matter is, what type of person your reader is. This will determine the particular form of writing you will use, whether it is a letter, a report, or a short story.

Effective writing means that the contents are relevant and appropriate to the particular situation. The ability to set out the contents in a clear and structured sequence is one of the basic skills on which all effective writing depends.

For effective writing, bear in mind the following:

- purpose
- topic or subject
- context
- audience
- language or technique.

## Purpose

For your written communication to be effective, remember to keep your purpose in mind at all times. Ask yourself, 'Am I informing, or looking for information?'

## Topic or subject

Think about what exactly you are going to say. Stick to one topic when you are writing.

## Context

Understand the relevance of what you are writing and where it fits in to the social context. For example, is it a magazine, a newspaper, a newsletter?

A knowledge of the context will determine the particular form or structure your writing will take.

## *Audience*

Consider your audience. It is important to take into account who your reader is and what their expectations are when reading your material. What exactly is motivating them in the reading process? Is it information or entertainment?

What degree of language competence does the reader possess? In other words, how accessible is this writing for my reader?

## *Language or technique*

What type of language will I use? How effective is my expression, and is this expression clear?

Writing an article for a school magazine will involve a different approach and style from a letter of condolence, or a sales letter, or a list of instructions.

Remember always to keep in mind both the purpose and the audience of the particular piece of writing. The particular context, the genre and the audience addressed will determine the style and language used. Therefore, always consider the following four points before you start to write:

- subject matter
- reader
- form
- language.

Successful written communication can be achieved by asking yourself the following questions:

(1) What do I want to communicate?
(2) With whom am I communicating?
(3) How can I best communicate?

Some of the principal functions of writing can be:

- to inform the reader about some topic: this is called the *language of information*
- to evaluate some topic: also called discursive writing or the *language of argument*

- to persuade somebody of something: this is persuasive writing or the *language of persuasion*
- to tell a story, to narrate something: this is called narrative writing or the *language of narration*
- to express oneself imaginatively using words and images as the medium: this is called the *aesthetic use of language*
- to describe or to share some personal experience: this is known as *descriptive writing*.

So, once you have worked out exactly what you want to say, go on to see what form your writing will take. Will it be written as a debate, or a narrative, or a dialogue?

Decide what style you will use. This can be factual or descriptive or imaginative, or perhaps a mixture of styles.

## THE HALLMARKS OF A GOOD WRITER IN ENGLISH

A good writer must have the ability to write clear and correct English and to choose language that suits the context. Good English is the use of language that is appropriate to the situation, in which the expression used is concise and clear.

Good writers have mastered the art of vivid prose. They possess the ability to see the ordinary extraordinarily well.

The following features are the hallmarks of good writing:

1. Unity: unity of tense, unity of thought, and unity of mood.
2. An originality and depth in content. An original approach is a personal or individual attitude to the subject.
3. A clear, accurate diction and sentence structure.
4. An ability to construct good paragraphs that have unity, emphasis, and coherence.

An integral part of the writing process is revising your writing. This is an easy and effective way to improve the quality of what you have written. It helps you examine and make judgments about what you have written.

In revising, consider the following points:

1. Does it address its intended audience?
2. Has this writing made a point?
3. Does it achieve its purpose through effective organisation of material and adequate support?

## Check-list for Precision in Writing

1. Know your audience.
2. Aim directly at a specific subject with a particular purpose.
3. Use exact words. Your words should be precise, concise, and specific. Choose a simple word in preference to a complex or ambiguous word. Use nouns and verbs meaningful to the senses. Use words that are familiar and not specialised. Choose short expressions in favour of longer ones. The main question to consider in your choice of words is, What is the purpose of this word? What is the particular context in which it will be used? A sense of purpose and a sense of audience are the chief guidelines in your choice of words.
4. Give exact figures and not imprecise generalisations. 'European women are generally more fashion-conscious.' 'Adolescents are perturbed and anxious people.' 'The Irish are a dirty and untidy race.' These are all generalised statements.
5. Take the same care with punctuation as you do with your choice of words.
6. Check all facts.
7. Avoid ambiguity: be careful of dangling participles and ambiguous constructions.
8. Omit extraneous or irrelevant material.
9. Point out clearly important aspects of the subject. This can be done through good paragraph structure.

## Style

Style is presenting or expressing the subject matter in a way that is best suited to achieving the writer's aim. As Aristotle wrote, 'A good style must first of all be clear. It must not be mean, or above the dignity of the subject. It must be appropriate.'

A forcible or terse style is compact, neat, concise, and precise. No superfluous statements are made. Every idea is expressed with a crisp brevity. Forcible style has an arresting impact on the reader.

Good writing presupposes a consistent and clear style that is matched or suited to the subject matter.

*Style is the particular way in which writers express themselves. Style is not something that is added on to the writing.*

There are as many styles as there are personalities.

The two most important ways in which you can improve your style are by familiarising yourself with the written word through reading a wide range of books and by writing regularly and learning from your mistakes. Examine how words work and how they combine to form sentences and paragraphs.

Write in a way that draws the reader's attention to the sense and substance of the writing rather than to the mood and temper of the writer.

Always write in a way that comes naturally.

## Rules for a good style

**Know exactly what you want to say, then decide how to say it.** Always write to communicate, not to impress.

**Put statements in a positive form, and make your assertions definite.** It is better to express a negative point in positive terms: for example, say 'dishonest' instead of 'not honest', 'forgot' instead of 'did not remember'.

Also, by putting negative and positive in opposition you can achieve a stronger structure. Look, for example, at the following statements:

> not honesty but simple justice
> not young, not renewable, but man
> not that she loved tennis less but that she loved reading more

**Choose a specific and concrete word instead of a general or vague term.** Look at the following statements:

> An air of frustration dominated the woman's actions, which was strange, as she was usually of a peaceful nature.

Say instead:

> The woman who was usually serene was frustrated.

> The children professed great joy as they took hold of their reward. They laughed as they were handed the money.

**Use an active verb rather than a passive one.** An active verb is more direct and vigorous than the passive. Writing is more forcible when the active voice is used in a habitual manner.

> Deirdre broke the window

is more forceful than

> The window was broken by Deirdre.
>
> At dawn the chiming of the bell could be heard.—The bell's chime could be heard at dawn.
>
> The reason she left home was that her relationship with her family was strained.—A strained family relationship caused her to leave home.
>
> There was a large amount of rubbish lying all over the city.—Rubbish lay throughout the city.

Look at the difference between the following sentences.

> Analysis of the language programme, together with its far-reaching consequences, must be made before a decision can be taken.—We must analyse the language programme, together with its far-reaching consequences, before we can make a decision.

In the first sentence the passive voice is used. This can make a sentence longer and more complicated; but readers absorb active sentences more easily.

> A study of the various acidic solutions was made, and the results were published in the monthly report.—When they had studied the various acidic solutions, they published the results in the monthly report.

**Avoid repeating yourself in the same words.** Repetition is bad when it is accidental, sloppy, or the result of poor vocabulary. On the other hand, when it is used well it can be a simple and effective means of creating the desired impression.

> We moved mesmerised through the museum. The whipping-block. The endless lists of names. The terrible, terrible photographs full of blank, empty and hopeless eyes. We walked on. Speechless, we paused between the ruins of the barracks.

Here the combination of short, terse sentences (and sentence fragments) with repetition of words such as 'the' gives a vigorous effect to the writing.

**Express co-ordinate ideas in a similar form.** In other words, expressions that are similar in content and function should be outwardly similar.

Blessed are the poor in spirit; theirs is the kingdom of Heaven. Blessed are the peacemakers; for they shall be called the children of God.

**Vary the length and structure of your sentences.** Use exclamation marks: 'What a wonderful idea!' Use question marks: 'Where did you find that?'

**Every sentence must have a subject, a verb, and an object.**

Each of the mass media | has | a different organisational pattern.

subject    verb    object

**Place whatever words you want to make prominent at the end of the sentence.**

Since then, society has advanced in many ways, but it has hardly advanced in fortitude.

**Always consult a dictionary when you are not sure how to spell a word, or to check the meaning of a word.**

**Get used to writing and rewriting.** Do not overwrite or overstate. Avoid ornate prose. Avoid using too much dialogue in a composition, as it breaks up the continuity and flow of thought.

**Learn thoroughly the basic rules of punctuation**—when to use a comma, how to use quotation marks correctly, and so on.

**Make sure the transitions between sentences are clear.** The section on paragraphs (page 142) gives examples of transitions and how to use them.

## THE ENGLISH COMPOSITION

The new syllabus for the Leaving Certificate offers the possibility of writing in a variety of specific styles or genres.

These will include writing in the *language of argument*. Under this heading comes the discursive or debate-style argument.

The *language of persuasion* will enable you to master the conventions of persuasive writing, to construct a persuasive article or composition on some topic that you feel strongly about.

The *language of information* will offer the opoportunity to write reports, instructions, reviews, memos, letters, or newspaper articles.

## THE ENGLISH COMPOSITION

There will also be the opportunity to write in such genres as autobiography or fable, or in a descriptive style. This type of writing falls in the category of the *language of narration*.

For this reason the topics cover a wide variety of different writing genres and invite a variety of approaches.

The art of composition-writing can be mastered with effort and practice. The composition is an attempt to present a reasonable and logical interpretation of the topic chosen. If you mean to do this well it is a complete waste of time to write a composition 'off the top of your head' without any preparation. If the result is to be a good composition, then certain approaches, such as pre-composition writing and a knowledge of the use of words and sentences, are indispensable.

The first principle of composition is to foresee and determine the shape of what is to come, and then to pursue that shape.

The process of composition-writing is a matter of probing ahead and forecasting the general outline or direction of the content. A composition-writer must see or visualise the composition's conclusion before they write the composition itself.

Therefore, pre-composition writing is important in that it determines what direction the composition is taking and what conclusions will be reached.

The composition must have a beginning, a middle, and a conclusion. The opening of your composition states your case: it establishes your stance or your particular commitment to the topic. The middle justifies this stance; and the end reflects on the beginning and the middle.

The composition should be an individual response to the subject. Compositions require content and ideas, and, particularly with the discursive composition, you must not only show that you have formed opinions and assimilated ideas on certain topics but must be able to organise and apply these ideas and opinions in a logical and fluent manner. Regurgitating material or merely learning compositions off by heart can be easily detected and can result in a severe loss of marks.

There must be deep reflection and thought on the content or subject matter at the composition's centre, and not merely a striking and colourful array of words and descriptions. Description is important in composition-writing, but it is always only a means to an end, a way of communicating your ideas in a vivid way to the reader. Sometimes the tendency to display or show off information in a colourful and highly descriptive mode can be a cover for a failure to think a little more deeply on a particular subject.

The composition is not a matter of repeating all you know on the subject: it demands a personal response and interaction with the chosen topic. The composition (and this is particularly so with the more factual or argumentative style of composition) offers an opportunity to generate ideas, develop a critical judgment on topics, discriminate between different standards, and draw conclusions. All this is a sign of the ability to think in an organic and creative way; and all these capacities are required in the Leaving Certificate composition at Higher level.

## *Pre-writing activities*

Many different activities preceding the actual writing can provide a means of generating ideas and producing a written result. Some examples of these activities include:

- pre-composition writing
- free writing
- brainstorming
- clustering
- cubing
- outlines.

All of these are methods that will help you to improve and polish the whole process of writing.

### PRE-COMPOSITION WRITING

Pre-composition writing is an indispensable part of the process of composition-writing. Remember that a composition must always be written and rewritten. Compositions need to be revised, refined, and rewritten. *Never* hand up the first draft of your composition.

The information in your composition must be sifted, edited and rewritten in a logical and organised manner. For that reason the process of brainstorming, drawing up outlines and working on rough drafts is an indispensable part of pre-composition writing.

Use *writing* as a way of working out what you want to say; so start writing immediately. Pre-writing activities are a useful strategy for getting started on the writing process. All pre-writing activities are designed to generate ideas and provide a focus for writing, thus preparing for the finished product. They do not produce a finished work.

## FREE WRITING

This is particularly helpful as a warming-up process before the stage of formal writing. The main idea is to put pen to paper and to get going on the writing process immediately.

The purpose of this activity is simply to practise the skill of writing anything and in any order whatever. Simply write about anything you choose and in whatever way you like, not caring about punctuation, spelling, or structure. Write without stopping. Do not stop to plan, organise, or edit.

*Focused free writing* helps you to focus on a particular topic and write freely about it. Take a topic, such as 'sports' or 'women and politics', and simply write as much as you can about it.

It can help to set yourself a time limit for this activity. Give yourself ten minutes, and then focus on writing about the competitive element in sports today, for example.

## BRAINSTORMING

This is the process of throwing your imagination into high gear and trying to trigger off as many ideas as possible on a topic.

Trigger questions serve a useful function, as they can provide fuel for ideas. Questions such as *why? what? where? how?* and *when?* can generate many different ideas on a topic.

## CLUSTERING

Clustering of ideas can help to sift your thought and put priority on your content. It helps you to put the most important ideas first. It is the process of developing the relationship between ideas as you record them or jot them down.

Begin by writing your topic on a blank sheet. Draw a circle around it. Write down at random the main ideas around that topic.

Draw a circle around each main idea. Connect each main idea to the topic with a straight line.

Jot down other ideas about the main ideas. Connect them to the subordinate ideas with a line.

In this way you will cluster several ideas around the general topic. The clustering of ideas can help to generate a multitude of ideas that later on can be joined together and interwoven in order to write the composition.

## EXPLORATIONS 2

Here are some examples of the clustering of ideas on the following composition titles:

(a) Is censorship necessary?
(b) The power of the press
(c) Drama and education.

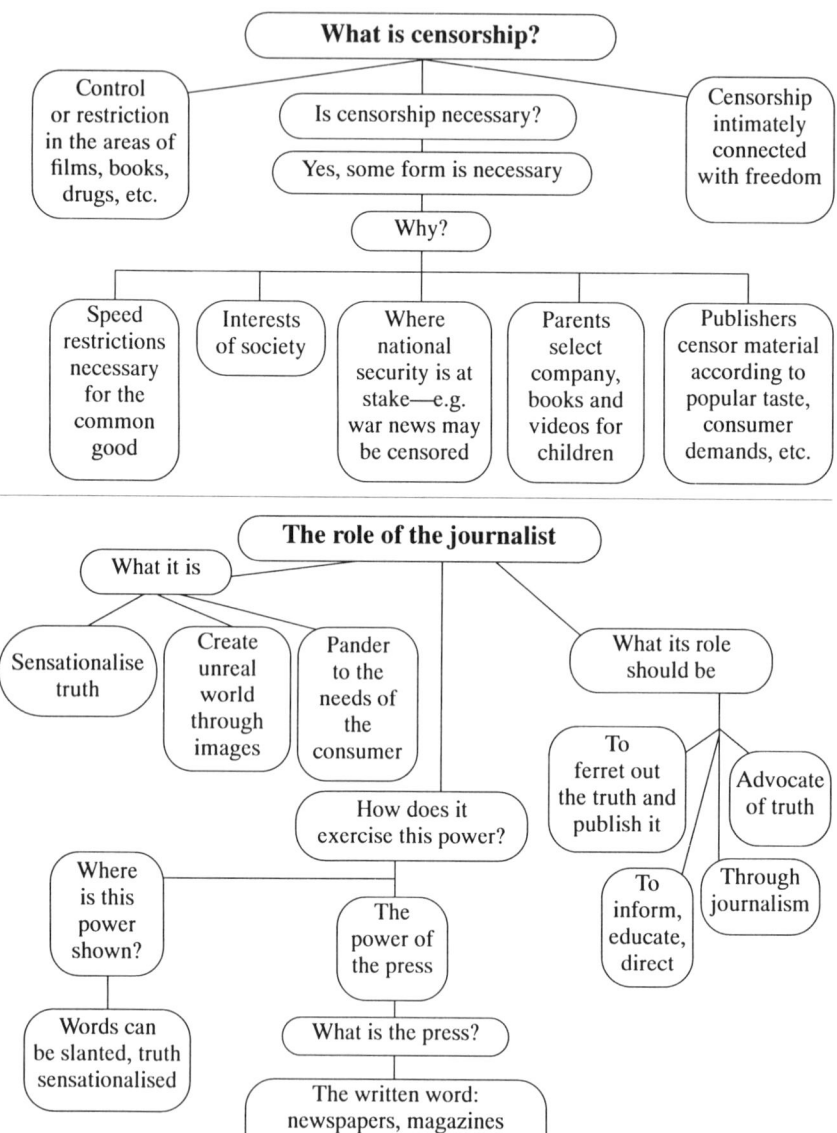

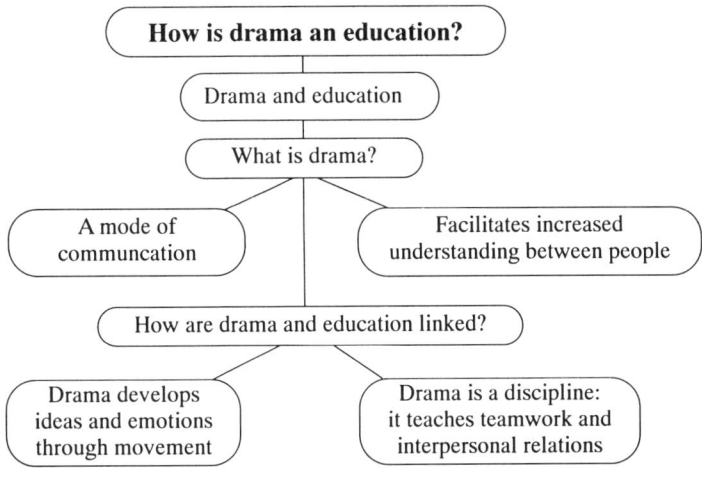

## CUBING

This is another pre-writing activity. Cubing means exploring a subject from six different angles: description, comparison, analysis, application, association, and persuasion.

Pick a topic, such as 'relationships', or 'sport', or 'religion'. Focus on the topic from these six aspects.

Start by describing it. For example, 'relationships': what exactly does the word 'relationships' mean? Describe the different kinds of relationships one can have in life. Compare relationships in the twentieth century with those in Shakespeare's time, for example.

Write on the application or value of relationships to society. Draw out an argument based on discussing relationships and how they affect the human personality.

## OUTLINES

Outlines are very helpful in planning the composition. An outline is a method of imagining the basic shape, order of sections and structure of argument in the composition. It forms the backbone of the composition.

In the process of constructing outlines, you are breaking the topic down into small stages. Each stage provides the scaffolding that will bring the composition one stage further. The outline is a means of getting organised and overcoming 'writer's block'.

Outlines have the following advantages:

1. The outline enables you to see the entire composition condensed into one page. It shows the main points, the supporting details, and the emphasis that should be assigned to each section.
2. A good outline will help establish coherence in your composition by showing the relationship between the main and subordinate points and between the subordinate points and the details that are introduced. It will give the reader a clear indication of the composition's central position and direction on the subject.
3. A good outline will establish the limits of the topic, the order of paragraphs, and the general direction of thought in the composition.

There has to be a certain flexibility in the approach to outlines, as all compositions do not demand meticulous outlines. However, to ensure clarity of thought and relevance, an outline of some type can be indispensable.

## Content

Check that all assertions made are supported by evidence. Your main stance or topic idea should be placed at the beginning of the composition.

## Direction of thought

Do the main divisions of your argument advance the central point? Have the main divisions got headings that show the direction of the argument?

## Structure of argument

Check the divisions and sub-divisions of the argument. Are they in proportion? Is there a proper and correct emphasis on central ideas? Are all details, examples and specific statements subordinated to general statements in the outline? Is there a good mixture of main ideas and subordinate points?

Does the outline give a sense of emphasis and an idea of the amount of space to be allotted to each section? Check for gaps or divisions of thought.

Outlines will help you to determine what your paragraphs are made up of and what ideas can be used in topic sentences. They will also help you to see what kind of transitions are needed in order to show a clear relationship between ideas. They help organise your thoughts and provide a direction for a flow of ideas in the composition.

Outlines can also help in overcoming exam paralysis. Staring at a blank page can be a daunting experience, and the outline can be a life-saver here.

Outlines also help you to structure and organise paragraphs. They help to refine your thoughts; they show what needs to be emphasised and what needs to be eliminated; they show where repetition occurs.

Many common errors can be eliminated by having a good outline, including

- gaps in the logical development of ideas
- excessive repetition
- the omission of central ideas and information
- going off the point
- insufficient evidence and examples.

As you divide your outline or plan into a series of sections or paragraphs, think carefully about the logical or rhetorical relationship between them. The section on paragraphing (page 142) deals with the different relationships between paragraphs in a composition and the relationships within paragraphs.

Here are some sample outlines on the following composition titles:

(a) Drama and education
(b) The power of the press
(c) Is censorship necessary?

## DRAMA AND EDUCATION
### Opening paragraph

Quotation:

> Life's but a walking shadow, a poor player
> That struts and frets his hour upon the stage,
> And then is heard no more. (Macbeth)

Discuss how, contrary to this quotation, drama is an art form that helps children grow as human beings and so helps to develop the whole person: body, mind, emotion, and spirit.

### Paragraph 2

Communication is at the essence of drama.
Drama is where people play or mimic human role models.
It increases understanding and depth in relationships.

### Paragraph 3

Acting necessitates teamwork.
Working with others develops the capacity to relate to others.

### Paragraph 4

Drama is a discipline: actors must stand still, know lines off by heart, move in a certain way, adapt to other viewpoints.

### Paragraph 5

Drama as education develops ideas and emotions through movement.
Example of theatre workshops, with children simulating real situations.

### Paragraph 6

Shows people how to think creatively, to use imagination and knowledge. This in turn increases potential to be creative and sensitive; it heightens powers of perception in the person.

### Concluding paragraph

Drama and education are interconnected.
Pupils are helped to become more lively, alert, self-confident.
Drama removes inhibitions, fosters spontaneity and creativity of approach; teaches how to work with and relate better to others.

## THE POWER OF THE PRESS
### Opening paragraph

Anecdotal opening on exposure of current political scandals.

### Paragraph 2

What is the nature of this power?
The power of the image and the written word—use of photography to slant truth—use of words to distort reality or to communicate the truth.

## Paragraph 3

How is this power shown?
Through propaganda—profit and commercial success a measure of the news and the mode in which it is presented.
Infringing on people's privacy, for example exposing the private affairs of people in public life.

## Paragraph 4

The role of the journalist today.
The difference between what it is and what it should be.
Examples from various sections of press—journals, gutter press, magazines, etc.

## Paragraph 5

How can this power be used to help society?
What happens when this power is abused?—corruption, lies, deceit, harassment of people. Examples from different areas: China, politics, lives of people who have been destroyed by media harassment.

## Concluding paragraph

Reference to anecdote in opening.
Discuss the power to influence for good and evil
—need to reassess its influence for good
—to educate and mould society
—need for truth in order to safeguard democracy
—need for role of press to be clearly defined and reassessed.

## IS CENSORSHIP NECESSARY?
### Opening paragraph

Answer the question in the title.
Yes, some form of censorship is necessary in certain areas of life.
Refer to mass murders, spate of violence, acts of terrorism sparking off need for certain censorship.

## Paragraph 2

The idea of freedom and how it is not an absolute.

Human freedom must be curtailed for the sake of the common good.
Examples:
—driving on certain parts of the road
—bus queues
—taxes, etc.

**Paragraph 3**

Discuss Bousset's remark on freedom: 'To be free is not to do everything one wants but to want everything one should want.'
Discuss how this involves the responsible exercise of freedom for society to function efficaciously.

**Paragraph 4**

Give examples of accepted censorship in certain areas, for example in wartime, news censored for the sake of security and diplomacy.
Health measures to protect people from disease, overuse of drugs, etc.
Publishers censor material according to public interest, taste, etc.
Parents protect children from dangers of bad company or from exposure to dangerous material on videos and television.

**Paragraph 5**

Discuss consequences of a lack of censorship:
—a purposelessness in the individual
—a certain reversion to the law of the jungle, as in the novel *Lord of the Flies*, where boys converted to barbarism when stripped of ordinary code of civilised values.

**Concluding paragraph**

Link a healthy attitude to censorship with the responsible use of freedom for the sake of the common good.

## *Problems and pitfalls in composition-writing*

1. **The wide choice of titles can be confusing.**
2. **Writer's block and exam paralysis.** The problem of knowing what exactly to write and overcoming writer's block or exam paralysis can be

very intimidating. Many pupils are overwhelmed by the process of starting an opening paragraph.
3. **Misinterpreting the title.** This can happen from reading the title carelessly. For example, if you are asked to write a composition on 'Killing time', you had better not start writing a composition on murder, unless you are sure that is what is meant: it is more likely to mean 'wasting time'. If you write before you think you are in danger of being penalised for irrelevance of content.
4. **Lack of unity or organisation of ideas.** This can occur when a composition is not planned properly. It is shown in obscure argument, woolly and incoherent thought, excessive repetition, and a general lack of direction in the composition.
5. **Content.** The content at Higher level must show a maturity of approach and good judgment. Poor content can be reflected in excessive repetition of ideas, digression of thought, or the introduction of irrelevant material.
6. **Repetition.** Do not repeat unnecessarily—but don't hesitate to repeat when repetition will increase clarity. A certain amount of repetition can be necessary in order to emphasise certain points. However, needless repetition can be the result of failure to plan a composition properly. Repeating the same word in sentences or the same sentences in paragraphs only weakens the basic structure of the composition.
7. **Faulty style.** Many marks are lost needlessly through carelessness in the mechanics of grammar, spelling, and handwriting, or through a sloppy and untidy style.
8. **Poor timing.** Time can be wasted in mulling over titles or in writing a draft. Give yourself the time required to plan the composition—neither to rush at it without a plan nor to spend too much time thinking about what to write.

OVERCOMING THESE PROBLEMS

1. **Identify your style early on**—whether it is descriptive, factual, or imaginative. The advice from your teacher can be invaluable here. Generally speaking, you will write best on a topic that you are interested in.
2. **Put pen to paper immediately.** Think first about exactly what you want to say; then go and say it in writing. Use writing as a means of working out what you want to say.

3. **Take account of every word** and the possibilities or connotations of each word.
4. **Begin by brainstorming the title.** Then proceed to draw up outlines.
5. **Pre-composition writing** (brainstorming the title and drafting an outline) will help you to draw out ideas on the subject. Think of suitable quotations, or any areas of literature (poetry, drama, fiction) that can be used to develop the content of your composition.
6. **Read your composition aloud if possible,** as it can alert you to unnecessary repetition. Check for repetition not only of words but also of ideas.
7. **Pay attention to detail,** in spelling, handwriting, and grammar. Correct all spelling errors, and check that every word you use is the right one.

## What examiners look for in the composition

1. **Understanding the issues of the question.** You need a good opening paragraph that focuses your stance and shows the direction your composition will take.
2. **Coherent argument.** Move from one point to another in a logical and coherent way. This is particularly important in the factual type of composition.
3. **Writing that is appropriate to the wording of the question.** Never reproduce in an examination a composition that you have learnt off by heart. You must frame the content according to the demands of the question.
4. **Originality.** Avoid writing the boring or stereotyped composition that lacks flair and originality. Use fresh language, and if possible adopt an original approach to the topic.

   Topics such as violence, war, sex, drugs, drunkenness and exam stress are now clichéd, and to get that better mark they should be avoided. However, if you must write on such a topic, write in an original way, or take a unique or more creative approach to the topic. Adopt a different slant on the topic, or use a variety of colourful phrases to offset the tedium that such themes can generate.

   Avoid at all costs writing pessimistic compositions. Many times a pessimistic approach only serves to frustrate your reader and may needlessly lose you marks.

Be careful in your choice of language. Avoid offensive and vulgar language. Such language contributes nothing to the skills of communication; it demeans yourself and your argument.
5. **Conclusion.** Draw together all you have said, and show what it adds up to.

## *Features of a good composition*

1. The content must have quality and an original approach. The ideas used should be relevant to the subject indicated by the title of the composition. At Honours level, a broad scope and richness in the ideas used is expected.
2. A composition must have good and if possible striking expression. Expression is good when a reader is able to understand and focus clearly on the content.
3. The composition should be structured correctly. Attention must be paid to the basic structure of paragraphs. There must be an overall unity within the composition: every paragraph must relate to the preceding one, and every paragraph must relate to the topic and develop it in some way. The overall impression of a composition at Honours level must be of a strong, co-ordinated unity. One technique that can be used to maintain unity and relevance within the composition is to stop after every paragraph and examine what exactly that paragraph says about the topic in question.
4. There must be correct sentence structure. A good composition should have a variety and strength in sentence structure in order to retain the reader's interest and to communicate the ideas effectively. The language, vocabulary and images used must be relevant and wide-ranging.
5. Care and attention must be paid to the basic mechanics of English: grammar, spelling, and punctuation.
6. The composition must have striking opening and concluding paragraphs, which serve the purpose of conveying an overall unity of impression to the composition.

## *Method of writing a composition*

1. Spend time choosing your topic, carefully working out the implications and meanings of each word in the title.

2. If the topic is not already in the form of a question, recast it in question form; this will help you to look at the topic from another angle or angles. Look at the following title, 'Blessed are the peacemakers', for example.

   —What is a peacemaker?
   —Why will peacemakers be blessed?

   Or in 'Things that still puzzle me':

   —What particular things in life puzzle me?
   —Why am I still puzzled or perplexed about such things?

   Be careful not to distort or misinterpret the title in this process.

3. Narrow the scope of your topic. For example, if you are writing on 'Freedom of the press', decide what areas of the press and what particular examples can be used. Naturally, broad, general examples can be given; but remember that you must treat the topic in some depth, and trying to tackle too many elements may leave the content vague and superficial.

4. Once you have chosen the topic, eliminate all other composition titles from your mind. Dedicate yourself fully to that particular title and try to soak yourself in the subject. Be decisive with regard to your topic. For example, in a composition on 'This technological age', you must decide what technology is in question and tackle the issues of positive and negative aspects of this development.

5. Use some of the pre-writing activities to start generating ideas on the topic. Brainstorm the composition's title. Jot down ideas as quickly as you can. Use trigger questions such as *how? why? where? what?* and *who?* on the title to trigger or spark off as many ideas on the subject as possible. You can then expand ideas into sentences, sentences into paragraphs, and paragraphs into longer sections.

**REMEMBER BEFORE YOU START TO WRITE:**

1. Rephrase the title as a question.
2. Brainstorm the topic by using trigger questions.
3. Cluster related ideas.
4. Select material for paragraphs.
5. Write out fully the topic sentence of each paragraph.

THE ENGLISH COMPOSITION

## HINTS ON COMPOSITION-WRITING

1. **Write every day.** Take a topic from a past Leaving Cert paper and write a paragraph to improve your expression.
2. **Develop the habit of free writing.** This involves writing whatever comes to your mind on any topic. Simply start writing freely; don't worry about grammar, style, or handwriting. The important thing is to put pen to paper in order to overcome writer's block.
3. **Gather information** by listening to good debate programmes on radio or television. Jot down new forms of expression. Read the work of professional writers in books or magazines, and write down phrases or new forms of expression in your notebook. Cultivate your own ideas on the topics raised and on current events: you can do this by having a notebook in which to collect ideas or to record interesting descriptions or anecdotes throughout the year.
4. **Use this material in class compositions** throughout the year.
5. **Understand your title fully.** Otherwise, don't write on it.
6. **Always draw up a rough draft first.** *Never write a composition 'off the top of your head.'*
7. **Avoid errors made in previous compositions** by learning spellings you have difficulty with and correcting grammatical mistakes.
8. **Identify your own strengths and weaknesses.** Work at eliminating the weaknesses and improving your strong points.
9. **Write simply.** Choose a simple word instead of a more obscure expression. Avoid using clichés, such as 'few and far between,' 'beat around the bush,' 'part and parcel'.
10. **Work at writing interesting opening paragraphs.**
11. **Draw up your own list of quotations and learn them off by heart.**
12. **Do not make general statements without supporting them with clear and specific examples.**

## CHECK-LIST FOR COMPOSITIONS

### Content

The ideas at Higher level should be rich and fertile. They should be capable of generating some insights as the composition progresses.

Ask yourself the following questions:

- Is the content original and lively?

- Is the main point of the composition clearly stated and developed sufficiently?
- Have I arrived at my own conclusions or relied too heavily on the interpretations of others?
- Does everything in the composition relate to the subject matter?
- Are there gaps in the logical development of ideas, or intrusions that sidetrack the argument?
- Have all general statements made been supported by evidence?
- Have I commented on the significance of quotations or examples in the development of my argument?
- In a factual or discursive composition, are the arguments presented in a balanced way?

*Organisation*

- Is the pattern of organisation clear? Does each paragraph fit in to the pattern of the composition and advance the main point?
- Are the points presented in the best order? Is there suitable emphasis and proper stress on the most important ideas?
- Are the transitions used effective? Do they unify a paragraph and provide a logical development of thought between each paragraph?
- Does the introduction give a clear idea of what the composition is about?
- Is the introduction or opening paragraph striking and relevant?
- Does the conclusion link to the opening and tie in all the ideas in an interesting way? Is the conclusion positive?
- Does the conclusion convey a strong unity of impression?

*Language*

- Is the language used clear and comprehensible?
- Are there words that are not properly defined?
- Have I avoided slang and jargon?
- Is the language concise, or are there redundancies, trite expressions, or awkward, difficult or ambiguous sentences?
- Are sentences varied in length and syntax?
- Have I used in every instance the exact word to convey the precise meaning?
- Is the same tone, the same level of language used throughout the whole composition?

- Have I avoided grammatical errors?
- Examine the use of verbs. Are the tenses inconsistent? Have I used the passive form instead of the active? Is there agreement between the subject and the verb? Have I used faulty co-ordination or subordination?
- Is the language economic and precise, appropriate to the subject being dealt with?

*Mechanics*

- Is the composition properly punctuated?
- Are all words correctly spelt?
- Are quotations introduced correctly?
- Is there unnecessary padding or needless repetition of ideas, words, or phrases?

## *The structure of a composition*

As we have seen, compositions are made up of ideas. These ideas are expressed in words, which join together to form sentences. Sentences combine to make up paragraphs.

The ability to master language demands a knowledge of how words work together to form sentences, and how sentences are combined to construct paragraphs.

## *Words*

Syntax is the particular order of words within a sentence. The syntax of a sentence can either

- balance the writer's arguments or
- disconcert the reader.

Words can be used figuratively, i.e. to appeal to the reader's senses and feelings. This is to use language in a vivid way.

Words used in this way can lend life and power to a piece of writing. Look at the following example of the vivid use of words.

---

The scullery was a mine of all the minerals of living. Here I discovered water—a very different element from the green, crawling scum that stank in the garden tub. You could pump it in pure blue gulps out of the ground, you could swing on the pump handle and it came out sparkling like liquid sky. And it broke and ran and shone on the tiled floor, or quivered in a jug, or weighted your clothes with cold. You could drink it, draw with it, froth it with soap, swim beetles across it, or fly it in bubbles in the air. You could put your head in it, and open your eyes, and see the sides of the bucket buckle, and hear your caught breadth roar, and work your mouth like fish, and smell the lime from the ground.

[Laurie Lee, *Cider with Rosie*]

It is important to be aware of the power of words and word connotations. The same word can have different meanings when used in different contexts. Look at the following statements:

(a) Intemperance is the failure to control or moderate one's actions.
(b) Intemperance cuts down youth in its vigour and manhood in its strength; it countenances the liar, respects the thief, and esteems the blasphemer. It violates obligation, reverences fraud, and honours infamy.

In the first sentence we are given a simple definition of the term 'intemperance', while the second example is an emotive or rhetorical commentary on the nature and effect of intemperance.

## WORDS AND HOW TO USE THEM

### Pictorial words

Here the word conveys a picture, image, or colour. A writer who uses pictorial words focuses on drawing a picture for the reader.

> The glow of a sinking sun was behind, and the mild glory of a rising moon was in front. All that remained of the day was a beamless amber light along the west, and I could see every blade of grass and every pebble on the path by the light of that splendid moon.

### Concrete words

A concrete word conveys a specific idea, a definite concept: 'heavy', 'round', 'fat', 'straight'.

## Abstract words

An abstract word denotes a quality or an intangible thing: 'kindness', 'loyalty', 'truth', 'goodness', 'beauty', etc. It is the opposite of a concrete word.

Many times the use of an abstract word can cloud the thought. For example, look at the following sentence.

> Goodness is an indispensable quality in the cultivation of virtue; however, magnanimity is often synonymous with strong character and greatness of soul.

The use of a number of abstract terms—such as 'indispensable quality', 'greatness of soul', 'magnanimity'—contributes to making the ideas in the sentence vague and obscure.

So the way words are used in writing, or the particular syntax of words, can affect the way in which something is communicated. The same word can be used to persuade and in another context to inform or to amuse.

Examine the different uses of the word 'expert' in the following sentences.

(a) The experts are always coming up with new ways to improve communication.
(b) He is an expert when it comes to dealing with computers.
(c) Experts were called in to dismantle the bomb.

In the first sentence the word 'expert' is used in a *persuasive* sense, the implication being that only the experts can show us new ways of communication. The second sentence uses the word 'expert' to make an *assumption* that in the field of technology this particular person is an expert. The third sentence simply *informs* the reader that experts dismantled the bomb.

## Sentences

Remember that a sentence is a group of words that makes complete sense.

### FEATURES OF A SENTENCE

1. **Sentences must be clear in their meaning.** The following sentence is an example of one that is ambiguous and confusing.

   > The bully attacked the schoolboy with an evil look in his eyes.

   Who exactly has the evil look, the bully or the schoolboy?

2. **Sentences must be correctly punctuated,** otherwise the meaning will be confusing. Look at the difference between these two sentences:

> Not everyone wants to go on a whistle-stop tour around India getting up at dawn packing and unpacking every day.

> Not everyone wants to go on a whistle-stop tour around India, getting up at dawn, packing and unpacking every day.

3. **Every sentence has a subject** (what the sentence is about) **and a predicate** or verb (what is said about the subject).

## *The paragraph*

A paragraph is very much like a miniature composition: it must have a beginning, a middle, and a satisfactory conclusion.

A paragraph is a cohesive unit, held together with appropriate links. It is the basic unit of any composition. All the paragraphs taken together in the composition are a vital demonstration of the thinking process by which the writer outlines and develops their attitude or stance on the particular topic. A problem may be discussed in one paragraph, and then the next paragraph will be structured or written in order to pursue a new direction or to take a further step in maintaining the argument.

Each new paragraph signals a shift in focus on the topic in question. This shift may be in time, or in place, or it could be one in approach to the subject being discussed. Each paragraph should begin with a sentence that relates what comes next to the last point you made and the structure of the composition as a whole.

A paragraph may underline a point made earlier by citing further evidence, or it may go on to explore the consequences of a point already made. It can also take a completely new direction towards the subject if necessary.

Each paragraph deals with one section of your subject and makes an important contribution to the subject as a whole. Paragraph follows paragraph in the order of presentation decided in your plan.

### THE LENGTH OF A PARAGRAPH

A paragraph can be of any length—a single sentence, or a passage of great duration.

Moderation is the main guide. A paragraph that is too long can be boring, difficult to follow, and a deterrent to the reader. The reader of a long paragraph will find it difficult to follow the flow of thought and the logical development of argument.

On the other hand, paragraphs that are too short can be frustrating and can easily go off the point. A very short paragraph can give the impression of haste, carelessness, or inadequate development of the content.

In general, good paragraph construction presupposes a good eye and a logical mind.

In writing, start a new paragraph simply by moving in a little from the margin (look at the paragraphs in this book), and start writing. Begin each paragraph with a sentence that shows clearly your main idea or one that helps the transition between the paragraph that went before. Make sure each paragraph develops the flow of thought in your composition.

There are three important things to bear in mind when constructing a paragraph:

1. Every paragraph must have a topic sentence or main idea.
2. Each paragraph must have a unity: all ideas (details, examples, explanations, statistics, etc.) must be related to the main point or topic sentence.
3. A paragraph must have coherence: the ideas must hang together so that the reader can move easily from one point to the next. Take special care with the last sentence of each paragraph, as it is the crucial springboard to the next paragraph.

## TOPIC SENTENCES

A topic sentence is the main sentence in the paragraph. All topic sentences relate directly to the central stance or main statement of the composition.

Topic sentences can come anywhere in the paragraph: they don't have to come at the beginning. Many times a writer can drive a point home much more forcibly by placing the topic sentence at the conclusion of the paragraph. Wherever you decide to place the topic sentence, remember there must be no doubt in your reader's mind about what exactly your topic sentence is.

Topic sentences are assertions: they need support, as many times they are not self-evident. The rest of the paragraph should be made up of examples or ideas that support the topic sentence.

## FEATURES OF A PARAGRAPH

The features of a paragraph include:

- unity
- emphasis
- coherence
- clarity.

'Paragraph unity' means that a paragraph has a topic sentence and that every other sentence in that paragraph has a direct bearing on that particular sentence. Anything that does not develop the main idea or topic sentence does not belong in the paragraph.

A lack of unity can occur in a paragraph when ideas or descriptions are introduced that interrupt the flow of thought in the paragraph and in the composition. It can also occur when a writer introduces digressions or irrelevant points into the paragraph. Two topic sentences in one paragraph can also cause disunity.

Placing the topic sentence at the beginning can help paragraph unity.

The following examples show lack of unity because of the introduction of one sentence. Can you identify the sentence that breaks the unity of the paragraph here?

> The teacher must be shown how best to prepare and present his lessons so that the pupils can most effectively learn. He must be made aware of the many teaching aids now available in addition to the blackboard. A teacher all too frequently considers himself a passer-on of information. He must learn to recognise the value of teaching aids in raising the standard of teaching efficiency.

The sentence 'A teacher all too frequently considers himself ...' is out of place in this paragraph.

Another example of disunity occurs from introducing unnecessary digressions or irrelevant points into the paragraph.

> It isn't only literature and history that should make us resistant to the suggestion that women have made no contribution to history. All around us, in public and private life, we find strong women, women who are as capable as any man, women who would know how to make their mark no matter what the social or economic situation in which they find themselves. War and politics have been the spheres in which there has generally been more male than female involve-

ment. The mothers and grandmothers of these women were surely of the same breed; it is an insult to their memory to think that they lived in complete and abject submission to men and never actualised any of their native talents.

The sentence 'War and politics have been the spheres ...' has nothing whatever to do with the paragraph, and so it breaks the unity in this paragraph.

## Emphasis

Emphasis begins at the stage of pre-composition writing. It means the correct positioning of all ideas, not only within a paragraph but within the composition in general. The general development of the composition will show that the more important ideas come first. The position of the topic sentence within the paragraph can contribute to this sense of emphasis.

A writer can choose to place the topic sentence first and expand the paragraph on the basis of this first sentence.

> A mocking-bird was singing near by. Its song was like pebbles being dropped one by one from a height into a pool of water. Then a quail began to call, using two soft guttural notes. Another quail answered, and the birds talked back and forth. Their call was not like the cheerful whistle of the Eastern bobwhite. It was full of melancholy and weariness, yet marvellously sweet. Still another quail joined the duet. This one called from near the centre of the field.

On the other hand, a writer may place the topic sentence at the conclusion of the paragraph in order to build up a climax or to sustain the reader's interest.

> For herself she lingered in the soundless saloon long after the fire had gone out. There was no danger of her feeling the cold; she was in a fever. She heard the small hours strike and then the great ones, but her vigil took no heed of time. Her mind, assailed by visions, was in a state of extraordinary activity, and her visions might as well come to her there, where she sat up to meet them, as on her pillow, to make a mockery of rest. As I have said, she believed she was not defiant, and what could be a better proof of it than that she could linger there half the night, trying to persuade herself that there was no reason why Pansy shouldn't be married as you would put a letter in the post office. When the clock struck four she got up; she was going to bed at last, for the lamp had long since gone out and the candles

burned down to their sockets. But even then she stopped in the middle of the room and stood there gazing at a remembered vision—that of her husband and Madame Merle unconsciously but familiarly associated.

[Henry James, *Portrait of a Lady*]

## Coherence or logical flow of thought

Writing is about joining. Everything in the sentence has to cohere or join. There must be co-ordination in a sentence, in a paragraph, and in a composition.

For a paragraph to read easily it must move smoothly from one idea to the next. It must have coherence: it must advance the main idea without losing the reader.

All the sentences in your paragraph must relate to one another. There must be a link between one sentence and another in such a way that your reader will see clearly a logical progress and development of thought from the whole paragraph.

The reader must be able to see how each sentence relates to the topic sentence and to the other sentences around it. Some devices for achieving coherence in a paragraph include using pronouns, repetition, and transitional phrases. Transitional phrases can join words in a sentence, sentences in a paragraph, and paragraphs in a composition. Transitions not only link ideas but also signal the logical relation between the ideas they link.

The use of linking or transitional devices can help to provide a relationship between the ideas and facts that they connect. In this way a smooth continuity is developed between the sentences.

Identify the linking devices in the following paragraphs and examine what the effect is in each case.

---

Generally, however, George Eliot's technique, in so far as it concerns the control of time, is successfully unobtrusive. This may be the reason why one of the most interesting and important aspects of *Adam Bede* has, so far as I am aware, gone completely unnoticed. This is the part George Eliot's control of time plays in the structure—moral and aesthetic—of the novel. The theme of the novel, with its strong sense of nemesis, its emphasis on consequences rather than motives, clearly demands the heavy stress on temporal evolution that is reflected in the precision of the narrative chronology. But a study of that chronology soon shows that the art of the novel, no less than its distinctive moral theme, is fundamentally concerned with temporal processes.

[W. Harvey, *The Art of George Eliot*]

---

Here, the repetition of the word 'this' reinforces the idea that her control of time in the novel is unobtrusive. The use of the word 'but' focuses on another aspect of the novel's concern with temporal processes.

Examine the linking devices in the following paragraph and their effect on the development of the thought.

---

Some acts are intrinsically evil, evil per se—always and everywhere, without exception: for example, the Pope cites homicide, genocide, abortion, slavery, prostitution, and trafficking in women and children. 'Though it is true that sometimes it is lawful to tolerate a lesser moral evil in order to avoid a greater evil or in order to promote a greater good, it is never lawful, even for the gravest reasons, to do evil that good may come of it.' Evil must never be called good, nor good evil. Here John Paul II takes on those moralists, including Catholic theologians, who say that an evil act may be justified by the end to which it is directed. It is never licit to do evil in order to achieve good. To those of a contrary view the question might be put: When is rape morally justified? Or the torture of children? Or Auschwitz? John Paul's answer is never. Intentions may be noble, people may claim that they are acting in good conscience, circumstances may mitigate personal responsibility, but the act remains, always and everywhere, evil.

[Richard Neuhaus, *The Truth about Freedom*]

---

In this extract, the repetition of the word 'evil', together with transitional devices such as 'here', 'it is', 'to those', serve the function of elaborating and developing the writer's argument.

Transitional words not only link ideas but also signal the logical relation between the ideas they link. They can show contrast, illustrate an argument, or emphasise.

To show contrast between different things or ideas, expressions such as 'however', 'conversely', 'although', 'but', 'nevertheless' or 'still' can be used.

To point out examples, use terms such as 'for instance', 'for example', 'like', 'such as', etc.

To show cause and effect or consequence: 'thus', 'hence', 'therefore', 'as a result', 'accordingly'.

To show relations of time or sequence: 'afterwards', 'next', 'then', 'as soon as', 'later'.

To show addition: 'furthermore', 'in addition to', 'also'.

To emphasise: 'indeed', 'in fact'.

To conclude: 'thus', 'therefore', 'finally', 'to sum up'.

To achieve coherence within a paragraph:

1. Avoid introducing two different ideas into a paragraph, as it can confuse the reader.
2. Don't digress or introduce irrelevant statements into your paragraph.
3. Don't dedicate two paragraphs to one idea, as this can interrupt the flow of thought in the composition. Each sentence should develop and advance the ideas that precede it.

## Clarity

Good writing aims at communicating effectively to—not impressing—your reader. The topic sentence or main idea in the paragraph must be evident to the reader. Clear paragraphing presents the contents of your message in a lucid and comprehensible manner.

The following paragraph can be taken as an example of clear expression.

> After St Edward's death, many of the people of England wanted Margaret's brother, Edgar, as king; but as he was young and had been born in a foreign country, he had neither the power nor the resources to withstand his rival, Count Harold. As is well known from this famous chapter in English history, the new king reigned for scarcely a year, since William of Normandy, who also had a claim to the English throne, defeated Harold at Hastings in 1066. Edgar realised that the lives of his family were not safe, and he decided to take his mother and sisters back to Hungary. Shortly after they had set sail they were caught in a violent storm, which drove the ship off course quite dramatically, and they landed eventually with some difficulty on the coast of Scotland.

Each sentence in the paragraph should relate to the one point or topic sentence. Whatever method is used, remember that all sentences play a role in developing the main or topic sentence and in turn developing the main idea or stance of the composition. Each sentence in a well-constructed paragraph develops the main point announced in the topic sentence. Whatever method is used to achieve this (analogy, contrast, comparison, explanation, etc.), it must keep the paragraph moving ahead to develop the central argument of the composition. It can also act as a signpost, showing where the idea or ideas are heading.

The introductory and concluding paragraphs are the most important ones in your composition.

The introductory paragraph has two main functions:

- to capture the attention of your reader
- to introduce your material and show your approach or stance to the composition topic.

Opening paragraphs should be short and should focus attention on where your writing is going. The opening paragraph is really a signpost of the route that your message is taking.

Introductory paragraphs may open with some striking description of something. Remember that in this case it must provide all the necessary information about time, place, atmosphere, mood, character, etc. A descriptive opening must also help the reader to get into the right frame of mind for the story that follows. In other words, it must establish the correct tone. It must also form a part of the story structurally.

A contrast introduction begins by presenting a commonly held belief or opinion about a subject; then the writer introduces a contrasting idea. This device will focus the composition and catch the reader's interest.

Look at the following examples of opening paragraphs.

> It is Sunday afternoon, preferably before the war. The wife is already asleep in the armchair, and the children have been sent out for a nice long walk. You put your feet up on the sofa, settle your spectacles on your nose, and open the *News of the World*. Roast beef and Yorkshire, or roast pork and apple sauce, followed by suet pudding and driven home, as it were, by a cup of mahogany-brown tea, have put you in just the right mood. Your pipe is drawing sweetly, the sofa cushions are soft underneath you, the fire is well alight, the air is warm and stagnant. In these blissful circumstances, what is it that you want to read about?
>
> <div style="text-align: right">[George Orwell, <i>Decline of the English Murder</i>]</div>

This opening paragraph on the 'decline of the English murder' adopts an anecdotal approach. The writer uses a series of short, terse sentences, together with some domestic and homely imagery, to arouse the reader's interest. The clever rhetorical question at the conclusion is naturally answered in the next paragraph and is a means of leading the reader on to find out more about the composition.

> My view of history is in itself a tiny piece of history; and mainly other people's history and not my own; for a scholar's life work is to add his bucketful of knowledge to the great and flowing river of knowledge fed by countless bucketfuls of the kind. If my individual view of history is to be made at all illuminating, or indeed intelligible, it must be presented in its origin, growth, and social and personal settings.
>
> [Arnold Toynbee, *My View of History*]

In this extract, the opening paragraph takes the form of a more discursive approach to the theme of history. The writer uses the first-person pronoun 'I' to give an individual flavour to the composition. The use of the original metaphors 'bucket of knowledge' and 'river of knowledge' add colour and vitality to the ideas.

> Lying in bed would be an altogether perfect and supreme experience if only one had a coloured pencil long enough to draw on the ceiling. This, however, is not generally a part of the domestic apparatus on the premises. I think myself that the thing might be managed with several pails of Aspinall and a broom. Only if one worked in a really sweeping and masterly way, and laid on the colour in great washes, it might drip down again in floods of rich and mingled colour like some strange fairy rain; and that would have its disadvantages. I am afraid it would be necessary to stick to black and white in this form of artistic composition. To that purpose, indeed, the white ceiling would be of the greatest possible use; in fact, it is the only use I think of a white ceiling being put to.
>
> [G. K. Chesterton, 'On Lying in Bed']

Here the writer adopts a humorous and surprising attitude to his subject. The colourful imagery and almost eccentric approach to the subject matter is clever and certainly attracts the reader and makes us want to read on.

Avoid opening paragraphs that are vague and general. The following paragraph is an example of one that is clearly leading nowhere.

> Success is ... what? What actually makes someone or something successful? Is it money, power, popularity? In my opinion being successful means being happy, being yourself and doing your best to achieve what you want out of life. Therefore my next question is, do we ever really achieve success, and if we do at what cost?

The impression here is that this paragraph was written hastily and with no attention to the organisation of ideas. It is repetitive and disorganised. There is very little content in it, and it is an example of a very weak opening paragraph.

An alternative treatment of the same title might be:

> If you can meet with Triumph and Disaster
> And treat those two impostors just the same ...
>
> The old adage that success and failure are merely impostors certainly deserves some consideration when we consider how equivocal the term 'success' is today. Many times we may wonder what exactly makes someone or something successful—whether it is money, power, or popularity. Is it possible to be successful in this life, given all the limitations of our nature and of life in general? I believe that personal happiness and self-knowledge contribute a lot to what success really adds up to.

Look at the following paragraphs (from actual pupils' work) and examine whether or not they are suitable as descriptive openings.

---

**The teenage cultural scene**
It's only really now, in the past year, that I've taken to going to the cinema again—and even at that I don't go too often. I've seen one show up at the Mayre, and that was a puppet show I took some children to see. (I did have a ticket to see 'Hamlet' when it was being performed in the Gate, but I lost the ticket and never got to see it.) Books I've always liked reading, but there are still those ones gathering dust on my shelves, with lots of paper marking where I stopped. (I found my ticket for 'Hamlet' a week after it ended, when I decided to finish one of those half-read books and discovered the piece of yellow card waiting for me in chapter 9.). And the reason I've never really paid regular visits to the big screen, or sat in front of a real, tangible performance, or stacked my shelves with fully read books? The answer is very simple: I had the choice when I was about fourteen—or rather when my

sister was sixteen—of either spending my pocket money on one of these three things or else using it for a more worthwhile cause—drinking and smoking and discoing on a Friday night. The decision wasn't really that hard to make. Friday nights from then on comprised urban bush-drinking, smoking in some corner of a disco, and strutting across a dance floor.

This opening paragraph gives the impression of having been written without proper organisation of thought or attention to the correct structuring of ideas. Attention to areas such as pre-writing strategies, drafting, brainstorming and constructing a composition outline would improve the flow of ideas here.

### Prejudice and tolerance

Prejudice is an ungainly weed that grows in the most exquisite gardens, and an infectious disease that knows no reason or boundaries. These irrational prejudices, whatever their origin, have wreaked havoc wherever they rear their ugly heads, as is demonstrated all too clearly in places such as South Africa and Northern Ireland. An unfounded, unjustified prejudice against people of a different skin and colour led to the foundation of the apartheid system. We are told that there is only one antidote to this omnipresent virus, and that is tolerance. Tolerance is a quality as praiseworthy as prejudice is deplorable. It is indeed a pity that we cannot inject certain people with a regular dose of it.

The writer here opens with a colourful metaphor and proceeds to develop the paragraph by means of some interesting and colourful illustrations. This is an example of a good opening, and it is substantial in length.

### Sounds in the night

As dusk falls and the blazing crimson sun sinks, to be replaced by the silvery-grey moon, the whole world undergoes a phase of metamorphosis. The mortal world is replaced by the supernatural, which reigns supreme in this infernal realm. Sometimes I wonder how prehistoric humans must have felt before the invention of fire, when they heard the wolves howling and the fearsome screeching of some unknown bird of prey. No wonder humans have always sought the protection of others! Protection—that is of vital importance. People have always sought for a sense of security against the unknown. Indeed that is what I seek when I snuggle up in bed, hugging my teddy bear and listening apprehensively to the sounds in the night. The very fact that your vision is hindered by this sense of darkness heightens your sense of hearing.

This is an example of a descriptive opening. The language is original and colourful; the writer moves on in the paragraph to ponder on humans and our need for protection.

**Confessions of a near-adult**
Shielding my face, I cried for help. This was a common occurrence in my house. He didn't care. He just laughed, feeling superior as he was three years older than me. We never got on my brother Brian and me. We were both as bad as each other between provoking and teasing, we always seemed to be at each other's throats. The one thing about my brother that sticks out in my mind is that he's never really able to hurt me physically, even though he has succeeded mentally. I am at present a wreck because of his verbal bullying. If it's not about my skin he's teasing, it's my weight or braces. Between the both of us, we have my parents driven crazy.

While the writer here adopts a fairly original approach to the subject, the paragraph has very little content. The language is largely repetitive, and there are basic errors in grammar and punctuation.

**Fashion: an indication of our time**
The dance floor was heaving with energetic bodies, mindlessly moving to the loud, pulsating music. As Jane awkwardly danced to the unfamiliar mix of Born Slippy—the club version, she had been informed—she felt totally out of place. There she was, dressed in a short lime-green dress, with unfamiliar make-up clogging her pores and reeking of Calvin Klein perfume. It was all Sarah's fault—her so-called best friend. Sarah was very fashion-conscious. She followed all the new trends and styles slavishly. She always knew where to go, what to wear, and what to do. 'Cosmo' was her bible, which kept her up to date on all the 'happening' places—places that would offer her the maximum enjoyment and pleasure, enable her to meet interesting people and, most importantly, change her image. But one thing was missing: a partner in crime. She needed someone who could accompany her around the night spots in Dublin—someone who would keep her company on dull nights when no-one better was out or about, but also someone who would not embarrass her by wearing last season's styles. In short, someone she could totally dominate. And that person was Jane.

The language here is varied and interesting. However, the subject matter tends to be too stereotyped and repetitive. Struggle to get that original angle on the subject.

### Breaking barriers

Andrew perched tensely in Pheasant's gleaming saddle, watching apprehensively as the rider before him crashed rather ungraciously through the bullfinch hedge and reappeared briefly on the other side before vanishing into the dim shadows of the wood. The butterflies that had fluttered around his stomach since early morning had disappeared, to be replaced by a sick, leaden feeling of dread and hopelessness. How had he let his mother force him into another one of these ghastly cross-country events? Surely she knew that he would fall off and humiliate her again, as he always did! She knew that he was petrified with fear, that he couldn't control Pheasant, that he had never once completed the course, despite six years of being forced to act out his mother's own unfulfilled ambition.

Peering nervously over his shoulder, Andrew could see her deep in conversation with the district commissioner of the pony club, a fearsomely horsy woman whose motto, frequently and thunderously proclaimed, was 'There's no such thing as fear.' He gazed apprehensively along the length of Pheasant's shining muscular neck with its row of tight plaits and tensed with fear as the horse began an irritable swishing of his tail, impatient at the long wait. The number attached to his tail was loose and looked as though it were about to fall off, but he was terrified to relax his grip on the reins. At any moment he knew the starting judge would raise his flag …

---

The opening paragraphs here take an original and interesting approach to the subject. The language used is rich and varied, and the sentences flow on from one to another in a vibrant and energetic manner.

Avoid definition-style openings, such as 'This technological era may be defined as …' or 'We may define man as …' These openings are far too dull and boring for your reader.

Avoid self-conscious expressions such as 'I hope to prove that …', 'I would like to deal with …', 'I feel that I have successfully …' Your opening paragraph should stand on its own and speak for itself, without this type of support.

One good way of introducing an opening to a composition is to use a quotation, or an anecdote, or a startling or unexpected statistic.

The following opening paragraphs are examples of actual pupils' work. Examine them under the following headings:

- unity
- coherence
- content and relevance to title.

**The power of love**
When thinking of the notion of love it conjures up romance and happy ever after endings, but love is so much more. Love in friendship brings about loyalty, parental love which is unconditional and their children's love which is impressionable is what ties families together and keeps them united, love in flings and relationships brings about passion and romance, unrequited love brings heartache. Love can be obsessive. Love gives fear, fear of commitment, fear of making the wrong decision, fear of being and remaining out of control with raging emotions and fits of passion, fear of giving too much of yourself away that you change, fear of depending on someone and being let down, but the strongest fear is giving someone the power to hurt you. By giving them your heart and they trod on it until all feeling dies and it goes numb and then they throw it back to you and walk away without a backward glance.

This is an example of a paragraph that is not structured correctly. There is no clear topic sentence and no paragraph unity. The writer makes several different references: the fear that love can bring, the notion of parental love, the hurt that love can cause. The sentence structure is awkward and ambiguous. The second sentence is badly punctuated and confusing. There is a great deal of needless repetition in the sentence beginning 'Love gives fear …' In general, it is an example of a very weak and poorly organised paragraph.

An alternative opening could be the following:

The whole notion of love can conjure up the idea of romance and fairy-tale glamour. The emotion of love, however, is far more powerful than this. The love that exists in friendship can generate a deep loyalty between people. The power and bond of family love can be seen in a reciprocal way between parents and children. It is the quality of unconditional love from parents that unites family life and binds its members together. Love can also cause pain and heartache, as can be seen in unrequited love, or the fear of betrayal on the part of the loved one.

### The magic of a smile

Old age had not been kind to Nelly. Her head hung low as her back was crumpled over. Pain crippled her stiff feet and made her once-nimble fingers clumsy and awkward. She dreaded the first Saturday of every month—the day she had to make the tiring journey to town to collect the pension. On the bus people pushed and shoved. She was lucky to be able to sit down. Today was no exception as she climbed the difficult steps onto the crowded bus. 'Here, take my seat,' chirped a young girl as she let her sit down. She smiled at Nelly, and they chatted for a while. No-one had smiled at her in years. That little expression warmed her heart and brought a tear to her eye. A magic happiness filled her, and the day was not such a burden after all.

---

This paragraph takes an anecdotal approach for its opening. The descriptions used are interesting and lively, and the sentence structures are varied.

### Failure

'What we have got here is failure, failure to communicate, failure of every sort.' These words by W. Axel Rose are only too true. At one time in your life you come into contact with failure. It may be profound or minute, but everyone goes through it.

---

This is an example of a poor opening paragraph. The quotation that opens the paragraph is feeble and says very little. The content of the paragraph is almost non-existent. Excessive repetition and poor expression weaken the paragraph considerably.

Here is a possible alternative version:

---

Failure seems to exist on every level and in every area of life. The words of Axel Rose ring true for our day: 'What we have got here is failure, failure to communicate, failure of every sort.'

When we speak about human life in general, it seems that people do seem to experience failure at some stage in their lives. This may be profound or mild. Failure is inseparable from our mortal nature; it is synonymous with the word 'humanity' and must be accepted as such.

### Hairstyles

Hairstyles play a huge role in modern teenage society. Hair has become the new medium of self-expression. Gone are the days of the conservative braids. If it's not bleached, permed, thickened, crimped and fried to within an inch of its life it's clearly not 'hip' these days. Instead of the customary flags that distinguish national groups, hairstyles now distinguish the complex groups that exist in teenage society.

This is an interesting opening, although it is a bit on the short side. However, the approach is lively and cheerful, and the language and analogies are varied and interesting.

**Doing one's own thing**
The educational system has no comprehension of what 'doing one's own thing' involves and definitely does not implicate this theory in its administration of schools. Regimental rules and ridiculous restrictions are rampant in these establishments. An immense amount of pressure is exerted by schools on the pupils to compete and conform to certain standards. It is my belief that schools suppress any form of self-expression and initiative.

This is an example of what not to do in an opening paragraph. The approach is too negative, and there is outright misuse of several words, such as 'implicate' for 'implement.' No clear stance is taken on the composition title.
Look at the following rewritten version:

The whole notion of 'doing one's own thing' certainly does not seem to be recognised by today's system of education. It may seem instead that there exists a system of regimental rules and rigid restrictions throughout various educational establishments. Doing one's thing connotes the expression of one's own style, liberation of movement, freedom of the personality. As the popular lyric states, 'Let your mind be free, do what you want to do, you got to live your life, do what you want to do.'

**A farewell to adolescence**
Monday morning, cool and cloudy, with frost carpeting the lawns of the university. I was finally here where I wanted to be. All those long, hard years of work had finally paid off; and yet the whole idea seemed like a dream. Nothing seemed real. I still couldn't believe that I'd reached my destination. I made my way towards the registration office, a tall, gloomy building. The gravel under my feet crunched as I sauntered dreamily over to register. I paused for a second before entering the building, took a deep

breath, and tried to take in everything around me. I looked towards the examination hall, and then over across the courtyard to the chapel and the dining-hall. I felt almost light-headed; but the butterflies in my stomach were there not from fear but from sheer anticipation. I turned towards the door and walked in.

---

The opening paragraph here is simple and conveys a feeling familiar to every student. The language chosen is precise and clear. The sentences follow on in a coherent manner.

## THE CONCLUDING PARAGRAPH

Your concluding paragraph is your final statement on the composition topic. It is the last impression left on your reader, and therefore it is vitally important.

A conclusion should exude a sense of control. What is important in the conclusion is not what one says but how one says it.

A good conclusion has two purposes:

- to round off the main ideas of your composition satisfactorily
- to provide an overall unity to your composition.

Avoid conclusions that repeat the main ideas of the composition in exactly the same words. On the other hand, do not go to the other extreme by introducing a completely different approach or new ideas in your conclusion, because this will only frustrate your reader.

One way of giving unity to the composition could be to present both the introduction and conclusion as a pair, to refer back to the introductory paragraph and develop the anecdote or statistic or simply the point that was made there.

Some phrases that can serve as a way of concluding your composition effectively are: 'To sum up, therefore ...', 'In conclusion we can see ...,' 'Finally it can be taken that ...'

Remember that your conclusion must show that you have complete control over your subject.

Analyse the following opening and concluding paragraphs (from actual pupils' work) under the headings *unity of impression, relevance,* and *length*.

## THE ENGLISH COMPOSITION

**Fashion: an indication of our times**
In the above story I have tried to illustrate what fashion means to the average person. Their definition of being fashionable means wearing the right clothes, going to the correct places, meeting the appropriate people, listening to the proper music, holding acceptable opinions and views, and forming socially desirable habits. To be blunt and to the point, this behaviour proves that people of today have developed a herd mentality. The desire to conform and to fit in exists with all of us. The need to be fashionable is only one example that illustrates this inherent quality in people.

The opening sentence is too self-conscious, and is redundant. It should be evident from the composition that the writer has illustrated what fashion means. It is not clear from the second sentence who exactly 'their' refers to. The concluding paragraph should tie up all the preceding ideas and present an overall unity of impression.

An alternative ending to a composition with this title could be:

For some people, being fashionable means wearing the right clothes, going to the correct places, listening to the proper music, holding acceptable views and opinions, and forming socially desirable habits. This type of behaviour, however, proves that people today have developed a herd mentality. This desire to conform and fit in exists within us all. Fashion, and the need to be fashionable, is simply one other example that illustrates this inherent element within people.

**Prejudice and tolerance**
Every evening on television we are provided with some light amusement in the form of Ian Paisley. He seems certain that every Catholic supports the IRA and hates Protestants. Catholics in the North of Ireland have endured discrimination in politics and jobs. Catholics are the children who are being reprimanded by a stern teacher without justification. Prejudice, wherever it might exist, be it in South Africa or Northern Ireland, has proved to be as destructive as guns. Prejudice can only be countered by tolerance. We must teach our children to 'live and let live.' It is really only by the imaginative effort of placing ourselves in the other person's shoes that we will arrive at an understanding of them. History is the greatest tool to show children how prejudice developed. And these young children will then be able to form their own opinions on such matters, even if it means rejecting their parents' views. I hope that gradually we can exorcise the demons of prejudice and ignorance.

The approach here is interesting and original. The length is quite substantial, and the language and examples used are relevant and colourful.

### Europe—long live difference!
We can, however, proceed on the road to political unity in Europe, if this is what is desired, without sacrificing any of the differences that make us what we are. But we must be vigilant—we must nourish and protect our individualities within Europe. Otherwise we will bequeath to future generations a clone of the United States of America. Only the name will be different: 'the United States of Europe.' As the French say, 'Vive la difference!'

The concluding paragraph here is not substantial enough to capture and tie up all the ideas. The quotation in the last line could be woven into the fabric of the paragraph more tightly and naturally.

### Confessions of a near-adult
A lot of us, having done our penance for our teenage years, will in fact venture out and take that step into the unknown world of adulthood. Although the demon drink may follow us on our journey, and we may only manage to cut down to ten cigarettes a day (a filthy habit picked up in first year), we will one day manage to get that job and take on the responsibilities of an adult. We will one day own that house with the white picket fence and the 2.5 children. Our teenage confessions will merely be stories (censored versions) to tell our grandchildren. Which reminds me of a time at my grandmother's when I took it upon myself to sell her finest ...

This is an example of quite a good conclusion. The last sentence, with its clever use of ellipsis, links in some of the preceding ideas used in the composition.

### The hand that rocks the cradle rules the world
Perhaps if their roles in history had been reversed, none of the consequences of wars would have occurred. If our cradle had not been rocked so vigorously our world and its future rulers might keep our world in peace at last.

This is an example of a very weak concluding paragraph to a composition that is obviously on the role of the woman. The paragraph is much too short and excessively repetitive: 'our world' is used twice in the last sentence.

**Hairstyles**
So it seems the modern teenager's obsession with hair dates back centuries, and the bleaching and teasing of hair is not a new revelation but simply one borrowed from our future ancestors. So, teenagers, unite, and join the universal sport of hairdressing (and don't worry—it can always be dyed back to its natural colour).

This paragraph is too short for a conclusion. It is an example of a humorous and fairly original use of language. You should tie up your ideas in the concluding paragraph, and perhaps refer back to the opening in order to attain that strong sense of unity.

*Sample concluding paragraphs with commentary*

**An Irish schooling**
If I were a child again and both schools stood, to which would I go? If not to some sterner, more ambitious school than either of them? It is a question of a 'hausser les épaules.' Certainly, if it is a matter of getting on in the world, to neither. But if one places more value on other things, then this type of school is ideal, and according as you value these other things the more, then the more reason to go to some old shack like mine where, although one learnt little about the world, one imbibed a great deal about life—and perhaps a little about the next life, too.
[Seán Ó Faoláin]

The writer begins his concluding paragraph with two effective questions, which he proceeds to answer. This is a positive conclusion and is substantial in length.

Here is the concluding paragraph from a composition entitled 'Machines and the emotions'.

Moral self-control, and external prohibition of harmful acts, are not adequate methods of dealing with our anarchic instincts. The reason they are inadequate is that these instincts are capable of as many disguises as the Devil in mediaeval legend, and some of these disguises deceive even the elect. The only adequate method is to discover what are the needs of our instinctive nature and to search for the least harmful way of satisfying them.

Since spontaneity is what is most thwarted by machines, the only thing that can be provided is opportunity; the use made of opportunity must be left to the initiative of the individual. No doubt considerable expense would be involved; but it would not be comparable to the expense of war. Understanding of human nature must be the basis of any real improvements in human life. Science has done wonders in mastering the laws of the physical world, but our own nature is much less understood, as yet, than the nature of stars and electrons. When science learns to understand human nature, it will be able to bring a happiness into our lives which machines and the physical sciences have failed to create.

[Bertrand Russell, 'Machines and the Emotions']

The conclusion of this composition is very well developed in a philosophical manner. It draws together very cleverly the main problems confronting human nature and technological development. It ends by proposing positive solutions to the dilemma of humankind and science.

**'A character sketch'**
He has red hair, very red, close and curling and a pale face long in shape with straight good features and little rather queer whiskers that are as red as his hair. His eyebrows are somehow darker, they look particularly arched and as if they might move a great deal. His eyes are sharp, strange, rather small and very fixed. His mouth is wide and his lips are thin, and except for his little whiskers he is clean-shaven. He gives me a sort of sense of looking like an actor.

[Henry James, *The Turn of the Screw*]

The effectiveness of this sketch is based on its use of carefully chosen detail: 'sharp strange eyes, thin lips, wide mouth, red curling hair.' The writer's choice is precise and apt: 'a long pale face, arched eyebrows ...' He is sensitive to fine details, and his description is vivid and striking.

The following paragraph is an example of a smooth and logical flow of thought from one idea to another.

The train presently arrived and Miss Stackpole, promptly descending, proved, as Isabella had promised, quite delicately, even though rather provincially, fair. She was a neat, plump person, of medium stature, with a round face, a small mouth, a delicate complexion, a bunch of light brown ringlets at the back of her head and a peculiarly open, surprised-looking eye. The most striking point in her appearance was the remarkable fixedness of this organ, which rested without impudence or defiance, but as if in conscientious exercise of a natural right, upon every object it happened to encounter. It rested in this manner upon Ralph himself, a little arrested by Miss Stackpole's gracious and comfortable aspect, which hinted that it wouldn't be so easy as he had assumed to disapprove of her.

[Henry James, *Portrait of a Lady*]

Now look at the following example of a paragraph that lacks total coherence in a composition entitled 'Sunlight'.

At the brightest moment, the Earth becomes entranced at its beauty. The gleaming reflections, the balanced and poised shadow movements, glittering and radiating water droplets glistening, purifying the smoky cities and glorifying the enhanced and aroused natural world becomes vibrant and exuberant on its arrival at earth.

Here is a writer who is misusing words and not thinking about their meaning and function in a sentence. The effect is one of incoherence and meaningless statements. Make sure you understand the meaning of each word you write; otherwise do not use it.

Here is an alternative version to this paragraph:

The Earth is now at its brightest moment and is becoming entranced at its own beauty. Water droplets glitter and glisten. Gleaming reflections from the trees highlight a balanced and poised movement, as the natural world becomes slowly aroused and enhanced.

*Check-list for paragraphs*

1. What is the purpose of the paragraph?
2. Is there one topic sentence that is easily identifiable?
3. Has the paragraph got clarity of thought, or is it woolly and convoluted?
4. Has the paragraph got substance, i.e. five or six sentences?
5. Is the content unified? Are all examples given relevant to the main or topic sentence?
6. Are the ideas organised correctly? Is there a proper emphasis on the order of ideas in the paragraph?
7. Has the paragraph got coherence? Is there an effective link between all the sentences in the paragraph?

8. What transitional devices are used?
9. Has the paragraph got an effective concluding statement?

*Remember!*

Each paragraph must begin with a sentence that relates what comes next to the last point you made and the structure of the composition as a whole. All sentences in the paragraph should develop the idea contained in the topic sentence.

Your paragraphs must be structured in the following way:

—**topic sentence:** This makes the main claim of the paragraph and tries to link with what goes before.

> Such preoccupations prevented Reverend Mother one day from examining the midday post until late evening.

—**together with subsequent sentences:** these justify or illustrate the claim or idea.

> She came to her study desk feeling a little tired, but content with the work of the afternoon. Dusk was advancing, but there was still enough daylight to work by. She laid her restless hands on the pile of letters and allowed her eyes to fall for an indolent second on the pleasant pathway outside with its ivy-niched Stations of the Cross and, beyond, through the gate, on the little black crosses of the convent cemetery.

—**together with the final sentence:** this sums up the paragraph with what will come next.

> 'Perhaps I shall have to lie there after all,' she thought resignedly. 'Perhaps I shall never see Brussels again—or Father.'
>
> [Kate O'Brien, *The Land of Spices*]

The following examples of topic sentences show the different methods by which the main idea can be developed.

(1) Illustration and example:

> A different kind of conservatism was represented by Robert Bridges, the poet. He was gifted with a sensitive and idealistic mind. Interested

in the sciences as well as in music and in language, he produced some finely chiselled lyrics.

(2) Enumeration:

There are many ways of studying for an examination. These can range from cramming to setting long-term goals and writing out copious study timetables.

(3) Cause and effect:

When people begin to take life easy they find it difficult to submit to a structured life-style.

(4) Comparison and contrast:

Prejudice can be seen to exist at many different levels, from apartheid in South Africa to victimisation of travellers in Galway.

(5) Definition:

A bore may be described as ...

## *Exercises*

*Exercises on the paragraph*
(Answers on page 237.)
Rearrange the following sentences to construct a logical paragraph.

(a) Southney would undoubtedly say that she saw them in that dreary light because she indulged in her fantasies—that the dangers he was alerting her to were already taking effect.
(b) The words 'flat and unprofitable', which she remembered from *Hamlet*, now rang out within her as the most apt description possible of her present surroundings and routine.
(c) Was this not a euphemism for the morbid mental state she had descended into, seeming sometimes to border on madness?
(d) 'Unfitted for the ordinary uses of the world ...'
(e) This could only mean that sooner or later—preferably sooner—she must summon up courage to cast out the beloved spectres of the nether world and turn her whole heart, mind and imagination to the surface world that others called the real.

(f) She must grasp this advice, written to her so generously by this famous and worthy man, and impale herself on it, whatever the pain, in order to retain her reason and her power to be of use to her family world.

*Exercises on coherence in paragraphs*
(Answers on page 237.)

1. Look at the following sentences, which are placed in random order; rewrite them in order to make a coherent paragraph.

    (a) Poe enjoys cheery subjects like premature burial, plague, the ghastly ruin of an old family, reincarnation, and walling people up in dungeons or vaults.
    (b) What are some of the usual themes of horror fiction?
    (c) A frequent motif is human metamorphosis into animal forms.
    (d) Stoker and King go in for the ugly perversion of vampirism.
    (e) Other odd obsessions are putrefaction, gore, cruelty, torment, sorcery, witchery, demonic possession, and madness.
    (f) Mervyn Peake favours degeneracy in labyrinthine castles, foul and cobwebby, slithery and sibilant.

2. The following paragraph has one sentence that breaks the unity. Identify this sentence.

> The African interior had waited many centuries for the coming of Christianity, and it was not until the late 1800s that missionaries from various European countries followed in the footsteps of explorers such as Livingstone. Portugal, Spain, Italy and France took the Catholic faith to the areas they colonised, while Holland and England spread Protestantism. About 1800 a group of White Fathers were sent by Cardinal Lavigerie from Algeria, which was under French rule, to Buganda, part of what is now Uganda. The missionaries quickly pointed out to Mukabya the error of his ways. The travelling conditions were appalling. They made the journey from Zanzibar on foot. Those who reached Buganda after several months of trekking through the jungle found the situation far from encouraging.

3. Identify the topic sentence of this paragraph.

> So it is. Once a book is fathomed, once it is known and its meaning is fixed or established, it is dead. A book only lives while it has power to move us,

and move us differently; so long as we find it different every time we read it. Owing to the flood of shallow books that really are exhausted in one reading, the modern mind tends to think every book is the same, finished in one reading. But it is not so. And gradually the modern mind will realise it again. The real joy of a book lies in reading it over and over again, and always finding it different, coming upon another meaning, another level of meaning. It is, as usual, a question of values: we are so overwhelmed with quantities of books that we hardly realise any more that a book can be valuable, valuable like a jewel, or a lovely picture, into which you can look deeper and deeper and get a more profound experience every time. It is far, far better to read one book six times at intervals than to read six several books. Because if a certain book can call you to read it six times it will be a deeper and deeper experience each time and will enrich the whole soul, emotional and mental. Whereas six books read only once are merely an accumulation of superficial interest, the burdensome accumulation of modern days, quantity without real value.

**4.** Identify the devices used to link the following paragraphs.

The decade will start with good economic news. The exchequer returns will show buoyant tax revenues, spending under control, and borrowing that has fallen by considerably more than the Government expected at this time last year. In a year of political uncertainty, short Dáil sittings, and a change of Government, economic management at least has remained on course. Through much of the eighties the state of the economy seemed to go from bad to worse. Profligacy in the late seventies, compounded in the early eighties, brought into being the extraordinary 25th Dáil, with its support for hairshirt solutions.

The hairshirt proved surprising in its effects. Although the electorate disliked the cuts, especially in health, the economy appeared to thrive on cutbacks; growth and employment picked up.

**5.** Write interesting opening paragraphs on the following topics:

   (a)  Love is ...
   (b)  The role of the media
   (c)  Cricket
   (d)  The dignity of human nature
   (e)  Jealousy
   (f)  Equality and the law.

**6.** Write a paragraph with the intention of informing the public about the traffic system in Dublin.

# EXPLORATIONS 2

7. Write a paragraph in which you try to persuade a group of schoolgirls to buy a particular cosmetic product.
8. The following are examples of main or topic sentences. Develop these into full paragraphs.

    (a) Nothing surprises anyone in Sarajevo any more.
    (b) As he stepped into the East Room of the White House, Bill Clinton looked like a platoon leader venturing into no-man's land.
    (c) The power of the information age descended on China in 1989.
    (d) If an ambassador is an honest man sent abroad to lie for his country, a statesman is a man who lies from the comfort of home.
    (e) Just then the little man hurried in by the gateway of the station.
    (f) In the early hours of the night it had rained, and the iron gate that led to the lightkeepers' houses had rattled loose in the wind. As it cringed and banged, it disturbed the dog that was lying on a mat in the dark, draughty hallway.

9. Develop the following quotations into interesting paragraphs:

    (a) Thinking about thinking leads to nothing.
    (b) A thing of beauty is a joy for ever.
    (c) Virtue is its own reward.
    (d) Grey hair often hides golden thoughts.
    (e) Revenge never repairs an injury.
    (f) Courtesy costs nothing, and pays for everything.

10. Now take some interesting quotations from your literature course and see how you can use them to make up a paragraph.
11. Look at the following paragraph. Identify the topic sentence; list the details that support the topic sentence; identify how the ideas in the paragraph are linked—through classification, explanation, proof, cause and effect.

---

Honesty is of pervasive human importance. 'I hate that man like the very Gates of Death who says one thing but hides another in his heart,' cries the anguished Achilles in Homer's *Iliad*. Every social activity, every human enterprise requiring people to act in concert is impeded when people aren't honest with one another. Honesty here is not just veracity—truth-telling— but the honesty of an 'honest day's work for an honest day's pay.' It is the honesty that the prophet Jeremiah sought. 'Run to and fro through the streets of Jerusalem, look around and take note! Search its squares and see if you can find one person who acts justly and seeks truth.' It is the honesty that the cynic philosopher Diogenes sought later in Athens and Corinth, an image that has proved remarkably durable. 'With Candle and Lanthorn, when the Sun shin'd I sought Honest Men, but none could I find,' as a seventeenth-century chapbook put it. Pinocchio's lie-lengthened nose is an image scarcely a hundred years old now, but it too has happily found a place among our enduring popular stories.

12. Develop the following statements into paragraphs by using contrasting statements:

    (a) Love is blind
    (b) Marriages are made in Heaven
    (c) All men are fools
    (d) Don't judge a book by its cover
    (e) Writing is easy
    (f) An apple a day keeps the doctor away
    (g) Better to have loved and lost than never to have loved at all
    (h) Power corrupts
    (i) City people are more in touch with reality than country people
    (j) Money makes the world go round.

*Exercises on pre-composition writing*

1. Rephrase the following composition titles as questions:

    (a) The power of the printed word
    (b) Rural Ireland still struggling to survive
    (c) Road rage
    (d) Life in a modern city
    (e) Let the punishment fit the crime.

2. Draft an outline on *one* of the following topics:

    (a) Modern woman has lost her charm
    (b) The end justifies the means—a theme for the modern age?
    (c) The joys of love
    (d) The sweet taste of success.

3. Brainstorm *four* of the following topics and write out a rough draft of the opening paragraph:

    (a) Sport and politics have little in common
    (b) Responsibilities

(c) Comedy touches something deeper in us than tragedy
(d) What a piece of work is man!
(e) My way
(f) Freedom is an illusion.

4. Free-write on *one* of the following topics:
    (a) The age of feminism
    (b) Roads
    (c) The relentless march of time
    (d) Stress—a symptom of our times
    (e) The forgotten war
    (f) Killing time.

5. Write an anecdotal opening paragraph on the following titles:
    (a) Failure.
    (b) Courtesy
    (c) 'As flies to wanton boys are we to the gods—they kill us for their sport.'
    (d) Music today—industry or art?
    (e) Words are all we have to go on.

## THE LANGUAGE OF NARRATION

### *Writing a narrative-style composition or a short story*

The section on comprehension (chapter 1) deals with the features of narrative writing. Here we will examine the way to construct a narrative-style composition.

In a narrative-style composition there needs to be a definite arrangement of ideas, and the story usually has a particular point of view. The writer leads the reader along, and there can be a degree of suspense.

When choosing this type of composition, bear in mind that it must be interesting to your reader. An interesting story is original, or at least takes an original approach to an ordinary topic or situation. A good story or narrative composition springs from your own personal experience; it has a flavour of authenticity and truth.

Writing a narrative-style composition demands the combination of a fertile imagination, a certain creativity, and the capacity to be inventive and adventurous.

The opening paragraph—ideally the opening sentence—should strike the keynote. Everything should follow on in the same spirit and be strictly relevant to the theme. There is no room for extra episodes or characters, superfluous description, or sub-plots branching out from the main one.

## *Method of writing a narrative composition or short story*

Narrative writing involves telling a story. The structure of a narrative composition can be straightforward and in chronological sequence. The story can be set in the past, the present, or the future.

A story can be told in many different ways. It can be told in dialogue or in the first person or third person.

Examine the following two accounts of the same incident.

> I noticed that there was a similarity between the man's way of eating and a dog's. He snapped up every mouthful quickly and looked around him all the time as if there was danger.

> I had often watched a large dog of ours eating his food; and I now noticed a decided similarity between the dog's way of eating and the man's. The man took strong sharp sudden bites just like the dog. He swallowed, or rather snapped up, every mouthful too soon and too fast; and he looked sideways here and there as he ate, as if he thought there was danger in every direction of somebody's coming to take the pie away.
>
> [Charles Dickens, *Great Expectations*]

The first account is just a reporting of what happened. The second conjures up the action: it shows it happening here and now before our eyes. This is what it means to write at first hand. Only by writing like this can one breathe life into one's work.

The following elements must be borne in mind when you are writing a short story or narrative-style composition:

- plot
- characters
- dialogue
- description
- atmosphere.

## PLOT

A narrative composition should have a story. This should unfold through a series of events that add up to what is called the plot.

Everything that happens in the narrative must be a development in the plot, which carries the narrative forward. Pace and progress of events are necessary in order to develop the story. There must be a clever and subtle mixture of action and description. At some stages the narrative may linger to set scenes, and at other times there may be suspense in the action.

Remember that the story must have a *shape*. For that reason it is important to have a definite beginning, middle, and conclusion.

The conclusion should depict a development of the opening situation or a different set of circumstances.

## CHARACTERS

The characters in a short story or narrative must be real, recognisable figures and not fantasy figures. Characters seem realistic and alive to you as a reader when you are able to realise them with your senses, react to them with your emotions, and follow them with your mind.

A good writer has to be able to get inside the skin of the chief characters. You must try to bring them to life, to describe what they feel, think, and do. Their natures can be revealed as much through their words as through their deeds. The writer has to give them motives for their conduct. To do this effectively you must be able to master the art of credible dialogue, together with the ability to describe scenes and narrate events.

When writing about characters, pick a basic trait or quality. If a character is insecure, don't tell it at once: show it; use implication. For example, the following lines reveal a character who is deeply self-conscious about the effect he is having on others.

> He would only make himself ridiculous by quoting poetry to them which they could not understand. They would only think that he was airing his superior education. He would fail with them just as he had failed with the girl in the pantry. He had taken up a wrong turn. His whole speech was a mistake from first to last, an utter failure.
>
> [James Joyce, 'The Dead']

## DIALOGUE

The ability to write effective dialogue is another requirement for good narrative writing.

The hallmark of good dialogue is its capacity to evoke relationships between people and to convey conflict in a realistic manner. The use of dialogue in narrative writing can convey realism or show conflict, or give pace and variety to the story.

A swiftly paced conversation can lead the reader on while at the same time keeping them in suspense. It can also make conversation seem real.

The main function of dialogue in writing is to reproduce live speech. The use of direct speech can either give a piece of writing variety and excitement or ruin it. Never allow dialogue just to slip into your composition: direct speech must have a purpose or object in a piece of writing.

When you use dialogue, make sure to punctuate it correctly.

- Use quotation marks at the beginning and end of each section of direct speech.
- Separate the dialogue from the narrative by means of commas.
- The first word in every piece of direct speech begins with a capital letter.
- Use a new paragraph every time there is a change of speaker.

To achieve an effect in using dialogue, concentrate on one aspect of personality. The vocabulary and imagery will reinforce the impression suggested by the dialogue.

Dialogue can be used to excellent effect in presenting a subject that is dominated by conflict, opposition, or duality of any type. However, if the content is linear and repetitive it can be self-defeating.

The following is an example of very weak dialogue (taken from a composition entitled 'The gang mentality').

> Jack turned to Bulldog and said, 'Why did you not kill him?'
> 'I had no butterfly knife,' said Bulldog.
> Jack replied, 'Where is the knife my brother handed you yesterday?'
> 'I don't know. It was in the holder, but now it's gone.'
> Jack shouted, 'Why didn't you tell me this before now?'

This dialogue lacks life and spontaneity. The language fails to show the type of characters and their moods.

Good dialogue must be clear and flow well. It should not need this kind of back-up:

'I know it,' he laughed,
'Don't tell me,' she sighed,
'They bore me,' he sneered.

Let the speaker's *voice* be angry or sad or ironic. When the writer uses devices such as 'he said,' 'he replied,' 'she laughed,' 'they chanted,' and so on, the rhythmic flow of ideas in the passage can be interrupted.

Another problem with dialogue is correct spacing. A mass of dialogue can interrupt the flow of thought and be jarring to the reader.

The following is a good example of dialogue that expresses anger:

'How dare you lie to me!' she screamed gaspingly. 'You saw the hen. I know you saw it! You stopped whistling. You called out. You called out. We were watching you. Isn't that right?' she demanded.

Examine the following piece of dialogue. Farrington has just been humiliated because of losing his job and has spent the evening trying to drown his troubles in the pub. He returns home in bad humour looking for his wife.

'Ada, Ada!'
'Who is that?' said the man, peering through the darkness.
'Me, pa.'
'Who are you? Charlie?'
'No, pa, Tom.'
'Where's your mother?'
'She's out at the chapel.'
'That's right ... Did she think of leaving any dinner for me?'
'Yes, Pa. I—'
'Light the lamp. What do you mean by having the place in darkness? Are the other children in bed?' The man sat down heavily on one of the chairs while the little boy lit the lamp. He began to mimic his son's flat accent, saying half to himself: 'At the chapel. At the chapel. If you please.'

When the lamp was lit he banged his fist on the table and shouted: 'What's for my dinner?'

'I'm going ... to cook it, pa,' said the little boy.

The man jumped up furiously and pointed to the fire. 'Look at that fire. You let the fire out! By God, I'll teach you to do that again!'

'I'll teach you to let the fire out!' he said, rolling up his sleeve in order to give his arm free play.

[James Joyce, 'Counterparts']

The dialogue here is racy and vibrant. Every word is precise and conveys a sharp image of the mood and atmosphere of the situation and characters.

## *The art of descriptive writing*

Mastering the art of descriptive writing is the essence of good narrative writing. The function of description in a narrative composition is either to form the background or atmosphere of the story or to conjure up images through concentrating on the senses.

Descriptive writing should not attempt to list every detail about the person, place or thing being described: rather it should focus on a number of small, significant details and on describing them with precision.

You must be clear about what impression you want to suggest to the reader, and then know what techniques will help to achieve this. Rely on the selection of vocabulary, the selection of imagery, and the selection of detail.

In good description, all the senses are intimately involved: we hear, see, smell, feel, touch and taste.

> The chief was a fat man with yellow brown skin who sat under an ancient nim tree in front of his hut, a loose chequered kikoi around his ample belly, naked children and chickens scratching around him in the dusty sand. He wore an embroidered Muslim cap and chewed betel nuts, occasionally spitting straight sprays of stained rusty saliva at dangerous angles. He was blind from sarcoma. Women with large velvety eyes came and went, some giggling shyly at our strangeness, others made bolder by age and experience. They wore amber or red glass beads around their necks, their heads were covered with thin coloured cloth, in Arab style, with minute silver earrings on their earlobes and rings through their thin Nilotic nostrils.
>
> [Kuki Gallmann, *I Dreamed of Africa*]

When writing description in a short story or narrative, make sure to keep it brief and blend it in naturally. Because descriptive writing involves giving a clear picture, select details with great care.

The following examples of description are based on a selection of precise and exact details.

The storm came rattling over the marsh in full fury.
The warm wind, which smelt of soda and of waterfowls' guano, blew through his straight fair hair streaked pale by the sun.
He had a narrow, clean-shaven face, with features evenly distributed and an expression of placid acuteness. Tall, lean, loosely and feebly put together, he had an ugly sickly witty charming face furnished but by no means decorated with a straggling moustache and whiskers.
The great still oaks and beeches flung down a shade as dense as that of velvet curtains, and the place was furnished like a room with cushioned seats, rich coloured rugs with the books and papers that lay upon the grass.

[Henry James, *Portrait of a Lady*]

It was late in a dull dark day in January. Huddersfield, far below Roe Head School, was lost in smoky fog. The wide lawns were snow-covered; the beautiful trees under which the pupils sat in summer were bare and weeping. Into this gloomy atmosphere, from the still darker interior of the covered cart which had brought her from Haworth, Charlotte's little figure emerged. She was helped down, and stood there, shrinking into herself from the raw air and from a misery and fear she could not conquer. Her box was lifted out, and the driver rang the doorbell of the school.

[Lynn Reid Banks, *Dark Quartet*]

The effect here stems from a careful selection of small details, which are woven together to form a picture of the arrival of this girl Charlotte.

Descriptive writing involves being both selective and specific in the choice of things that it depicts.

Broaden your vocabulary in order to avoid stereotyped descriptions. For example, look at the shape as well as the colour of the eyes:

   narrow, slanting dark eyes
   lively, sharp grey eyes
   large, oval blue eyes

## PERSONIFICATION

The use of personification to heighten description can bring an otherwise lifeless piece of writing to life. For example, instead of saying that the idea suddenly occurred to him, a writer can use an expression such as 'the idea sauntered up to him and tapped him on the shoulder, wanting to know the cause of all the uproar.' Through the use of personification here the writer achieves a more vivid and dynamic effect.

Look at the effect of personification in the following sentence:

> The cathedral, which was one of the most powerful modes of communication in the fifteenth century, told time for the benefit of all Paris, and through the stained-glass windows displayed the intricacies of Christian theology and adverted to the existence of highly unpleasant demonic winged creatures, while at the same time referring diplomatically to the majesties of political power.

Remember that in descriptive writing you are concentrating on colour, shapes, and relationships between objects. So practise writing sentences, focusing on description.

## ATMOSPHERE

A writer needs a vivid and controlled imagination in order to build up an atmosphere that will make an impact on a reader and draw them into the story. Atmosphere is created in narrative writing by a blending of people, events, and setting.

Look at the following lines, which build up an atmosphere of tension and fear.

> Not the faintest sound of any kind could be heard. You looked on amazed and began to suspect yourself of being deaf—then the night came suddenly and struck you blind as well. About three in the morning some large fish leaped, and the loud splash made me jump as though a gun had been fired. We had a glimpse of the towering multitude of trees of the immense matted jungle, with the blazing little ball of sun hanging over it all perfectly still. Then a muffled rattle, a cry, a very loud cry as of infinite desolation soared slowly in the opaque air. A clamour modulated in savage discords filled our ears.
>
> [Joseph Conrad, *Heart of Darkness*]

> The grey warm evening of August had descended upon the city and a mild warm air, a memory of summer, circulated in the streets. The streets, shuttered for the repose of Sunday, swarmed with a gaily coloured crowd. Like illuminated pearls the lamps shone from the summits of their tall poles

upon the living texture below which, changing shape and hue unceasingly, sent up into the warm grey evening air an unchanging unceasing murmur.

[James Joyce, 'Two Gallants']

The atmosphere here builds up a sense of warmth and comfort.

To sum up, therefore, a short story or narrative composition should have a blend of plot, sharply delineated characters, a clash or conflict, and a certain time or place. There should also be a definite mood. The story should conclude with a final action or the resolution of a conflict.

The conclusion of a story must also satisfy the reader by being logical and fit into the mood and subject matter of the writing.

The following composition (from an actual pupil's work) is an example of a narrative style with a strong focus on description.

**The life of Reilly**

I loathe and detest the morning. Especially at eight o'clock. It's the same every single day. The incessant beeping of that infernal alarm clock as it stretches its tentacles into my brain and rudely wrenches me from a deeply satisfying dream. It always manages to wreck everything. This morning, for example, I had been let loose in Brown Thomas's with a gullible and indulgent rich man's credit card. I was just about to purchase a wildly expensive designer evening dress when the ringing of the cash register somehow metamorphosed into the beeping of that ugly, square and squat alarm clock.

A drowsy arm slowly emerges from underneath the pillow and blindly swipes at the top of the bedside table. Tubes of moisturiser, loose change and a pile of tapes are swept to one side as five fingers clumsily seek out the source of that infuriating sound, which is attempting to reel me into the land of the living. Triumphantly the button is pressed, the noise is no more, and silence reigns again. The victorious arm steals back underneath the pillow, leaving a trail of destruction in its wake but with its mission fully completed.

But, alas, the damage has been done! Although I wrap the covers snugly around my curled-up body and nestle into the soft pillow, my mind is no longer shopping in Brown Thomas's. It is now contemplating the weather, a shower, and what to wear to school. I refuse point blank to open my eyes. I am determined to go back to sleep, and I will have that dress. But my efforts to return to my comatose state are futile.

I become aware of the frosty nip in the air. My nose tingles with the cold. Lethargically I turn over onto my stomach and bury my head in the pillow, but to no avail. I can hear my room-mate in the bathroom gushing water, muttering curses, and clinking bottles. The door slides open and she stands there fully dressed and says what she says every morning.

'Miriam, it's twenty past eight ... Are you going to get up or will I have to drag you out of bed?'

And I respond, as I do every morning, with a loud drawn-out groan of resignation, as I realise that there is no escape. I have to get up and face the world again ...

She strides over to the window and abruptly tugs open the curtains. The sudden intrusion of light into the room has an air of finality to it. The night has turned into morning, and now it's time to get on with the day. I sluggishly sit up in bed with bleary eyes, hair like a furze bush, and a glum expression. Groggily I clamber out of bed and scuttle crablike across the room and into the shower.

Eight minutes later I stumble down the stairs and into the dining-room, only to slump onto the chair. Not capable of communication, I stare into the distance, my mind a total blank. Around me, amid the clatter of plates and cups, snatches of conversation over my head ... 'Great—microwaved toast again ...' 'Donna, can I borrow your physics papers? ...' 'Lucy, had we any French homework? ...' I sit there oblivious to everything, slightly disoriented, slowly gathering my scattered thoughts together.

And then it arrives. The elixir of life, the source of all vitality and vigour ... a large, steaming mug of black coffee. Liberally laced with sugar, the smell alone seeps into my subconscious and revives my dormant zest for life. Slowly, like a smouldering piece of wood bursting into flame, my glassy stare disappears. My leaden limbs begin to feel normal, and gradually I become a member of the human race once more.

Thus fortified, I find the strength to start the long, agonising trek to school—all twenty minutes of it. Walking over the Blitz Bridge, the fresh wind buffets my face and chases away all the lingering cobwebs of sleep and doziness. Fully alert, I look at all the patiently queuing cars of the nine o'clock rush hour and wonder where they're all going. Sober-suited men cross the road carrying bulging briefcases and furled umbrellas. Morose teenagers trudge reluctantly to school, dejected at the prospect of another mundane day of classes and homework. Young women with flawlessly painted faces and short skirts hurry to work, passing the primary school children who, stress-free, skip happily to school. Everyone is on the move, rushing to their day's occupation.

I glance at my watch and quicken my pace. Can't be late again, or the principal will surely tear out my internal organs and show them to me. Amazingly, I manage to avoid verbal vivisection and reach my first class unmolested. The day passes in a blur of classes, study, gossip, lectures, and veiled threats from teachers on what will happen if Work Is Not Done. People rush along the corridors with varying expressions of despair. There is an occasional smile, defeatist shrugs, lots of scowls, and a few sulks.

The study is never silent, with papers rustling, bags unzipping, pencil cases rattling, and books opening. Yearning glances are thrown into the yard, where the memory of a cigarette before study lingers on. Heads are in studious positions but minds are far away in places where homework and exams don't exist. A smothered giggle rouses the wrath of the supervisor. Outraged, he struts up and down the hall like a peacock on steroids, looking for the culprit. Once discovered, the sinner is banished to the principal's office, and a collective sigh of sympathy for that poor unfortunate is exhaled by classmates.

At 8:55 p.m. impatient eyes stare at the study clock, willing the second hand to move faster. Books are surreptitiously slid into bags, yawns are stifled, and coats are soundlessly slipped onto weary shoulders. The remaining five minutes seem like a lifetime to those intently gazing at the unhurried clock. At last the clock reaches nine. The supervisor's usual cautions about picking up paper etc. are drowned as a turbulent mass of humanity surges towards the exit door.

Eleven thirty p.m. is my favourite time of day. I am curled cosily in my bed, swamped in blankets, pillows, and jumpers. All the woes and worries of the day diffuse slowly out of my brain. My eyelids begin to feel heavy, my head begins to droop. There is a small vengeful smile playing on my lips as I lose consciousness ... I'm thinking of the last day at school, when that malignant alarm clock becomes redundant and when I gleefully smash it to pieces with a hammer. Sweet dreams ...

---

The approach here is realistic and authentic. The writer registers ordinary details of everyday life in a vivid and precise manner. The autobiographical approach makes it more interesting and arresting in effect.

The following composition (from an actual pupil's work) is an example of descriptive writing.

---

### Unemployment

A vicious gust of wind blew down the dilapidated street, whipping the raindrops before it. Claire shivered and clutched the hood of her shabby anorak more tightly around her face, partly to protect herself from the driving rain but also partly to hide behind it. The wheel of the baby-buggy jammed in the broken paving-stone just outside the door of the post office, and two-year-old Christopher began to howl as she wrenched it free with a tired jerk. His roars seemed to increase in volume as she pushed her way into the post office to join the end of the social welfare queue. Half-heartedly,

## THE ENGLISH COMPOSITION

Claire attempted to hush her son in response to the sour look from the woman behind the glass partition. To tell the truth, she felt like screaming herself, and had she done so none of the equally depressed people standing in front of her would even have glanced around.

Familiar figures, most of them, the same old hopeless bunch every week: the same down-turned faces, shabby coats, harassed-looking women, unshaven men. The same disease affecting every one of them—the epidemic of the dole queues, the plague of Ballycree.

Apathy. Hopelessness. The grinding misery of poverty wore them down: the telly sold, new shoes for the kids a distant memory, the terror of Christmas approaching, the menace of moneylenders ... Somehow it all seemed worse in the rain.

This is unemployment. It's real. It doesn't go away. Yes, we can turn off the television or the radio when the monotonous old statistics are broadcast: 'Current unemployment figures are up by 0.7 per cent on last year. When seasonal factors are taken into account, the rate has increased by 1.3 per cent ...' Yes, we can shake our heads mournfully at the newspaper headlines: 'Jobs axed in Unichem'—that's easy. But the true victims of unemployment, the anonymous and seemingly forgotten masses, cannot deny the reality of switching off the television or the radio. They probably haven't even got a television or a radio. They are the reality.

Ballycree is one of the worst unemployment black-spots in Ireland. There's a cliché for you: black-spot. It's more like a cloud, really—a black, poisonous, sulphurous, choking cloud that presses down on people and suffocates them. It is not only the depressed and depressing ghetto of Ballycree that is overshadowed by this cloud: each lucky person who happens to live there and who happens not to have a job has their own personal little black cloudlet, which floats miserably about six inches above their heads. Even the written word Ballycree has a faint dark mist around it. Can't see it? That's funny. Interviewers and prospective employers detect it a mile off. 'Sorry,' they say. 'You're unfortunately not quite the person we're looking for.' They might as well say you don't live in the right place or you have no qualifications.

There's another evocative word—qualifications. For residents of Ballycree and other economically depressed suburbs, qualifications don't mean university degrees. They don't mean Leaving Certs. Usually they don't even mean Junior Certs. Did you know that early school-leavers under twenty-five have a national unemployment rate of over 45 per cent? This drops to 39 per cent for those with a Junior Cert. That's a fair lot of raindrops. These figures are even starker if, like Claire, you are an early school-leaver aged over twenty-five; in this case the struggle to fill in application forms is simply not worth it.

Claire left school at thirteen. An intelligent girl, she bitterly resented her family's monstrous assumption that she would automatically and effortlessly take over her mother's role when she became ill. As a surrogate mother she was a poor substitute, and the care of her own ill mother, together with four younger brothers and sisters, as well as endless mounds of housework, threatened to overwhelm her. At first she attempted to keep up with her school work by asking her former school friends what homework they had, but with scarcely a minute to herself her secret plans soon fell by the wayside, and with them all her hopes for the future.

Unemployed and unemployable, Claire is now a frustrated single mother. Once she dreamt of emigration, packing her bags and escaping from the prison of her wretched life. She now knows that this is a joke. Without the money even for a bus fare, and with the inescapable burden of a child to care for, she is trapped.

Chris began to scream again. Still strapped into his buggy, he'd dropped his soother onto the grimy lino floor. Wearily bending to pick it up, Claire went to the sink to rinse it. A hairy spider scuttled to safety as she turned the tap with an effort. A thin trickle of brownish water spluttered out, accompanied by the rough clanking of the pipes. She shuddered as she thought how near she came to hating her crying child. She could smell his dirty nappy and knew he needed to be changed. Instead, however, Claire sank into the oily chair in the dim little room. Slumping over the table with her head in her hands, she began to sob hopelessly. The raindrops trickled down the filthy glass of the window.

---

The writer here uses some vivid description: 'vicious gust', 'dilapidated down-turned faces', 'shabby coats', 'unshaven men'. There is a strong focus on colour and registering small details in a vivid manner: 'black-spot', 'poisonous choking cloud'. The writer links the opening and concluding paragraph very well.

## THE AESTHETIC USE OF LANGUAGE

## *Writing an impressionistic or imaginative composition*

This is a style of writing that seeks to describe a feeling or experience rather than to communicate factual information.

It is important when undertaking an impressionistic style to maintain a balance between being spontaneous and being systematic. The composition demands an inherent order and organisation of material;

however, an impressionistic approach presupposes sometimes that the particular order is not always traditional and conventional.

This type of composition demands the ability to write with a great deal of perception about human feelings. An impressionistic style is the opposite to a factual or discursive approach.

## *Imaginative writing*

The imaginative composition always demands that the writer puts their own personality into the writing. This style demands some striking powers of imagination and creativity. A writer of this style must have the capacity to capture the subject in a highly imaginative way. Generally, the links between ideas in this type of composition will be conveyed by means of clever and subtle images and not directly through logic, as in the discursive composition.

Compositions that are written in this style demand creativity, an innovative approach in the use of subject matter and language. An ability to write poetic language and striking description is important when undertaking this type of composition.

The following composition (from an actual pupil's work) is an example of an impressionistic style. The ideas are woven together in a novel and fluid way. Here the writer has taken a distinctly original approach to the composition title.

**Confessions of a near-adult**
God love them all, he thought to himself. So many papers, so many dreams and aspirations. Just how many of them would be realised!

He knew, or at least he told himself, that correcting Leaving Certificate English was a job. Just like any other job.

For God's sake, he told himself, what could be easier! The marking criteria were in front of him—albeit under a coffee-ringed mosaic. But it was not easy.

He knew that he should not let it get to him. That it was no concern of his. But this year, for whatever reason, it was.

Perhaps it was the title of the composition—'Confessions of a near-adult'. It framed a vague notion of his.

All that could be seen was a brown cloth bag with a brass padlock. Fairly unimpressive. But as it lay there, despite its small dimensions, it filled the room.

To him over the days it assumed life. Living and breathing. A wonderful marvel.

Scripts. Two hundred and forty scripts. He had never become entirely comfortable with that word. To him it was too meaningful, too emotional a word to use, too close.

To him, however, the word quite aptly summed up the essence of what they were. Scripts. Two hundred and forty lives and people. Some men and women, most just boys and girls still. These strangers with whom his life was inextricably tied for an instant.

A coffee break gave him time for a few moments of idleness and personal thought. He lit a cigarette. Boiled the kettle and added some coffee and sugar to a mug, stirring away the dark stains.

In the hall the clock chimed, reminding him that it was three in the morning. The world was slumbering and at peace. He was the only consciousness in a world of sleepy minds, or so he liked to feel.

Upstairs, Catherine lay between the warm sheets of their bed. Little Ruth would be lying motionless in her arms. Jason would be snoring gently, wrapped up in feathers, down, and Thomas the Tank Engine.

He wanted to go upstairs. To join them all. To kiss Catherine as she slept. To say sorry and apologise for losing the cool over breakfast. To hold her close and smell her hair. But he could not.

Between the kitchen door and creaking stairs, the bag of scripts glowed in the moonlight. Emitting its own energy. Radiating.

What was this presence he had allowed into his home and into contact with his family? Of course there were some entertaining confessions. Some rampant imaginations. That boy who said he was an English-teacher and was only doing the paper to satisfy his own curiosity. A ludicrous idea; however, it was well written, sharp and enjoyable. A little gem. A2. A boy with—or was it a boy at all? Did it really matter? This year it did.

Then there was the boy ... candidate whose mother had meningitis, and he had to spend all his time looking after her. A likely story. An excuse for inadequate expression and poor spelling. Not to mention punctuation! He had barely remembered to use full stops. A cheat and a user.

He had lived with illness himself. The candidate had misspelt meningitis—a dead give-away. Even at the age of seven he could spell that terrible word nobody was allowed to say. Dealing with illness every day changed you. It robbed you of your innocence and growing-up time. Into a child's heart it inflicted you with a knowledge that was unbecoming of your age.

All he had ever wanted—his sole ambition—was to marry Catherine. After all these years he loved her even more. Time had replaced the initial tempestuous passion with something deeper, with more feeling.

They both now relied on each other completely. He felt unsure and anxious when away from her and the children for more than a day.

Actually, when he said marrying Catherine was his sole ambition he was mistaken. It was so long ago he had nearly forgotten. He had wanted to be a writer. A silly fancy. Her parents would never have consented if they thought they were gaining a writer. Come to think of it, he was never better off after swearing never to pick up the pen in anger again.

He had been constantly unwell—headaches, flu, and colds. Coming back from school, correcting homework, then starting to write well into the night.

Enough of that! It was so easy to let the mind wander. Time for another paper. Back to the bag.

As he opened the kitchen door and his eye took in the radiant bag, it now looked empty and slouched. It no longer seemed a menacing presence.

He lifted the coarse cloth bag to his nose. Inhaled deeply the smell. Who were these people?

The bag was no longer a teeming, choking presence. It was two hundred and forty lives distilled. It encompassed feelings from bitter hate and love to apathy and indifference.

There were two hundred and forty voices, anxious and relaxed, but all full of hope for the future.

How many of them would realise their dreams? How many of these voices would identify exactly what they were striving for? It didn't really matter. They would set out with enthusiasm and vigour and take as big a bite of life as they could. That was the essence of it all.

Enough for tonight. So what if he did his best correcting between midnight and four o clock!

He would go up the creaking staircase. Slip between the warm sheets and wake her, or perhaps not.

Regardless, he would lay his lips on hers and kiss her. Knowing that he had achieved more that he could ever have imagined, even if at the robust age of thirty-seven.

---

The approach to the subject here is original and interesting. The vocabulary is fresh and simple. The writer uses the flashback technique in a clever way, and there is a naturalness and rhythm in the movement. Paragraphs are loosely structured to fit in with this type of confessional approach to the subject.

The following composition is written in a highly imaginative and witty fashion. It is an example of a unique approach to the subject.

## Teenagers

The life of a teenager, condensed and speeded up, would probably make a richly funny cartoon to the impartial observer. A sadistic streak, however, would be essential to gain full enjoyment from watching the plight of a hapless innocent child whirled onto the rollercoaster of 'teenagerhood'.

Being a teenager is a fate you would hardly wish on your worst enemy. Very few adults will acknowledge this. They reminisce about the 'good old days', when they themselves were young, and assure us that we are having the time of our lives; now if only we wouldn't wear those dreadful clothes and listen to that terrible music! The same old platitudes are trotted out over and over again, accompanied by sighs of fake nostalgia. But in reality, what adult would return to the struggle of being a teenager? You know as well as I do: few, if any.

Why do you imagine that thirteen is considered an unlucky number? The answer is obvious: it is at this stage that children who are unfortunate enough to have survived to this stage are thrown into the deep end of the pool of life, to sink or swim! Sometimes I imagine life as a swimming-pool. Up to the age of thirteen, children paddle and splash in the kiddies' pool, guarded and sheltered from the big bad world. Then, without warning, they are removed and flung headlong into the deep end of an enormous, apparently endless pool of horror. The water is dark, murky, and freezing, infested with icebergs, sharks, and sea monsters. The only other inhabitants of the deep end are members of what is ridiculously called the teenage peer group. They are too overwhelmed by their personal struggle for survival even to sneak a sideways glance at a fellow-sufferer, let alone to peer at him!

Apparently if one manages to dodge the icebergs and escape from the sharks and sea monsters, the water does get warmer as one swims along. By the mid-twenty mark, conditions are quite pleasant. Having been a teenager for four years (only two more to go!), I am a fairly experienced dodger, ducker, and diver. One has to be to survive the metaphorical icebergs, sharks and monsters that make the life of anyone aged between thirteen and nineteen a very dangerous place.

It has been said that there were no teenagers in Ireland until the sixties, when the term was imported (presumably from the United States); and this is a false statement. Perhaps there was no term for this stage of acute suffering—i.e. adolescence—but that is no reason to say that it did not exist. However, I do believe that the dodgers, duckers and divers of a generation ago did not need to be so adept as we are today. We have bigger, fiercer icebergs, sharks and monsters to contend with.

Adolescence is a time of change and a time of pressure. Teenagers must endure a hormone-induced physical, mental and emotional upheaval that is enough to knock even the most stable and self-confident person out of sync.

Girls seem to grow up faster than their male counterparts. Often, far from sticking together as fellow-sufferers of teenagerhood, adolescents retreat into their own little cocoon of insecurity, emerging only to antagonise adults and verbally bash each other. Neither side can win a verbal bashing contest: boys may scoff at girls' new bumps and curves, but what can be more cringingly embarrassing for the same boys than a voice that stubbornly refuses to remain on an even keel! Sports probably deserve a paragraph to themselves, but I am determined not to give the malignant little entities that satisfaction! Suffice it to say that only someone who has gazed despairingly into the mirror at a face closely resembling a pepperoni pizza can know the true meaning of adolescent angst.

Not only is adolescence a time of change for the teenager, it also seems to be a time of change for their parents and families. What is it that causes an apparently normal set of parents and siblings to metamorphose into something resembling the Addams family—a gang of dangerous weirdos whose main aim seems to be the utter humiliation of the unfortunate teenager? I am sometimes convinced that I was switched at birth and that somewhere there is a reasonable, rational, normal family where I *really* belong. Somewhere there is a father who understands about the need for pocket money and new clothes, a mother who doesn't care about school reports, and siblings who don't complain that I come back half an hour after curfew on a Saturday night. All that remains is to find them, convince them, by DNA tests if necessary, that I am their true daughter, and all will be sweetness and light. But by that time I will probably no longer be a teenager, and so the exercise will have been in vain.

The mental and emotional trauma that accompanies adolescence is largely related to moral issues. Group peer pressure encourages experimenting with alcohol, drugs, and sex. It is astonishing that there are not more teenage suicides—but then, we are a pretty resilient bunch. We need to be to cope with the greatest pressure of all that blights the lives of all teenagers: the Leaving Certificate examination, and its menacing sidekick, the 'points race'. It is all very well to criticise the undoubtedly dreadful human rights abuses committed in far-flung lands such as Bosnia and Tibet; but were Amnesty International to discover the true extent of the torture imposed by the points system they should be clamouring for it to be abolished. Not only do teenagers have to contend with their own tension and strain but they are bombarded with advice and admonitions to work harder from parents and schools. Meanwhile the peer group pulls strongly in the opposite direction. Who would be a teenager?

The two characteristics that stereotype teenagers most are their clothes and general appearance, and the music they listen to. They are what often make them appear as members of some other species. In reality they are coping methods—a little like inflatable armbands in the murky cold pool. Trying to establish a sense of personal identity while simultaneously dealing with mental, emotional and physical turmoil, stormy personal relationships, agonising moral decisions and overwhelming academic pressure is a mammoth task. Teenagers, more than most others, need to belong to some group in order to feel secure. Fashion trends can be considered as age-old methods of self-assertion; whether the individual chooses to wear leather and chains, platforms and flares, or a grotty mixture of tangled hair, ragged denims and clumping boots is not as important as the sense of 'belonging' that the look imparts. Belonging to the unhappy band of duckers, divers and dodgers, that is. What right-minded teenager would even contemplate being seen to belong to their own family?

If adults would take the time to listen to some of the music teenagers listen to, instead of bellowing abuse, they might gain a little more insight into the outlook of the younger generation. Wistful, mournful love ballads, angry resentful rock and metal, and rhythmic optimistic dance music—these convey some of the emotions of every teenager, while celebrating the natural resilience inherent in virtually all of us.

Adults are in no position to wag disapproving fingers at the younger generation. I have been shocked to overhear some things my own mother has said. Contrary to popular belief, teenagers are people too. One may wear peculiar garments, listen to unintelligible music, get sloshed or stoned, rage, rant and rebel occasionally—but we do have a tough time, except in the view of adults who gaze into a rose-tinted rear-view mirror. 'It wasn't like that in my day.' Ever heard that phrase? I'm sure you have. Perhaps you've even used it yourself. Of course things were not the same in your day. We're not going in reverse. The teenagers of today are the adults of tomorrow, and I think we're doing a pretty good job.

---

The writer here uses some interesting metaphors. The 'water' metaphor of icebergs, dodgers and duckers is both interesting and original. The approach is colourful and lively, if self-indulgent. The language moves forward in a vigorous and energetic fashion.

## THE LANGUAGE OF ARGUMENT

### Writing a discursive composition

A discursive composition is one in which the writer arrives at a conclusion by means of facts and argument. Some other terms for this type of writing are 'argumentative' or 'controversial' writing.

# THE ENGLISH COMPOSITION

A good discursive or debate-style composition involves convincing your reader of the validity of your argument, and this can be done through clear logic, sound argument, and the correct organisation of ideas. Argument is at the centre of this type of composition. What is important in a composition of this type is the organisation of facts, together with the proper arrangement of ideas so as to produce a lucid and persuasive argument.

Facts can be developed by means of definition. For example, a composition on apartheid could define the nature of apartheid in one paragraph. Facts can also be developed through analogy, illustration, cause and effect, or classification.

In a discursive composition you divide the issue you are dealing with into conflicting sides or points of view.

This type of composition demands the use of assertion, justification, and presupposition.

An **assertion** is where you claim that something is true, for example that apartheid is still a problem in South Africa.

**Justification** is signalling clearly the significance of the ideas you are presenting and the attitude you are adopting towards them. It means supporting or substantiating the points you are making with clear, factual evidence.

**Presupposition** means that you take certain facts for granted and that your reader is already aware of various aspects of your topic. For example, in a composition on apartheid you could take for granted that your reader is aware of the existence of apartheid in South Africa for many years, how it was opposed by the liberation movement, and how it has been overturned.

The outline will play a major part in developing the argument in a discursive composition. (The section on outlines on page 127 shows how to structure the ideas in a composition of this type.)

Your opening paragraph or opening statement must reflect the restrictions imposed by the topic, besides establishing clearly your approach or stance to the subject in question. This means that before you start writing a discursive composition you must know clearly your own stance on the topic. You cannot change your mind on the topic half way through!

Clarity is important so that your reader can follow your train of thought. State your argument clearly and simply, and make sure you have not left out any essential points in your argument.

Sometimes a short, terse sentence can help to establish clearly your point, and this can be corroborated later on in your composition.

It is important to recognise and to be able to use the different skills involved in writing an argumentative composition. Bear in mind the selection of evidence, the structuring of thought, and the need for coherence. These are all higher thinking skills that involve the exercise of discrimination, evaluation, and synthesis.

## *Techniques in writing a discursive composition*

1. Use pre-writing strategies to get started: writing in a journal, free writing, focused free writing, cubing, and clustering of ideas. All these techniques will sharpen your skills.
2. Identify your audience and the tone or point of view you will use.
3. Develop a controlling idea or stance that will propel you through the composition. This idea will clarify your position on the topic and generally indicate the direction in which your composition is heading. For example, in a composition entitled 'Freedom of the press is a basic right' you might adopt the idea that slavery and repression are contrary to the dignity of the human. The composition's title can thus be defended by showing the negative effects of slavery and restrictions on the human spirit and on society in general. A good opening statement or standpoint will establish your purpose clearly in both your own and your reader's mind. Restrict and narrow your topic by taking a definite stance or position on the topic.
4. Make sure there is priority in your argument: put the most important ideas first. Give your reader a clear expectation of how your argument will develop and which ideas are more important. For example, in a composition on 'Violence and the media' you might discuss how the media can depict violence and so aggravate it.
5. Cultivate the technique of writing persuasively. Treat any arguments against your viewpoint in a balanced way. Give plenty of examples to support your position. Such examples should be woven into the body of your composition in as natural and fluid a way as possible. Gather support in order to ensure a clear focus on your composition and to support your points.
6. Avoid a sensational or exaggerated approach to the subject, such as: 'It is time that women stopped being slaves and started to assert their long-overdue rights and began to fight against male dominance.'

7. Avoid a one-sided presentation. You must reflect an awareness of other aspects and opinions on the topic. Balance of presentation in ideas is an important feature of the discursive composition. Make sure to present your ideas in a detached and objective manner; avoid a subjective or prejudiced approach in a discursive-type composition. A writer of this type of composition must be able to move steadily through conflicting arguments and present a clear, logical conclusion at the end.
8. Never use emotional language when writing a discursive composition. When you have convincing material to offer as evidence, present it as vividly as you can and let your readers draw their own conclusions. If the argument has flaws, it is better to strengthen it by reasoning and facts and to collect more evidence than to try to mask its weaknesses by name-calling or overdramatising your position. The chain of evidence and reasoning must be easy to follow in a well-written discursive composition.
9. Beware of using words or groups of words that denigrate or victimise people. References to people's sex, race, nationality, religion, class or physical ability should be treated cautiously. Avoid discriminatory language, such as 'male nurse', 'woman doctor', and so on.
10. Clear and concise writing requires the avoidance of jargon and the elimination of redundancy. Repetition, clichés, emotional and offensive language, euphemisms and double-speak are inappropriate and in fact weaken an argument. In clichéd writing, commonplace ideas and worn-out wording take the place of careful observation and original thinking. Clichés render an argument slack and lifeless and drain away all credibility.

Most written arguments require complex thinking but not necessarily complicated expression. The more difficult and complex the ideas are, the more need there is for a simple and clear expression. Work to produce clear, orderly sentences. Group related ideas together, and emphasise essential points. Always try to write concisely.

## THE LANGUAGE OF PERSUASION

The features of the language of persuasion are dealt with in the section on comprehension (chapter 1). In this section we will discuss the method of constructing a persuasive argument or composition, and the particular features involved in this type of writing.

To write a composition or article and use the language of persuasion means to convince your reader of something that you personally believe in.

It is important to distinguish between the language of argument and the language of persuasion, because they are quite similar. While the language of argument will rely on a rational and logical approach, the persuasive writer must be able to advance their argument as eloquently and as convincingly as possible. A good persuasive writer must be able to express their viewpoint clearly and logically, while at the same time disposing of any contrary opinions.

## *Features of persuasive composition or writing*

1. Know your audience. Identify carefully their level of knowledge, their motivations and interests. Remember that an article on 'examination stress' will have little relevance for a group of housewives. Similarly, a persuasive composition on changing fashions will be wasted on a group of schoolboys.
2. Once you have ascertained who your audience are, adapt your message and tone accordingly. State your purpose clearly and confidently. Establish the correct tone with your audience. It can help sometimes to inject a note of humour or irony into your writing in order to gain the attention of your readers more readily. Do not use colloquial language or slang if you are addressing a group of academics or the Minister for Education. Similarly, do not use formal language if you are writing on pop music for a teenage magazine.
3. Use techniques such as effective images or anecdotes to support your viewpoint. These can also serve the function of arousing certain emotions about your topic in the reader.

Look at the following paragraph from an article on the Chernobyl accident, where the writer makes effective use of images and anecdotes to illustrate the emotion of fear.

> Head against the fogged-up window, which couldn't be opened because of the fear of radiation dust; numbed, sweating, terrified underneath my radiation protection suit, I began to question my very sanity. What in the hell was I doing in the world's most radioactive environment? Inner cries of 'Help!' rushed to the surface. I felt engulfed by a strong sense of panic. I couldn't breathe. My heart raced and felt as if it might burst. I looked at

the Geiger counter in my hand and—my God!—I saw the needle rise beyond what it was capable of registering. My fear was overwhelming. Feelings of sinking into a deep black hole rushed forth like a torrent of evil. I screamed silently. I was in my own private world of terror. I had just entered 'Death Valley', the exclusion zone surrounding Chernobyl.

Looking at my companions—an Irish film crew sent with the task of filming a documentary which would tell the world the truth about the aftermath of the Chernobyl accident—I felt ill with the weight of responsibility. The bravery we had felt earlier had evaporated. Each of us was now afraid to divulge our inner horror. We stayed locked in our private worlds. My mother's promise to light a church candle daily failed to ease me. Frantically, my mind fled into its darkest recesses to find something to sustain me. Images of my parents and closest ones flashed in and out. Prayers and words of laughter squeezed their way in between the blackness. With all of this rush of emotion my personal story of Chernobyl unfolded.

[Adi Roche, *Children of Chernobyl*]

---

This is an example of emotive or persuasive writing, where the message is conveyed at the level of the emotions or feelings. The fear of being buried alive is conveyed sharply through the sentence structure. The short, terse sentences, together with the emotive 'I' throughout, convey this effect of near-hysteria and nightmare very sharply. The anecdotal reference to the film crew and to the mother lighting candles intensifies the emotional impact of this piece.

Because persuasive writing relies less on facts, remember the power of the image and the need for striking expression to convey the message.

When writing a persuasive composition or article, bear in mind the following points:

- Avoid making sweeping statements or vague generalisations, such as 'all examinations should be scrapped,' 'all women need to be liberated,' 'all teenagers take drugs.'
- Do not make unsupported statements. Support each argument you make with sufficient evidence or effective illustrations.
- Avoid using an aggressive tone, as it will only serve to alienate your reader.
- Do not distort the truth. While a certain amount of hyperbole or exaggeration is permissible in persuasive writing, it is never justifiable to distort or pervert the truth.

## EXPLORATIONS 2

Look at the following extract, which adopts distinctively persuasive devices to communicate the arguments.

> There was once a town in the heart of America where all life seemed to live in harmony with its surroundings. The town lay in the midst of a checkerboard of prosperous farms, with fields of grain and hillsides of orchards, where, in spring, white clouds of bloom drifted above the green fields. In autumn, oak and maple and birch set up a blaze of colour that flamed and flickered across a backdrop of pines. Then foxes barked in the hills and deer silently crossed the fields hidden in the mists of the autumn mornings. Even in winter the roadsides were a place of beauty, where countless birds came to feed on the berries. The countryside was in fact famous for the abundance and variety of its bird life, and when the flood of migrants was pouring through in spring and autumn people travelled from great distances to observe them. Others came to fish the streams which flowed clear and cold out of the hills and contained shady pools where trout lay.
>
> Then a strange blight crept over the area and everything began to change. Some evil spell had settled on the community: mysterious maladies swept the flocks of chickens; the cattle and sheep died. Everywhere was a shadow of death. The farmers spoke of much illness among their families. In the towns the doctors had become more and more puzzled by new kinds of sickness appearing among their patients. There had been several sudden and unexplained deaths.
>
> There was a strange stillness. The birds for example—where had they gone? Many people spoke of them puzzled and disturbed. The few birds seen anywhere were moribund: they trembled violently and could not fly. It was a spring without voices.
>
> On the farms the hens brooded, but no chicks hatched. The apple trees were coming into bloom but no bees droned among the blossoms, so there was no pollination and there would be no fruit.
>
> The roadsides once so attractive were now lined with browned and withered vegetation as though swept by fire. These, too, were silent, deserted by all living things. Even the streams were now lifeless. Anglers no longer visited them, for all the fish had died.
>
> In the gutters under the eaves and between the shingles of the roofs, a white granular powder still showed a few patches; some weeks before it had fallen like snow upon the roofs and the lawns, the fields and streams.
>
> No witchcraft, no enemy action had silenced the rebirth of new life in this stricken world. The people had done it themselves.
>
> [Rachel Carson, *Silent Spring*]

The approach here is very dramatic. The writer uses the narrative method very cleverly to convey the point about the progressive decay in animal and plant life. In persuasive writing, the power of images is predominant. The language and imagery used here are powerful and effective yet very simple and comprehensible. Strive for that direct and lucid style of writing.

The following is a sample composition (from actual pupils' work) written in a persuasive style on the topic 'A society can be judged by the way it treats its minorities'.

> I agree with the motion that a society can be judged by the way it treats its minorities. Don't blame the Government, teachers, parents or anybody else for the way in which minorities are treated. It's not their fault really. I believe the young miscreant responsible for the whole lot goes by the name of Mr Pericles. Unfortunately, however, I am led to believe that bringing him to justice would be impracticable, because of the fact that the wretched malefactor died some years ago—a few thousand, to be precise—in Ancient Greece.
>
> For it was this smart young fellow's idea to come up with a thing called democracy. To be fair to the man, he probably didn't understand the full consequences of what he started. In fact he probably thought it was a darned good idea at the time. I'm sure the system worked like clockwork and was a roaring success when it was first introduced. 'Hands up, those who think we should pick a fight with the Persians. One, two, three ... okay, the act is passed.'
>
> Unfortunately, things are not as simple nowadays as they were then. Today we have countries with populations numbering millions. Politicians and those who rely on being elected don't concern themselves with people any more: there is simply no need any more.
>
> Take, for example, that fine and noble institution and pillar of world democracy the American government and, in particular, the presidency. Why should a presidential candidate have to carry out such a useless and degrading act as going out and meeting the average man on the street when he has demographics? No longer should a politician put up with the banal and frankly unhygienic act of kissing babies at random. Thanks to demographics, he needs now only to kiss a selected and representative assortment of babies. Not only does he know what cheek to kiss and what hand to squeeze but he also knows where to be seen doing it too. Giving a little something for everyone, pleasing all. Show up at a few coincidentally televised bar mitzvahs for sons of leading Jewish citizens. Attend a St Patrick's Day parade: that should secure the Paddy vote. Praise some really

pitifully young black director-producer-writer-actor sort of fellow and get the world (or at least the black community) vote and hopefully not the KKK vote. Admit to being his number 1 fan and to knowing where he's 'coming from.' Kiss a retarded baby for the 'Everybody loves that stuff' bonus point. Say things like 'Ich bin ein Berliner.' Know that the year you were born was the Chinese year of the worm.

That's what present-day politics comes down to. A few sympathetic words, a firm handshake, and a few lucky photo opportunities—that's what it's all about nowadays. That is how the politicians, the elected representatives, the leaders of our modern society do it.

But what if you, as a person, don't rate very highly in the demographics? If you are part of a community of people that just don't matter in terms of overall importance? Then what? One of two things can happen to you, one bad, the other worse.

First, it may be decided to forget about you, your needs and rights, altogether. Bad, yes. Unfair, true. But the worst case? Not so.

Example scenario: an island 250 miles south of somewhere. It's called Paradise Island. Ninety-seven per cent of the population consists of racist, bigoted supporters of less severe gun laws, all of whom are white, underpaid, and angry. The other 3 per cent are black teenage single mothers who are Jewish and who control the industry of the island and don't like white people too much. The man running for president could do one of two things: leave the 3 per cent alone, because they won't influence the vote; or victimise the 3 per cent, much to the satisfaction of the 97 per cent, and ensure his election. Which option will he take?

The whole story may sound bizarre and outlandish, but I hope it proves a point (in an admittedly silly but simple way) for you. Such an obvious and easily understood way as this helps us to consider that such a process is taking place in Ireland today, for it is. But it is doing so in a much less dramatic and more subtle fashion.

I refer to the travelling community. It may seem on a national level that the travelling people are not being 'got at.' Instead, travellers are just for the most part forgotten about. If they can't read or write and have no fixed address, and therefore, more importantly, can't vote, who cares about them? Only a few token halting-sites (themselves being built regardless of the travellers' actual needs and wishes) and a few serviced stops remain as the Government's token gestures of support for the travelling people. However, the story changes at 'grass roots' level. At this level, local authorities and councillors quite openly tell travellers that they are unsavoury and unwanted. This is done at this level because only in these circumstances can elected representatives be so sure of the wishes of the majority of their constituency.

> But if this is the practice in small local councils, then is the effect not the same as if it was Government policy? It is even worse, because at this level it is a lot more insidious and harder to fight.
>
> The travelling community is only one minority group, and they are the only group I have decided to deal with. But replace the word 'traveller' with any other minority and the story will be the same.
>
> A society can be judged by the way it treats its minorities. Human nature means survival of the fittest, and so when one group of people is so much more dominant than the other, weaker one, the 'put the boot in while he's down' attitude comes into play.
>
> And so, to sum up, not just society but the way humankind has evolved and indeed human nature can be judged by the way the majority in society treat the majority, how the strong treat the weak.

The approach to the topic here is lively and interesting. The writer adopts a humorous approach to the subject, which is a skilful weapon of the persuasive writer when it is used cleverly. Also, the use of an anecdote to support a point, as in the rather ironic reference to Paradise Island, is a clever tactic of persuasive writing.

The style is easy and colloquial, the language and imagery used are familiar and accessible to everyone. The sentence structure is terse and varied. However, as is typical of much writing at this level (senior cycle), the scope and range of ideas is limited. The ideas lack penetration and depth in places.

## THE LANGUAGE OF INFORMATION

This type of communication may also be described as *functional writing*. As we have seen in the chapter on comprehension, the language of information is the basis of all report-writing, as well as the writing of a list of instructions, a memo or a letter, or a newspaper review.

Mastering the skills of these different genres will be discussed in detail in this section. Let us examine first the features of functional writing.

For your communication to be effective in writing, remember to keep your *purpose* in mind at all times. Ask yourself: am I informing, or looking for information? Understand the relevance of what you are writing and where it fits in to the social context.

Functional writing can have as its objective some of the following purposes:

- to supply information
- to give instructions or make requests
- to persuade or influence the reader to adopt an attitude or to act on a particular matter.

One common fault in technical or functional writing is a failure to select information appropriately. Writers can be irrelevant: they can digress and introduce unnecessary points, and they can give superfluous information. This can happen because of a lack of focus on the part of the writer. Failure to accurately assess questions such as the purpose of the writing, the audience or the subject matter can contribute to these problems.

Once you have worked out exactly what you want to say, go on to see what form your writing will take.

Some examples of functional writing are:

- reports
- memos
- letters
- summaries
- bulletins
- instructions.

The following considerations must be taken into account when you are engaged in this form of writing:

1. What are the reader's expectations? Who is my reader? What job have they?
2. What am I trying to achieve in writing this message or information?
3. What exactly do I need to include in this message to achieve this result from this particular person?

Functional writing tests your ability to use language

- clearly
- appropriately
- concisely.

The style, therefore, should be factual and clear.

## Features of functional writing

1. **Clear organisation of information.** All arguments and information must be expressed in a logical and coherent manner.

2. **Relevant content.** There must be no digression from the point and no introduction of useless or irrelevant information.
3. **An appropriate style and expression.** Different situations and circumstances call for different styles of writing. In general, for functional writing the style should be unobtrusive—like a windowpane through which information can be clearly seen.
4. **Short sentences.** The intelligent use of sentence length is an important ingredient of effective style for functional or informative writing. Flexibility and variety in sentence length make writing easier to read. Short sentences can be used to make complex or important information arresting and make it stand out. Generally, long sentences should be avoided.

FEATURES OF STYLE

1. **Avoid overlong sentences.**
2. **Use precise and simple vocabulary.**
3. **Avoid jargon, slang, buzz-words, and 'commercialese'.** *Jargon* is the inappropriate use of the terminology of a specialised profession. *Slang* is extremely informal language, generally confined to casual speech, especially among uneducated people. *Buzz-words* are temporarily fashionable expressions, designed to appear like technical language but often with no real meaning and frequently ungrammatical (such as 'ongoing' for 'continuing' or 'continuous'; 'at this point in time' for 'at the present time' or 'now'; 'pro-active' for 'active'; 'nationwide' and 'worldwide' used as adverbs). *Commercialese* is the use of dated and stereotyped formulas of a type once common in business correspondence ('Enclosed herewith' for 'I enclose'; 'I refer to your letter of …' instead of 'Thank you for your letter of …' etc.).
4. **Limit the use of the passive voice.** Use the active form of the verb.
5. **Use concrete words rather than abstract ones.**
6. **Use each word in a way that clearly illustrates its meaning.** For example, does 'Check undercarriage locking-pin' mean remember the information, or record it, or verify that the locking-pin is in place? Remember that words can have different meanings according to their context.
7. **Use factual rather than emotive words.** Use words that are clear, concise, precise, and objective. The word you choose must clearly

represent what you want to say. Do not use words figuratively, as many times they can obscure or dim the facts. The literal use of words concentrates the mind on one meaning, whereas a figurative use of words invites the reader to elicit secondary meanings. The raw material of functional writing is

- factual, not emotive;
- informative, not descriptive or narrative.

So an objective and detached tone must be used. Avoid the subjective 'I' as much as possible. Choose words that carry plain, objective meanings; pin down the meaning as closely as possible.

8. **Use the precise number of words.**
9. **Use a shorter rather than a longer word.**
10. **Use a shorter sentence rather than a longer one.**

## *Objectives of functional writing*

Every document—memo, report, bulletin, summary, letter or press statement—has an objective. Some of these objectives are:

**—to inform:** to provide information on something;
**—to explain:** to justify information and to give reasons for your opinions and conclusions;
**—to convince:** going beyond explanation and trying to bring your reader over to a certain viewpoint. In explaining, you say why you believe certain ideas are valid. Convincing involves informing, explaining, and then providing incentives for action to your reader;
**—to illustrate:** to explain something by using one or more examples. For example, to show the need for political structures between North and South, the following illustration can be drawn:

> A million people will use the Belfast–Dublin rail service this year, compared with 250,000 in 1993.

**—to elaborate:** to add more information on the topic:

> Bytewise is Ireland's eighth-largest computer company, with sales last year of £17 million, an increase of 17 per cent on the previous year. Bytewise distributes Apple computers and Unix work-stations as well as a range of computer printers.

—**to request information:** the writer may ask questions that will motivate the reader to carry out some action:

> Please let me have the accounts that are outstanding for last month.

—**to research information** and come back with specific answers:

> Please study how much an extension to the west wing will cost and supply me with written details, including cost, labour, and time involved, by 5 October.

—**to provoke thought:** this type of writing may pose a rhetorical question that will get the reader to think more deeply about something rather than to reply immediately;

—**to confirm:** to clarify and document information already known to the reader:

> Please confirm that the wages of all employees have been paid this month.

—**to remind:** the writer is confirming while also asking for action to be carried out:

> Remember that the order for oak furniture must be sent by Monday at the latest.

—**to summarise:** this is to draw conclusions from information that preceded.

## WORDS

To improve your power of written communication it is important to examine closely the nature and structure of words, sentences, and paragraphs.

A sense of audience is a key to successful word choice. Knowing exactly who will read your document, what kind of person is being addressed, is vital in the writing process. Place every word and expression in a context that makes your meaning clear to the reader. When necessary, provide an immediate, explicit explanation or definition as soon as you have used the term.

In technical writing, the words that are used must be exact and objective. Only the required number of words should be used that make the meaning instantly clear. The following sentence is an example of a long-winded or verbose style of writing:

> In the light of your failure to make the last three payments on the car you purchased through us, we are taking immediate steps to repossess the vehicle.

Write instead:

> Because of your failure to make three payments on the car, we have no other option but to repossess it.

Again, do not write:

> Thank you for your order of 21 April for filing-cabinets, which are now ready.

Write instead:

> The filing-cabinets you ordered on 21 April are now ready.

## SENTENCES

Words must be built into straightforward and concise sentences. Short sentences hold the reader's attention. Avoid complex sentences: use a simple sentence instead.

Look at the following sentences as an example of confusion in presenting controversial ideas.

> An essential prerequisite of peace in the industrial world is the maintenance of prices at a constant and unchanging level. It is not a solution to increase workers' pay packets to coincide with upward trends in prices. We must ask the following questions: can we have at one and the same time full employment, prices held at a steady and even level, and negotiations entered upon for increases in workers' wages? It is my opinion that the aim of seeing each and every member of the community being employed should be removed from the sphere of party politics. If we are unable to achieve all three of these very desirable goals that we are aiming at, let us at least achieve that one.

By making these sentences shorter and more punchy, a more vigorous piece of writing can be produced.

> Prices kept at a consistent level will maintain stability in the business world. The solution does not lie in increasing workers' pay to coincide with price increases. Is it possible simultaneously to

have full employment, a consistent level of prices, and negotiations for an increase in workers' wages? Our main objective should be the attainment of full employment.

Avoid using stock phrases and stereotyped formulas, which are time-wasting and imprecise.

|  | *Use instead:* |
|---|---|
| in the event that | if |
| with regard to | concerning |
| under active consideration | being considered |
| in respect of | concerning; in relation to |
| in the majority of cases | in most cases; usually |
| currently | at the present time; at present; now |
| sufficient | enough |
| canteen facilities | canteen |
| weather conditions | weather |
| on a regular basis | regularly |

## PARAGRAPHS

Each paragraph should deal with one aspect of your subject matter. Restrict each paragraph to one topic. Paragraphs should have a topic sentence, and every sentence in the paragraph should relate to that one point or topic.

This topic sentence may be placed at the beginning, as it can act as a signpost and help paragraph unity.

Pick out the topic sentence in the following paragraph.

> The rate of inflation remains moderate, despite the high level of economic growth, according to the latest official figures. They show that prices rose by just 0.1 per cent in March, less than expected and indicating that Ireland remains well placed to meet the Maastricht inflation rules.

The topic sentence here is clearly set out at the beginning of the paragraph. The remainder of the paragraph gives examples of the increase (0.1 per cent) and how that will affect Ireland's relationship to the Maastricht conditions.

Clear paragraphing presents the contents of your message in progressive and readily comprehensible stages. Links or transitional devices help to provide unity between paragraphs. These links can be provided by the use of transitional devices, such as the following:

- 'subsequently'
- 'afterwards'
- 'formerly'
- 'if'
- 'unless'
- 'because'
- 'in addition to'
- 'as well as'
- 'besides'
- 'therefore'
- 'consequently'
- 'thus'

**'If'** shows a relationship of to time:

> The company will expand its market if its sales of coffee increase this year.

**'Because'** shows a relationship of cause:

> Because the Central Statistics Office has only begun to publish monthly figures this year, there is no comparable figure for March 1996.

**'Unless'** outlines conditions:

> Unless the company reconsiders its refusal to pay the agreed increase, it will be necessary to examine what further steps can to be taken to bring about a resolution.

**'Subsequently'**, **'formerly'**, **'afterwards'**, **'then'**, **'later'** and **'now'** all indicate a time relationship:

> The managing director invested in a further thousand shares, and subsequently the profits boomed.

**'In addition to'**, **'as well as'** and **'besides'** show additional evidence:

> An important function of the state is the issuing and certifying of money. In addition, it is convenient to have a single, trustworthy authority producing money in order to carry out everyday transactions. Besides, people prefer money that is certified by an authority.

'**Therefore**', '**thus**' and '**consequently**' indicate that what is being said is a logical consequence and a direct result of what was said before:

> The safeguarding of water quality costs millions of pounds each year. Money has to be got from additional sources to pay for this. Consequently, the Government is worried at the state of the finances and the probability of increasing taxes.

Links between paragraphs can also be provided

—**spatially:** The emphasis here is on the position occupied by each item of the contents. For example, the following set of instructions is based on spatial order:

---

**Connecting the power adapter**
1. Plug the power adapter connector firmly into the printer's power socket.
2. Plug the other end of the power adapter cable into an earthed electrical outlet.
3. If the electrical outlet is on the same side as the parallel port on the printer, fit the power cable into the cable track so that the printer's power cable is neatly housed in place.

---

—**by chronological order:** this method deals with the time sequence in which events take place. The following example is a set of instructions in chronological order for cleaning the filters in a washing-machine:

---

1. Turn off the water tap.
2. Switch the machine on, and set the programme selector to 'Easy care 30'. Start the machine.
3. After approximately 40 seconds, switch the machine off, using the on-off button.
4. Unscrew the hose from the tap, and rinse the filter under running water.
5. After ten minutes, reconnect the hose.
6. Unscrew the hose from the back.
7. Use a flat pliers to remove the filter. Clean it, then replace it.
8. Reconnect the hose.
9. Open the tap, making sure there is no water leakage.
10. Leave it for 30 minutes, then close the tap.

---

—**by functional order:** in this method, the items are grouped together according to their function, i.e. what they actually do or what they can be used for. The following list of instructions for sending faxes from a computer is based on functional order:

1. Open or create a document with any application.
2. Open the 'Print set-up' dialogue box, and choose 'Superfax' as your active printer.
3. Print the document by selecting the application's 'Print' command, making the appropriate selections in the application's 'Print' dialogue box and clicking on 'OK'.
4. When Superfax's dialogue box appears, fill in the name, organisation and telephone number fields in the 'To' selection.
5. Click on the 'Start fax' button to send your fax.

## Reports

The differences between a report and other kinds of functional writing are that

(a) reports classify, analyse and present material clearly;
(b) the subject matter of a report is divided into sections, which are usually further sub-divided.

In writing a report for an examination, you must supply enough details and information to make your report convincing. Your report must also be long enough to show that you can organise material effectively.

When you are writing a report, ask yourself the following questions:

1. What is the purpose of this report?
2. What objectives am I hoping to achieve with this report?
3. What is the theme of the report?

A report is effective when

(a) it is understood without undue effort;
(b) the findings of the report are acknowledged to be valid and are acted upon.

## Preliminary check-list

1. What would be a suitable title for the report? Giving the report a title can help to establish the main theme or topic being dealt with.

2. What information needs to be included and what needs to be disregarded in the report?
3. Is the report to be a detailed one, or is it to be written in summary form?
4. What resources have I got at my disposal? For example, what equipment have I got? What budget have I been allocated?
5. What time limits am I subject to in producing the report?
6. How will the report be structured?
7. Who will read the report? Assessing exactly who your readers are will determine what particular style you will use. Writing a report for the management of a company will demand a style different from one suitable for a report for your colleagues or for the public.

## *Objectives of the report*

The purpose of a report can be

- to inform
- to evaluate a situation or set of circumstances
- to instruct
- to describe
- to provoke debate
- to persuade
- to explain.

An information report simply gives give the facts: it does not interpret them or comment on them in any way. An interpretative report, however, gives facts and interprets them for the reader.

An analytical report gives facts, and interprets and comments on them. It goes on to suggest reasons or to explain the significance of these facts. It also draws conclusions or makes recommendations.

## *Organisation of information in a report*

A report will usually have the following elements:

- title
- introduction
- main body of the report, usually divided into sections

- conclusion
- recommendations (where appropriate)
- references (if any were used)
- glossary (where appropriate).

Make liberal use of headings and sub-headings. These will act as signposts, signalling routes and announcing the content of sections. Headings and sub-headings in reports are usually numbered, often in the **compound numbering** style (1.1, 1.2, etc.).

A text laid out in the form of a report invites the reader to expect an argument. It moves from the statement of a problem, through evidence with discussion, to a statement of implications or conclusions.

## *Sample headings in a report*

- Terms of reference
- Introduction
- Work carried out
- Findings
- Conclusions
- Recommendations
- Summary
- Acknowledgments
- References
- Appendixes

### TITLE

The title of a report must inform the reader about what is in it. A good title helps to focus the report. Avoid long-winded titles as far as possible, such as 'A Study to Determine the Usage of School Canteen Facilities at Lunchtime'. Write instead: 'Report on the Use of the School Canteen'.

### TERMS OF REFERENCE

The terms of reference are the detailed instructions given to the writers of the report about what they are to investigate. The terms of reference may also include the date on which the report was commissioned. An official report on the number of pupils taking Irish in the Leaving Certificate might be entitled 'Number of Pupils Undertaking the Leaving Certificate Examination in Irish', while the terms of reference might be something like this:

> At the request of the Minister for Education and Science, the Chief Inspector of the department, Mr Éamann Ó Dálaigh, was instructed on 9 April 1998 to prepare a report on the number of pupils who will sit the Leaving Certificate examination in Irish in 1999.

## INTRODUCTION

In the introduction you should state fully the problem you are aiming to solve or the aspect of the question you are setting out to investigate. Give the reasons for carrying out this report, together with the time limits, details of those carrying out the investigation, the materials and methods used, and any other relevant details.

## WORK CARRIED OUT

This will consist of detailed information on what has been done in order to find information, for example surveys or interviews. Statistics and other data may also have been collected. All accounts of work carried out in gathering the information must be recorded here.

## FINDINGS

Under this heading will come the main body of the information you have gathered on the subject.

It is important in this section to organise the information that has been obtained both clearly and well. Understand clearly the relationship between the different parts of the information.

At this stage, it is important to distinguish between what information is useful and what can be thrown away.

## CONCLUSIONS

The conclusions of your report should link your terms of reference with your findings. Conclusions should flow naturally from your evidence and arguments. They should be clear, simple, and objective.

Where *conclusions* refer to the past, *recommendations* point to the future.

RECOMMENDATIONS

These are often best presented as a list. For example, in a report entitled 'Keeping Localities Tidy: Improving the Environment', the recommendations might be presented as follows:

1. Competitions should be organised regularly—for example monthly—to create incentives for improvement.
2. More rubbish bins should be installed in areas such as parks and picnic-sites.
3. Youth clubs and other local groups should provide the initiative by organising a 'tidy town' campaign.

SUMMARY

The summary of a report should reflect the findings, together with comments from the main body of the report. The summary must be a true account of the report and should emphasise any areas requiring special emphasis.

A good summary will

- outline the main points of the report by providing a précis of what the recipient is going to read
- provide an outline of the main conclusions, with recommendations, for those recipients who are not going to read any more of the report.

## *Style of report-writing*

The language of reports should be *factual and objective.* Do not use emotive or ambiguous words. Avoid any tendency to impress: write to express facts, clearly and logically. Reports are generally written in the past tense.

## *Sample reports*

**Report on Staff Dissatisfaction at Sligo Distilleries Ltd**

**1  Terms of reference**
On the instructions of the personnel and works director (9 May 1998), to report on staff dissatisfaction and to make recommendations.

**2  Introduction**
The employees of Sligo Distilleries Ltd have expressed their concern at the management's rejection of the recommendations of the Labour Court for resolving the continuing problems over pay and conditions. Employees are dissatisfied with working conditions and with certain changes in the company. The management wishes to reconsider its policy and to assess the exact grounds for complaint by employees.

**3  Procedures**
  **3.1  Questionnaire**
  A detailed questionnaire on working conditions and changes within the company was circulated to all employees.
  **3.2  Interviews**
  All supervisors were interviewed. Twenty other employees, selected at random, were interviewed.

**4  Findings**
  **4.1  General**
  Some of the comments from supervisors indicate a strong sense of grievance among employees. Many feel bitter over loss of earnings over the last two months. Other employees are angry with the company because of the substantial changes in structures and work practices.
  **4.2  Causes of dissatisfaction**
  Resentment is felt by for the following reasons:
    **4.2.1  Training**
    Not enough training time is allocated to informing employees about new technology.
    **4.2.2  Lack of mobility**
    Employees are being kept too long in one area or section.
    **4.2.3  Conditions**
    1. Not enough equipment has been allocated to dealing with the work load.
    2. There is not enough work space for the present number of employees.
    3. A backlog of work has accumulated because of the introduction of new technology and changed office procedures.

### 4.2.4 Pay
1. Wages have not been increased in line with the increase in work load over the last three years.
2. Overtime rates are below the norm.

## 5 Conclusions
### 5.1 Training
There is evidence that the complaints about a lack of adequate training are justified.

### 5.2 Conditions
The present number of workers exceeds the amount of equipment available.

Machines are being repaired on time, but because they are old they break down more often.

There is an increase in the amount of written work, though enough people are available to complete this once the problems with office technology are resolved.

### 5.3 Wages
Wages are lower than the average available from other employers in the region.

## 6 Recommendations
1. That a new training programme be introduced to allow employees to gain knowledge of new machines.
2. That money be allocated in the budget for the purchase of new equipment, in accordance with the number of employees.
3. That wages be increased by 6 per cent to bring them into line with present standards.

William O'Brien,
Personnel officer
9 May 1998

---

## Comment

The structure of this report is a standard one. Headings and sub-headings are clearly laid out and numbered, giving a clear indication of the structure and content. The terms of reference are clearly spelt out; the findings are arranged in logical sequence and are clearly outlined by means of sub-headings.

The language is formal and objective. The conclusions spring logically from the preceding points; the recommendations point to realistic areas for improvement.

## Report on Students from Inner-City Areas who Pursue Third-Level Education

### 1 Terms of reference
On 4 April 1998 the Minister for Education and Science instructed the Chief Inspector of the department, Michael Bowles, to report on the number of students from inner-city areas who attend third-level colleges.

### 2 Procedures
**2.1** Surveys were carried out in second-level schools in Dublin, Cork, Limerick, Waterford and Galway to ascertain the number of pupils from inner-city areas who qualified for entry to third-level education.

**2.2** Questionnaires were issued in university colleges and certain other third-level institutions to ascertain the proportion of students from the selected areas attending courses there.

### 3 Findings
**3.1** A greater number of students (relative to population) attend third-level institutions in Dublin than in other cities.

**3.2** Cities with higher rates of unemployment, especially Cork, have a lower rate of participation.

**3.3** The proportion of inner-city residents achieving higher grades is not appreciably different from that of students from other areas.

**3.4** In the last five years there has been an increase of 10 per cent in the number of women students from these areas.

### 4 Conclusions
**4.1** In some cities, notably Cork and Waterford, the proportion of school-leavers attending third-level institutions has increased by only 0.1 per cent in the last five years.

**4.2** Students from inner-city areas who manage to complete courses have a high success rate.

### 5 Recommendations
**5.1** More employment and work incentives should be provided in relatively disadvantaged cities to provide motivation for students from these cities to attend third-level education.

**5.2** Grants and scholarship facilities should be made available at second level to facilitate families from these areas.

## Exercises

Write a report of 300 to 350 words on the following questions. Define the terms of reference yourself, and do not worry about constructing accurate facts. The important thing to bear in mind is using the correct layout.

1. As secretary of a foreign-language school, you have been asked to write a report on a trade fair that you attended in Geneva.
2. You are the personnel manager of a large department store. You have been asked by the managing director to make a report on the number of employees, the quality of their work, and suggestions for improvements.
3. You are employed as secretary in a secondary school. Prepare an information report on the effects of severe weather during December and January.
4. You are chief librarian in a university where the facilities cannot provide for the large number of students. Write a report on the library, with recommendations for possible improvements.
5. You are the secretary of a youth club. You have been offered premises at a low rent, for three years only. Write a report for the committee on the situation of the club and on the need for a new venue.
6. As secretary of a tennis club you have been asked by the committee to write a report on facilities in the club and to recommend improvements that would bring about an increase in membership.
7. Write a report on the number of schoolchildren who watch television during the week. Include the number of hours and the type of programmes watched, and make recommendations.
8. As secretary of a large hospital, you are asked to prepare a report on the hygiene facilities in wards B and C. Include recommendations.
9. You are the head of the sales department in a publishing company. The managing director has requested a report on sales for the present year and a comparison with last year's figures.
10. As secretary of the Department of Health, you have been asked to draft a report on the number of children under fifteen who are using drugs.

## Final check-list for reports

1. Does the title indicate the nature of the report?
2. Are the objectives of the report clearly stated?

3. Have these objectives been met in the report?
4. Is the language of the report clear? Are there obscure phrases or expressions?
5. Is there evidence of bias, of intemperate language or of emotive terms in the report?
6. Are all the terms that are used clearly defined?
7. Is the report written in the correct tense?
8. Are all the claims that are made clearly substantiated by fact?
9. Are the conclusions based on evidence?
10. Are the recommendations that are made feasible?

## *Operating instructions*

The ability to write and understand a set of instructions also falls into the category of the language of information.

A well-written set of instructions begins with a statement of the general aim of the procedure, or an outline of the various steps or stages in the instructions.

1. Choose a sequence for your information. Work from the main points downwards to details, and not the other way around.
2. Use the imperative form of the verb.
3. Avoid ambiguity: instructions must be clear-cut and complete.
4. Avoid negative instructions.
5. Be flexible in your organisation of information and layout.

Generally, instructions consist of

- introductory explanations
- information about tools required
- information about materials required
- definitions
- warnings.

Look at the two following sets of instructions on the handling of incoming post, then answer the questions.

1. **Instructions for dealing with incoming post**
    1. Open all letters. Check for enclosures and place in tray marked Encl.
    2. Stamp letters with current date. Place in tray marked L.

3. Cross all drafts and cheques with name of company's bank.
4. Make note of amount in cheques and pass them to cashier.
5. Record all registered letters and addressees in appropriate book.

**2. Instructions for dealing with incoming post**
1. All envelopes should be opened completely, so that no enclosure is missed.
2. Enclosures should be placed in the tray labelled "Encl."
3. Letters should be stamped with a date and placed in the tray labelled "L".
4. Check that all bank drafts and cheques are crossed with the name of the company's bank.
5. Make a note of the amount of each cheque, and pass cheques on to the cash department.
6. Registered letters should be recorded in the registered letters book, and a note should be made of who the letter is addressed to.

## Questions

(Suggested answers on page 238.)

**1.** Which set of instructions is clearer? Give reasons for your answer.
**2.** Compare the use of language in each set of instructions, and comment on the effect in each case.

## Check-list for writing instructions

1. Clarity is an indispensable feature of good instructions, so make your statements specific.
2. There must be a logical sequence in the different stages of your instructions.
3. Make sure that the different stages or steps are manageable. Say one thing in each sentence.
4. Put the most important item in each sentence at the beginning.
5. Use the imperative mood of the verb.
6. Use short sentences and short paragraphs.
7. Avoid jargon.

THE ENGLISH COMPOSITION

## *Exercises*

1. Write a list of instructions on how to use an electric kettle.
2. As principal of a school, write a list of instructions on
   (a) examination procedures;
   (b) the importance of punctuality in the school;
   (c) the procedures to be adopted in the case of a fire in the school.
3. As gym teacher, write a list of instructions on how to use the equipment in the gym.
4. Rearrange the following list of instructions on installing a toner cartridge in a printer:
   (a) Open the printer door.
   (b) Press the 'Change cartridge' button.
   (c) Close the printer door.
   (d) Remove the toner cartridge from its box.
   (e) Press the power button to turn the printer on.
   (f) Insert the toner cartridge into the holder at such an angle that the green top is tilted towards you.
   (g) Gently remove the tape covering the ink nozzles.
   (h) Push the green top in until the cartridge snaps into place.
5. Discuss the differences between the two following sets of instructions. Take into account the structure, tone and style used in each.

---

**1. How to light a hotplate burner**

1. Push in and turn the control to the large flame symbol.
2. Press in and depress ignition button.
3. When the burner has lit, release the ignition button.
4. Turn the control anti-clockwise and adjust to the setting you require.
5. You may be able to hear the hotplate burners on full setting. This is normal and is a useful indicator of the setting you have chosen.
6. The section 'Lighting your cooker' in your owner's handbook will give you more details.
7. If the hotplate burner will not light you may have misplaced the burner parts after cleaning. Section 3 gives you details on how to replace them correctly.

---

**2. How to light a hotplate burner**

1. Turn the control button to the flame symbol.
2. Press in the ignition button.

3. When the burner has lit, release the ignition button.
4. Turn the control to the setting you require.
5. If the hotplate burner will not light, adjust the burner parts by turning to the right. They will click into position.

## Letters and memos

Every letter carries not only information but an image of the writer and the organisation they work for. It is important to be aware of the power of this image.

There are different kinds of letters; for the most part, however, we think of them as either formal or informal.

Formal letters, which include business letters, demand the ability to choose the appropriate tone and language for the particular occasion. Informal or personal letters are not much written nowadays.

Before you start writing a letter, know what you want to say. Set out your information logically, and organise it into paragraphs. In a letter, paragraphs are signposts to your reader to help them follow your message.

Examinations on the writing of letters and memos are testing

(a) the coherent organisation of information;
(b) the use of appropriate expression;
(c) accepted standards of layout.

## The layout of a letter

1. The sender's address is usually written in the top right-hand corner. However, a letter from an organisation or a company will be on a printed letter-heading, which can present the name and address in a variety of ways. Many private individuals have a printed letter-heading also.
2. The name and address of the person the letter is addressed to is usually written on the left-hand side, a little below the printed heading.
3. The date—which can be under the recipient's address or on the opposite side of the sheet—is written out fully, in the form *5 July 1999*. All letters must be dated, as they are retained and become a record of the transaction.
4. Any reference number is written either above or below the recipient's address.

5. You can begin a letter with 'Dear sir or madam,' but it is far more acceptable to find out beforehand the name of the person you are writing to; you would then begin 'Dear Mr Murphy,' 'Dear Dr O'Brien,' etc.
6. The first sentence contains the main point of your letter.
7. You can close your letter with the expression 'Yours sincerely,' 'Yours faithfully,' or 'Yours truly,' according to preference. There is no difference between these terms: they are just standard formulas. Most formal and business letters nowadays have 'Yours sincerely.'
8. Remember:
   —'Yours' begins with a capital letter;
   —'sincerely' has an *e*;
   —'truly' has no *e*.

## *Characteristics of a letter*

1. A formal and courteous tone. Delicacy as well as courtesy is required when you are conveying unwelcome information.
2. Correct layout. Use the best style, and make it pleasing to the eye.
3. Correct spelling and punctuation.
4. A choice of vocabulary suitable for the person being addressed.
5. The absence of clichés. Use fresh and concise language, free of jargon. Avoid verbose formulas, such as the following:

---

Dear Mr O'Brien,
 Thank you for your letter of 27 April, which we have received. With regard to the matter that you mention in your first paragraph, you will be pleased to know that the filing-cabinets you ordered are now available.

---

The phrase 'which we have received' is clearly redundant, and the rest of the letter is long-winded.

Dear Mr O'Brien,
 Thank you for your letter of 27 April.
 The filing-cabinets you ordered on 27 April are now ready.

Generally, both letters and memos involve

- getting the reader's attention
- making a claim

- supporting it—justifying or explaining the claim
- calling for action—indicating what you want the reader to do, what you will do, or both.

## Types of letters

### JOB APPLICATIONS

Use a form of expression that is clear and straightforward. Explain clearly such important details as dates and names.

Even if you are enclosing your CV, mention the reasons why you are suited for this particular job.

Give the times when you are available for interview, and (if possible) include a telephone number.

### Some phrases for letter-writing

- I wish to apply for the position of ...
- I am applying for the post of ...
- In reply to your advertisement of ... I would like to apply ...
- I am available at any time for interview.
- I wish to apply for the course in ...

### LETTERS OF COMPLAINT

A letter of complaint has to be written with a lot of care, and the control of emotion is essential in order to get the desired result.

When writing a letter of complaint, first make sure that you are complaining to the right person.

Keep letters of complaint short. Focus on the results you want rather than on the incompetence of the person or organisation involved.

Outline your problem clearly, without giving way to anger. Propose a specific solution: suggest something that can be done to remedy the problem. Make sure to keep a record of all contacts.

Here is an example of a letter of complaint:

# THE ENGLISH COMPOSITION

13 Clonliff Square
Dublin 7

14 November 1997

Mr Seán Graham
Henderson Brothers Ltd
Youghal Road
Cork

Dear Mr Graham,

    I am writing to you about the washing-machine that I bought from your firm last month. I am very disappointed with this machine, as it has been out of order since it was bought. The filter has not been working, and as a result the water is not filling up inside the machine. It seems to me that the motor is faulty.
    The result of this damage has been enormous inconvenience to the household, as all the dirty clothes have piled up in the last few weeks. I feel that the machine should be replaced, and I would be grateful if you could take immediate action to solve the problem.

Yours sincerely,

Siobhán Murphy

## Comment

In writing a letter of complaint, you must give exact details of the transaction carried out. Explain the faults clearly. Ask what action will be taken to rectify the matter. Mention the deadline required.

When writing a letter of complaint, bear in mind the following guidelines:

1. Address the letter to someone who can do something about the problem.
2. Keep the tone polite.
3. State the problem clearly and simply.
4. Give definite details that explain the *who, what, when, where* and *how* of what has happened.
5. Include a photocopy of invoices or receipts, as well as information about prices and any other important details.
6. Suggest a solution.

## Answering a letter or complaint

A great deal of tact and sensitivity is needed when answering a letter of complaint. At all times keep the tone courteous, whether you are wrong or not.

Begin by acknowledging the letter and the complaint. Keep your letter clear and factual. Acknowledge the fault if you are to blame, and accept the consequences.

Mention the steps you are taking to rectify the matter, and declare that the problem will not happen again. Conclude with a renewed apology.

## Features of a reply to a complaint

- Statement of regret: acknowledge that the letter of complaint has been received.
- Cause of problem: give an account, after an explanation of why it happened.
- Action to be taken: explain whatever action will be taken to remedy the complaint.
- Restatement of apology, together with the hope that good will can be retained.

## LETTERS OF CONDOLENCE

Letters of this type need to be sensitively written.

Address the person directly and offer your sympathies sincerely and simply. Mention your availability at any time if the person needs help or support.

## SALES LETTERS

Letters of this type are designed to win your readers over, to get them to buy your product.

Start a letter of this type by dramatising a problem. Go on to present your product or service as the solution to this problem.

Speak directly to your readers about how they will benefit from dealing with you. Quote some independent sources of authority, such as the medical profession, to enhance your credibility.

To create a note of urgency, offer a discount or a special offer to prompt the reader to act. Create or include a reference to time, as this will intensify the sense of urgency.

## FORM LETTERS

Form letters are stereotyped letters that are prepared with standard wording that can be sent to many people. They are designed to suit all routine occasions.

This type of letter can be impersonal, or it can be used as the basis of a more individually tailored letter, in which some paragraphs are standardised and others are customised.

## *Exercises*

1. Write a letter to the newspaper about some issue you feel strongly about.
2. Write a letter of application for a summer job in a restaurant.
3. Write a letter of sympathy to a friend whose mother died recently.
4. Write a letter to the Minister for Education and Science about what you think of the examination system.
5. Write a letter of complaint to a local TD about the state of the footpaths in your area.

## *Memos*

A **memo** (short for 'memorandum', meaning a reminder) is an internal letter, with a fixed structure and usually written on a printed form, to someone within the same organisation. They are usually handwritten.

A good memo should be brief and to the point. It should be unambiguous and clear. It should be relevant and have no digressions.

Memos must be polite and courteous, even when demanding that instant action be taken.

Here are some sample memos:

---

**O'Brien and Flood Ltd**

**From:** John Armstrong, sales director
**To:** Aisling Griffin, office manager
**Subject:** Collecting delph from airport
**Date:** 4 May 1998

Arrangements have been made to collect delph (order no. IL 632) from the airport on Friday at 11 a.m.

---

**From:** Mary Downey
**To:** Head Office
**Subject:** Returning jeans
**Date:** 30 April 1999

1. Returning jeans, wrong colour and size, as discussed on phone.
2. Please replace with model specified in order 406613, dated 2 Feb. 1998 (size 14, colour blue).
3. If this is not in stock, please credit this branch.

*Exercises on composition*

1. Write a short story on *one* of the following topics:
   (a) Confessions of an armchair sportsman/sportswoman
   (b) Tomorrow and tomorrow and tomorrow
   (c) Seize the day
   (d) Strangers in the night
   (e) Dreams.
2. Write a debate or a discursive composition on *one* of the following topics:
   (a) Ireland is still a great country in which to live
   (b) Television has destroyed family life
   (c) Is there any future for amateur sport?
   (d) Censorship is good for society
   (e) The greatest of evils and the worst of crimes is poverty.
3. Take each of these opening sentences and write a narrative-style composition:
   (a) It was Sunday evening and he was settling down peacefully beside the fire, paper in his hand and pipe in his mouth. Suddenly he heard an ear-piercing scream.
   (b) There it came again, thundering through the air at an extraordinary speed. She moved forward to investigate.
   (c) He struggled wildly, tearing his clothes in shreds as he moved in the undergrowth, when …
   (d) Liam recognised the swimmer and raced in to save her, but would he be in time?
   (e) When I walked in over the threshold I suddenly felt an uncanny feeling that I had been there before.
4. Take a person you know and think of some difficulty they have to confront, either in themselves or in a relationship. Write this in story

form, making sure to bring in some conflict the person experiences, and draw out a necessary climax and conclusion.
5. Write a story about a character who has to confront a radically different situation from what they have been used to (or facing a serious illness, or experiencing a personal crisis). Develop the story on the basis of this person's interaction with this situation.

*Exercises on writing in the language of persuasion*

1. Write a persuasive article for a school magazine on the value of and the need for more select reading.
2. Select an issue about which you feel strongly. Write a persuasive composition on that topic, using any one of the following selection of audiences:
   —teachers
   —your parents
   —adolescents
   —old-age pensioners
   —the Government.
3. Write a persuasive article for a newspaper on the need for more law enforcement in the area of crime.
4. Write a persuasive composition on the topic 'The value of politics today'.

*Exercises on descriptive writing*

1. Write four separate paragraphs on a building. In each case create an impression of
   (a) gloom
   (b) joy
   (c) untidiness
   (d) an old-world style
   (e) modernity and comfort.
   Select carefully the images, vocabulary, and details.
2. Add words that appeal to the sense of taste, hearing and touch to make the following sentences more specific. For example: 'Along the hedge by the roadside the sun glinted on the bicycle wheels.'—'Along the hedge bordering the road the weak sun glinted on curves and ellipses of bicycles wheels.'
   (a) Our mother's house needs cleaning.
   (b) My granny's special pie is tasty.

(c) The drive through the valley was relaxing.
(d) My uncle painted the front door.
(e) The car made a noise as it moved down the street.
(f) Her dress was flattering.
(g) Peppermint has an interesting taste.
(h) The price of crisps is appalling.
(i) The noise of the drill drowned the lecturer's voice.

**3.** Rewrite the following sentences using active verbs and descriptive adjectives to make the writing more specific and detailed:
(a) My house is a mess.
(b) The girl rode her bicycle on the footpath.
(c) The old woman walked down the lane.
(d) Our park is very untidy.
(e) My pet cat can do a number of tricks.
(f) It's easy to understand why she gets angry.
(g) My county has many historic sites.
(h) The dinner we got there was not tasty.
(i) Our campsite was unappealing.
(j) There are many professions that interest me.

**4.** Select a small object—for example an apple, orange, pen, or watch. Spend five minutes recording on paper its shape, colour, and size. Make *four* detailed observations about this object. Record less prominent features, such as indentations, minor gradations in colour, smell, taste, feel, and sound of the object.

**5.** Rewrite the following sentences to include *four* descriptive details and to make the expression more vivid:
(a) My father, a butcher, had rough hands.
(b) The garden had a nice colour in spring.
(c) My old bicycle has an unusual colour.
(d) I opened several parcels on my birthday.
(e) The animal crawled across the road.

**6.** Rewrite the following sentences to include a strong focus on description:
(a) The girl crawled under the bed.
(b) The car moved out from the kerb.
(c) Men generally sleep a lot easier.
(d) The garda moved away from the building.
(e) Night fell quickly on the land.
(f) Darkness crept up silently.

(g) Sarah had a short walk.
(h) Miriam left the library at four o'clock.
(i) The man moved slowly away from the house.
(j) The cat remained motionless on the wall.

*Exercises on writing styles*

**1.** Choose a topic on which you have a strong opinion. Write out this opinion, using *two* of the following styles or approaches:
   (a) a discursive composition;
   (b) a passionate speech to your class;
   (c) a descriptive anecdote;
   (d) a letter to the newspaper;
   (e) an article for a teenage magazine.
**2.** Write on *one* of the following topics in *three* different forms or genres: imaginative, descriptive, and narrative.
   (a) Airports
   (b) That Monday morning feeling
   (c) Fragile Earth
   (d) Poverty in an age of affluence
   (e) People power
   (f) An age of change
   (g) 'He who makes no mistakes does not usually make anything.'
**3.** Examine the following sentences under the headings tone, audience, and purpose. (Suggested answers on page 238.)
   (a) I own an oul' Ford Capri, but it doesn't go that well, 'cos the wheels are off and I have to put it up on concrete blocks.
   (b) If Merson's first-half influence had been little, his influence on a spirited Boro second-half fight-back could not be underestimated.
   (c) Figures coming in from the first new house sales campaigns of the year show that private investors now comprise up to 35 per cent of all enquiries for new three-bedroom houses, up from about 20 per cent late last year.
   (d) Straddling the Meath-Westmeath border, the lough is regarded as one of Ireland's best wet and dry fly-fishing lakes, with brown trout of up to six pounds being the most popular catch here.
   (e) Adult learning has become very flexible, adapting itself to the needs and life-style of all potential students.
   (f) The Labour MP Martin Linton, who is part of the Home Affairs Select Committee, which scrutinises gambling and law and order,

said the idea of selling scratch-cards bearing Diana's name was 'too tacky for words.'

**4.** From the following topics, write four opening paragraphs using the following styles: informative or factual; imaginative or dramatic; humorous or entertaining; satirical or ironic.
   (a) Exams are not an end in themselves
   (b) Changing fashions
   (c) We are what we eat
   (d) Rock music: an indication of our times?

**5.** Identify what style is appropriate for the following situations. Write on *one* of these topics in *three* different styles: informative, imaginative, and descriptive.
   (a) A letter of application for a job
   (b) A description of a street fight
   (c) A meeting with a famous person
   (d) A speech to a class about a voluntary social project that you are involved in.

**6.** Pick *one* of the following topics, then write out fully your opinions on it. Justify your opinion with evidence.
   (a) 'Soap operas are the opium of the people'
   (b) Judgment Day
   (c) 'Young people are slaves of fads and fashions'
   (d) Illusion and reality
   (e) Refugees
   (f) 'Freedom must be limited in order to be possessed'
   (g) 'There is no such thing as complete happiness'
   (h) 'Laws are like cobwebs which catch small flies, but let wasps and hornets through' [Swift].

*Exercises on objectives*

(Suggested answers on page 238.)
Briefly describe the main objective of the writer of each of the following pieces. Identify the sentences in which that objective is stated clearly. Describe the order of presentation used in each extract; say, with reasons, why you think (or do not think) that the order of presentation is suited to the writer's subject matter and objective.

(a) Membership has been the same for the last two years—approximately three thousand. This figure is disappointing, bearing in mind that the membership fee has not been increased. For this reason we have launched an advertising campaign in both national and local newspapers. We have also organised the distribution of a thousand leaflets in the locality. The growth of our golf club depends also on the enthusiasm of our individual members; we have therefore included four detachable membership application forms at the end of this bulletin for your own use. Please distribute these to relatives and friends. We are asking you to try to bring at least one new friend before July, so that we can get a fairly substantial increase in our numbers in order to support this summer's campaign.

[From a quarterly bulletin published by Fedamore Golf Club]

(b) Disruption to other students because of latecomers is now increasing. I recommend to the committee that access to the examination hall be prohibited, and that the doors be locked, fifteen minutes after the examination begins.
I hope for the full support of the committee on this matter.

[From an examination board's report]

*Exercises on word precision*

Select the precise word to fill the gap in each of the following sentences. (Suggested answers on page 239.)

(1) If this new sub-committee functions as planned, the committee will be able to ... members' suggestions much more quickly. [adopt/adapt/operate/fulfil/carry out/implement]
(2) Much of the blame for the ... of the British economy has been placed on the attitude and performance of managements. [plight/situation/dilemma/state/degree]
(3) Diagrams are often useful for ... the physical relationship of the components of the environment. [showing/outlining/describing/clarifying]
(4) The work-place ... problem has become acute in recent years. [relations/safety/engineering/plants]
(5) The client's ... to settle his claim within a month is reasonable. [pledge/promise/claim/guarantee]

(6) Send drafts of all pages on which errors occur so that ... can be made in any future reports. [additions/substitutions/alterations/corrections]
(7) The results should be of great interest to you, and we plan to send you a ... of our principal findings. [résumé/précis/report]
(8) When you exceed your overdraft limit, the bank automatically ... a surcharge. [organises/fixes/imposes/carries out]
(9) We think that to ... payment is inappropriate at present. [defer/cancel/stop]
(10) Long-distance travel out of Ireland has ... in price over the last ten years. [lowered/increased/plummeted/jumped]

*Exercises on ambiguous or verbose statements*

**1.** Rewrite the following sentences in a more vigorous and succinct style. (Suggested answers on page 239.)
   (a) You will not catch a cold walking in the park.
   (b) At the close of the season, the company found that trading had not only decreased alarmingly but also major exports.
   (c) There is no reason to think that what was written is not true.
   (d) It is my considered opinion that there never was and never will be such a demonstration again.
   (e) Youth today are slaves of fashion, and nearly all young people follow the latest fads in fashion, especially girls.
   (f) Very little or even no changes occurred in the last year.
   (g) Older children take drink because they think it makes them look older.
   (h) Destruction of the entire central section of the building took place as a result of the conflagration.
   (i) It is a proven fact that at this time of year there are more deaths on the road caused by drunken driving than at any other time of the year.
   (j) In this modern world of today too many people devote their leisure to things like videos and television, where they have everything laid on for them.

**2.** Draft a questionnaire based on the hypothesis that television has damaged the literacy level of school-going children. Include a list of specific questions that require short answers. Pay attention to
   (a) the people who will be answering the questions;
   (b) the size of the questionnaire (twenty to thirty questions should be enough);

(c) the issues you want to identify;
(d) possible solutions.

*Exercises on 'loaded' or subjective language*

Express the meaning of the following sentences in precise, factual and objective language. (Suggested answers on page 240.)

(a) A soft light spreads across the polished aluminium control panel, illuminating the combined CD, radio and cassette player in readiness for your decision.

(b) A superb three-year unlimited mileage warranty makes it very, very safe.

(c) Relax and get ready to succumb to the purity of sound as your chosen piece of music envelops you.

(d) Nothing penetrates deeper, while the formula replenishes from root to tip, to bring out your hair's true potential.

(e) The bottom line is that all this technology and expertise puts reliable and more affordable international communication in your hands.

(f) Now wearing heels—even high heels—can be a painless pleasure with these unique new insoles.

(g) It's a personal touch that not only conveys a professional image to your callers but also ensures that all your calls are captured.

(h) The highly acclaimed stylish and sporty Supra combines thrilling performance with the sort of traffic-stopping good looks of a classy sports car.

(i) It's a stupendous award-winning mechanism that utilises a positive electromagnetic charge, which as a result produces about 90 per cent less ozone than other organic drums.

(j) These wide-leg, flat-fronted jeans with authentic styling details are available in many sizes.

# Four

# ANSWERS TO EXERCISES

## CHAPTER 2

EXERCISES ON THE SENTENCE

*Exercise 1 (page 108)*

(a) Complex.
(b) Complex.
(c) Compound.
(d) Balanced.
(e) Complex.
(f) Compound.
(g) Simple.
(h) Compound.
(i) Balanced.
(j) Balanced.

*Exercise 2 (page 108)*

(a) Pupils get bored easily in the summer holidays, so they should get jobs.
(b) If you cannot see how serious this issue is, I think you should consider retiring.
(c) Life is at best a wonderful experience, although it involves both suffering and happiness.
(d) The worst and most tremendous fear is failure.
(e) This great story would both darken the mind and open one's eyes.
(f) Big cities are dirty, disease-ridden, and overpopulated.

(g) How can these people know anything else when they have nobody to teach them?
(h) What we've got here is failure at every level.
(i) Our society today tends to accept these problems as everyday occurrences, without doing all it can to prevent them.

## Exercise 3 (page 109)

(a) I have nothing to offer but blood, sweat, tears, and toil.
(b) The manager described the department's problems succinctly, clearly, and candidly.
(c) It is as important to review the records daily as it is to collect accurate information.
(d) Law-abiding citizens who have a speeding fine are an exception to the rule in modern society.
(e) Charles Jarvis is an excellent lecturer, a personable conversationalist, and a good writer.
(f) Sport has been popular for a long time, and it looks as if this will continue.
(g) People who were never interested in soccer were overjoyed when Ray Houghton scored in the one-nil victory over Italy.
(h) Life has an abundance of obstacles; the greatest one at present is my parents.
(i) While I was cleaning my room that night, I saw the same man throwing stones and shouting at the same time. Luckily, no-one was outside.
(j) The number of young people dedicating their time and skills to youth work is striking.

## Exercise 4 (page 109)

(a) Sentence fragment.
(b) Sentence fragment.
(c) Sentence.
(d) Sentence.
(e) Sentence.
(f) Sentence fragment.

*Exercise 5 (page 110)*

(a) Over the years, I have been enriched by a wide variety of people from different races and creeds.
(b) Enclosed is a copy of the annual report for the fiscal year 1996.
(c) I believe that the co-operation shown by employees and the management was responsible for the increase in sales last year.
(d) We must decide soon whether or not we are going to build the new extension.
(e) We will withhold making a decision until we have the necessary data.
(f) Love is widespread, and it cannot be challenged by any other emotion.
(g) The writer's purpose in the passage is to show that most people today are careful to maintain the status quo in society.
(h) The sound of horns beeping, the screeching of brakes, the sounds of bags, briefcases and boxes clattering, together with the high-pitched noises of people, were to be heard as they made their way down O'Connell Street.
(i) The writer's use of statistics, facts and references is persuasively communicated.
(j) Expansion occurred in new areas; it then slowed down, until it reached a peak in 1998.

## EXERCISES ON GRAMMAR

*Exercise 1 (page 110)*

(a) 'Jane': proper noun; 'France': proper noun; 'group': collective noun.
(b) 'Women': common noun; 'Madrid': proper noun; 'fear': abstract noun.
(c) 'Team': collective noun; 'courage': abstract noun.
(d) 'Mrs Smith': proper noun (noun phrase); 'crowd': collective noun; 'Lisbon': proper noun.
(e) 'Charity': abstract noun; 'virtue': common noun.

*Exercise 2 (page 111)*

(a) After I had researched the topic for five months, my supervisor cancelled the project.

## ANSWERS TO EXERCISES

(b) After I had been rejected by three companies, my employment counsellor suggested that I should rewrite my CV.
(c) The first three exercises must be completed in order to learn the technique thoroughly.
(d) John is the cleverer of the two.
(e) As I was entering the golf course, the lightning struck.
(f) There is no hatred between Jack and Mary.
(g) Each of the boys must wear his uniform.
(h) The art of conversation is needed now more than ever before, in order to enrich our lives.
(i) Will anyone be there?
(j) I cannot work as I used to.

*Exercises 3 (page 111)*

(a) The town's main street is very narrow.
(b) The boys' ties are in a bad state.
(c) After yesterday's events, I feel very hopeful.
(d) The typist finds Dr Thornton's letters very hard to understand.
(e) Women's rights in this century have been a point of contention.

*Exercises 4 (page 111)*

(a) Wouldn't it be marvellous to go!
(b) It's not going to rain yet.
(c) You'll find it in the press under the stairs.
(d) Hurry up, or we'll never get there on time.
(e) I didn't say they're mad.

*Exercise 5 (page 111)*

(a) for.
(b) out.
(c) out ... for.
(d) from ... since.
(e) on.
(f) at ... on.

## Exercise 6 (page 112)

(a) but.
(b) but.
(c) but.
(d) or.
(e) and.
(f) but.

## Exercise 7 (page 112)

(a) Now that I am working too hard and playing too little, my ulcer is acting up again.
(b) Before I leave for Africa I will have to get a new visa stamped in my passport.
(c) As I was waving frantically, the taxi went right past me.
(d) The manager spoke harshly to the secretary.
(e) The new product, which doubled the company's gross sales, was developed in two weeks.
(f) The main problem is the emphasis placed on programmes about satellites, which are launched on boosters.
(g) The safety director decided to revise procedures after she had inspected the plant.
(h) The meat was tough, and the pie was tasteless.
(i) She arrived in tears at the school and in a Ford Capri.
(j) He adored both his French teacher and biology.

## Exercise on punctuation (page 114)

(a) And now, ladies and gentlemen, we come to the most interesting exhibit of all.
(b) 'Your dinner is on the table!' she shouted. 'All right,' he replied. 'I'm coming now.'
(c) He entered the room, locked the door, took out his papers, and seated himself at the desk.
(d) Faith, family and football—in that order—are the most important things in my life; but keeping the balance is not easy.
(e) 'Has she injured you?' he asked.
(f) Eat more meat; otherwise you will regret it.

(g) He said, 'I'm going out now, and I will be in by nine. Don't wait up for me.'
(h) My younger brother, who is a tax inspector, knows all about this matter. He will advise you best.
(i) 'We're waiting for the school bus,' said the children. 'It's late again. We've made a terrible mistake to wait so long.'

# CHAPTER 3

*Exercises on the paragraph (page 165)*

1. (c)
2. (a)
3. (b)
4. (d)
5. (f)
6. (e)

EXERCISES ON COHERENCE IN PARAGRAPHS

*Exercise 1 (page 166)*

1. (b)
2. (a)
3. (d)
4. (c)
5. (f)
6. (e)

*Exercise 2 (page 166)*

The sentence beginning 'The missionaries quickly pointed out to Mukabya ...' breaks the unity in this paragraph.

*Exercise 3 (page 166)*

'Once a book is fathomed, once it is known and its meaning is fixed or established, it is dead.' This is the topic sentence in the paragraph.

## Exercise 4 (page 167)

The writer develops the argument by means of comparison in the phrases 'in a year' and 'through much of the eighties.' The argument is developed by means of analogy, with the word 'profligacy' and repetition of the term 'the hairshirt.' Contrast is shown through the word 'although.'

## Exercises on instructions (page 216)

1. The first version is long-winded and verbose, while the second is crisp and comprehensible.
2. The vocabulary and sentence structure in the second version are simple and clear and easy to follow. The use of the imperative form of the verb in this version makes the meaning much more clear, terse, and direct.

## Exercises on writing styles (page 227)

(a) Tone: colloquial; audience: friends and acquaintances; purpose: to provide information about a car.
(b) Tone: informative; audience: sports fans; purpose: to provide information on sports personalities.
(c) Tone: factual; audience: house agents; purpose: to provide information on house sales.
(d) Tone: persuasive; audience: tourists; purpose: marketing of tourist areas.
(e) Tone: informative or persuasive; audience: adults interested in further education; purpose: to promote adult education.
(f) Tone: colloquial or informative; audience: the general public; purpose: the condemnation of scratch-cards.

## Exercises on objectives (page 228)

(a) The writer's main objective here is to motivate members to join in the recruiting drive. The last sentence—'We are asking ...'—expresses this objective clearly. The writer uses an ascending order of importance, ending with the main point. The method

## ANSWERS TO EXERCISES

here is persuasive, and therefore the order and structure of ideas are significant. The writer supplies evidence that the committee has been doing its utmost to recruit new members. The extract concludes by requesting members to take action in order to remedy the situation. In the last sentence the members are requested to bring along a friend as part of the recruitment campaign and as a way of giving their support.

(b) The writer's objective here is to get the committee's agreement to the proposed action. The information is presented in descending order of importance, with the main points first. The order of presentation is well suited to both the subject matter and the objective of the writer. The problem is clearly outlined in the first statement; the remaining sentences provide reasoned arguments to support the recommendations set out in the first sentence.

### Exercise on word precision (page 229)

(1) implement
(2) state
(3) outlining
(4) safety
(5) pledge
(6) corrections
(7) report
(8) imposes
(9) defer
(10) plummeted

### Exercise on ambiguous or verbose sentences (page 230)

(a) You will not catch a cold while walking in the park.
(b) At the conclusion of the season, the company found that both trading and major exports had decreased alarmingly.
(c) There is no reason to think that what was written is untrue. There is every reason to think that what was written is true.
(d) It is my opinion that there never will be such a demonstration again.
(e) Youth today, especially girls, follow the latest fashion trends.

(f) Little or no change occurred in the last year.
(g) Older children take drink to make them look more grown-up.
(h) Fire destroyed the entire central section of the building.
(i) It is a fact that there are more deaths on the roads from drunken driving at this time of the year than at any other time.
(j) Today too many people devote their leisure to television, videos, and computers, which costs them little effort.

## Exercises on 'loaded' or subjective language (page 231)

(a) There is a CD-player, a radio and a cassette-player inside the aluminium control panel.
(b) A three-year mileage warranty makes it very safe.
(c) Relax with your favourite music.
(d) This shampoo penetrates deeply and will make your hair shiny.
(e) With this technology you can get cheaper and more reliable communications internationally.
(f) With these insoles you can even wear high heels.
(g) Your calls will be answered in a professional manner.
(h) The Supra is a sports car that operates very well.
(i) It's a mechanism that employs a positive electromagnetic charge, which produces about 90 per cent less ozone than other organic drums.
(j) These jeans, which are wide-leg and flat-fronted, are available in many sizes.

# ALSO AVAILABLE

Cognitive Research Trust
Ed de Bono.
8 up 103 yrs!

6 hrs    instead of all 10 yrs.
NCUA
Inservice
19/20¢ for 25 deaf people Belfast

Thinking as a skill
Set programme & attach it to subject.
Ed doesn't want people to teach
12 mcess Leclests to feel
'Sin rget jeise wrong' de Bono.
Joyce dd — Earl Ern leader pilots
PMI — b
Plus minus Interesting
Constructive Thinking — Scissors
allow still
                PO Box
                2917
                OS
Package    WW Ed de Bono
            Menlo. Ca
01- 82504266  feedback +
   ann lynch   student rates